The Inner Journey
Views from the Buddhist Tradition

Series Editor: Ravi Ravindra
Associate Series Editor: Priscilla Murray

The Inner Journey
Views from the Buddhist Tradition

Edited by Philip Novak

PARABOLA Anthology Series

MORNING LIGHT PRESS

Published by Morning Light Press 2005.

Editor: Philip Novak
Series Editor: Ravi Ravindra
Associate Series Editor: Priscilla Murray

Morning Light Press
323 North First, Suite 203
Sandpoint, ID   83864
morninglightpress.com
info@mlpress.com

Printed on acid-free paper in Canada.

13 Digit ISBN: 978-1-59675-005-0
10 Digit ISBN: 1-59675-005-7
Philosophy
SAN: 255-3252

Library of Congress Cataloging-in-Publication Data

The inner journey: views from the Buddhist tradition / edited by Philip Novak.

     p. cm. -- (Parabola anthology series)
   Selected from Parabola magazine.
   Includes bibliographical references.
   ISBN 1-59675-005-7 (978-1-59675-005-0 : alk. paper)
   1. Buddhism. I. Novak, Philip. II. Parabola (Mt. Kisco, N.Y.) III.
Series.
   BQ4055.I46 2005
   294.3--dc22
                              2005020091

To the path makers
and the pilgrims on the path

General Introduction to
The Inner Journey: A Parabola Anthology Series

When *Parabola: Myth, Tradition, and the Search for Meaning* was launched in 1976, the founder, D. M. Dooling, wrote in her first editorial:

Parabola has a conviction: that human existence is significant, that life essentially makes sense in spite of our confusions, that man is not here on earth by accident but for a purpose, and that whatever that purpose may be it demands from him the discovery of his own meaning, his own totality and identity. A human being is born to set out on this quest. ... Every true teaching, every genuine tradition has sought to train its disciples to act this part, to become in fact followers of the great quest for one's self.

For over thirty years, *Parabola* has honored the great wisdom traditions of every culture, turning to their past and present masters and practitioners for guidance in this quest. Recognizing that the aim of each tradition is the transformation of human life through practice supported by knowledge and understanding, *Parabola* on behalf of its readers has turned again and again to Buddhist and Christian monks, Sufi and Jewish teachers, Hindu scholars, and Native American and other indigenous peoples, evoking from each of them illumination and insight.

Over the years *Parabola*, in each of its issues devoted to a central theme of the human condition as it is and as it might be, has gathered remarkable material. "The Call," "Awakening," "Food," "Initiation," "Dreams and Seeing," "Liberation," "The Mask," "Attention": in these and in scores of other issues, a facet of the essential search is explored, always with the aim of casting light on the way.

The purpose of the *Parabola Anthology Series* is to gather the material published in *Parabola* during its first thirty years in order to focus this light, and to reflect the inner dimensions of each of these traditions. While every religious tradition has both external and inner aspects, the aim of each is the transformation of the whole being. The insights and understandings that ring true and carry the vibration of an inner meaning can provide guidance and support for our quest, but a mere mechanical repetition of forms which were once charged with great energy can take us away from the heart of the teaching. Every tradition must change and evolve; it has to be re-interpreted and re-understood by successive generations in order to maintain its relevance and application.

Search carries a connotation of journey; we set out with the hope for new insight and experience. The aim of the spiritual or inner journey is transformation, to become more responsible and more compassionate as understanding and being grow. This demands an active undertaking, and insights from those who have traveled the path can provide a call, bring inspiration, and serve as a reminder of the need to search.

For this series, selections have been made from the material published in *Parabola* relating to each of the major traditions and teachings. Subtle truths are expressed in myths, poetry, stories, parables and, above all, in the lives, actions, and expressions of those people who have been immersed in the teaching, have wrestled with it and have been informed and transformed by it. Some of these insights have been elicited through interviews with current practitioners of various teachings. Each of the great traditions is very large and within each tradition there are distinct schools of thought, as well as many practices, rituals, and ceremonies. None of the volumes in the present series claim to be exhaustive of the whole tradition or to give a complete account of it.

In addition to the material that has been selected from the library of *Parabola* issues, the editor of each volume in the series provides an introduction to the teaching, a reminder of the heart of the tradition in the section, "The Call of the Tradition," as well as a list of books suggested for further study and reflection. It is the hope of the publishers and editors that this new series will surprise, challenge, and support those new to *Parabola* as well as its many readers.

—*Ravi Ravindra*

Contents

THE CALL OF THE TRADITION

*Just as the great ocean has one taste, the taste of salt, so also this Dhamma
and Discipline has one taste, the taste of liberation.*[1]

*It is through not realizing, through not penetrating the Four Noble Truths
that this long course of birth and death has been passed through and
undergone by me as well as by you. What are these four? They are the noble truth
of dukkha; the noble truth of the origin of dukkha; the noble truth of the cessation of
dukkha; and the noble truth of the way to the cessation of dukkha.*[2]

*All that we are is a result of what we have thought: it is founded on our thoughts,
it is made up of our thoughts. If a man speaks or acts with an evil thought, pain
follows him, as the wheel follows the foot of the ox that draws the wagon.
All that we are is a result of what we have thought: it is founded on our thoughts,
it is made up of our thoughts. If a man speaks or acts with a pure thought,
happiness follows him, like a shadow that never leaves him.*[3]

*The extinction of greed, the extinction of hate, the extinction
of delusion: this indeed is called Nibbana.*[4]

*Who sees Dependent Arising sees the Dhamma; who sees
the Dhamma sees Dependent Arising.*[5]

*To refrain from evil,
To achieve the good,
To purify the mind,
This is the teaching of all Awakened Ones.*[6]

—the Buddha

There is no difference between Samsara and Nirvana.
There is no difference between Nirvana and Samsara.[7]

—Nagarjuna

The Way is not difficult for one who has no preferences.[8]

—Seng Ts'an

In Buddhism, practice and Enlightenment are one and the same.[9]

—Zen Master Dogen

We are here for a short time. We must try to do something good
with our lives. Try to be at peace with yourself and help others share that
peace. If you contribute to others' happiness, you will find the
true goal and meaning of life.[10]

—His Holiness the 14th Dalai Lama

The Inner Journey: Introduction

That the Buddha begins his teaching with a frank recognition of human life as inevitably subject to pain, illness, decay and death is well known. Yet Buddhism's gospel, the good news responsible for its longevity and world-historical influence, is not the important but finally secondary observation that life hurts. It is rather that within this impermanent, perpetually perishing, indeed death-dealing world, a flow of happiness remarkable for its depth and durability is entirely possible. Throughout its literature and on virtually every page of the legend of Gotama's life, Buddhism affirms that human beings aim for a greater fullness of quality in their experience, and that they do not do so in vain. Every woman and man, it teaches, embodies a profound capacity for attending to the rich flow of quality which arises spontaneously in the passing moments of our lives from a place just beyond the ego's reach. Nirvana, described by the Buddha as "freedom from greed, freedom from aversion, and freedom from the 'self' confusion," it is not totally unknown to us before it is fully realized, but a reality less and less obscured as interferences to our reception of it are dissolved. Long before the 'yonder bank' appears intimations of it reach awakening shores.

It is clear therefore that when the Buddha counsels reduction of our craving for sensual gratification, it is not to please some dour god or punish ourselves, but rather to enable a qualitatively richer trend of feeling to arise, distinct from its cruder counterpart in that it leaves no hooks in our flesh, no compulsion to repeat. Buddhism aptly calls the refinement effected by its Eightfold Path "the purification of emotions," and no one has ever caught its spirit better than William Blake:

He who binds himself to a joy
Does the winged life destroy
But he who kisses the joy as it flies.
Lives in Eternity's sunrise.

As our emotional circuitry is refined through the moral and meditative practices of the path, what begins to arise in us more regularly are extraordinary sensibilities — equanimity, lovingkindness, fellow-feeling, joy — so plenary in beauty, serenity and delight that the Buddha himself referred to them as divine abodes *(brahmaviharas)* capable of limitless extension. Important as these are, they are but emblems of a broader ethical unfolding suffused by the intention to lessen the suffering of others. The end of this process, nirvana, represents a psycho-emotional reconstitution so advanced that not only do baser feelings stemming from greed, aversion and the 'self' confusion no longer arise, they *can* no longer arise. It was to discover all this — and to create a map to guide others to the discovery — that Gotama turned his back on palace life. Buddhism is therefore not about the abandonment of life, but about the exchange of life-as-usual for life in a new key. Professor Corless, no doubt aware of the frequency with which Buddhism is still misunderstood as pessimistic, calls it as a profoundly positive vision whose key experience is the experience of joy.[1]

Alas, human psychophysical locations tend to be ill-attuned to the satisfying flow of quality freely available in the fleeting now. We find ourselves blinkered by *dukkha*, or "suffering," a kind of static which blocks our capacity to feel and see things as they are. While some *dukkha* stems from the normal shocks to which all flesh is heir, by far its greater portion stems from correctable mistakes — as per the Buddhist quip, "pain is inevitable, suffering optional." Broadly put, these mistakes are our chronically inept reactions to the normal difficulties of life: being separated from what we want, being tied to what we don't want, getting what we think we want only to watch its capacity to satisfy decline, and, deepest of all, clinging to a false notion of self. The net effect of a life's worth of these perfectly natural but unskillful reactions to everyday pleasures and displeasures is a habit-hardened tangle of tendencies, a dispositional miasma which cuts us off from the reality that Buddhism says is always already there to enjoy. The Buddhist path therefore is not so much about growing wings as it is about discarding chains. It is about an inner change that requires an inner journey.

And the inner work is three-pronged. First it is moral. Whatever else the Buddha was, he was an ethicist who taught that an amendment of conduct was the indispensable beginning of and constant accompaniment for the Path he charted. Second, it is intellective. It requires a cognitive effort to pierce the depths of the cause and effect logic behind the Buddha's diagnosis of human sorrow and his prescription for its alleviation. But third, and perhaps most distinctively, it is meditative. The Buddha discovered that the subtlest, most recalcitrant root of our *dukkha* is the mistaken view that my "self" is a permanent entity separable from the interdependent, co-conditioning and ever-changing psychosomatic processes that comprise me. Comprehending this error with our frontal lobes is comparatively easy. Undoing it all the way down to our reptilian brain, as it were, is considerably more difficult and much more than a matter of hatching new thoughts. It requires a different strategy altogether, one which involves the entire sensorium of the body as deeply as it involves the untapped potentials of the mind. It requires, in a word, meditation — the sustained practice of special modes of attention that lead to liberating insight. It is not an accident, after all, that one of the most powerfully resonant images in the psychic inventory of the human race is one that represents a person, the Buddha, sitting still in silence. It is perhaps because somewhere in its deepest recesses the human mind has always known that this symbol anticipates the noblest possibilities of our evolution that the Buddha's teaching should remain so alive and so relevant twenty-six centuries on.

The articles collected in this volume were first published in the journal *Parabola* between 1976 and the present, a time of extraordinary growth of Western interest in Buddhism. In this period, to cite but one statistic, the number of Buddhist practice centers in the United States mushroomed from 21 in 1964 to well over 1000 today. The pieces presented here can credibly claim to be both causes and effects of this remarkable efflorescence.

Chapter One invokes 'Turning Points.' When in the early hours of a May morning long ago the Buddha reached a level of insight that convinced him nothing essential had been left unlearned, his joy was such that he broke into a quiet song to celebrate the reality of freedom. The chapter's epigraph attempts to capture the exultation of this pivotal moment in the great teacher's life. It is drawn from Edwin Arnold's *The Light of Asia*, which was itself something of a turning point in the coming of Buddhism to the West. Published in 1879, it sold nearly a million copies and sent the first wide wave of Dharma awareness rippling across the North American continent. Of the two articles contained in this chapter, one is a key passage from Hermann Hesse's famous novella, *Siddhartha*, in a new translation by S. C. Kohn. Hesse's work, first published in 1922, is only indirectly about Buddhism, but its evocation of the timeless challenges of the spiritual path has brought countless readers to inquire further into the Buddha's teaching. In this excerpt the young Siddhartha confers with the Buddha, convinced of the latter's matchless wisdom but equally sure that he must discover his own path to awakening — a not uncommon conundrum.

The other article comes from the pen of the Catholic monk and writer, Thomas Merton, and requires an extra word of introduction. Back in the 1930s when the twenty-ish Merton entered the strictest contemplative order in the Catholic Church and embraced a life of silence behind monastery walls, one might not have predicted he would come to exert an incalculably large influence on Western interest in Buddhist thought and be remembered as a founder and patron saint of Buddhist-Christian dialogue. But as Merton's soul ripened in the silence of his Kentucky monastery, it turned increasingly toward the light of Buddhist and Taoist thought. In 1968, at 53, Merton was finally granted permission to travel to the native lands of these traditions. The opening pages of his *Asian Journal* shimmer with excitement: "The moment of take-off was ecstatic ... We left the ground, I ... with a great sense of destiny, of being at last on my true way after years of waiting and wondering and fooling around ... I am going home, to the home I have never been in this body."[2] Yet of all the moments in Merton's Asian pilgrimage none was more important than the one excerpted here. It is nothing less than Merton's own *satori*, an experience of deep, inner awakening on suddenly beholding the great Buddhist rock sculptures at Polonnaruwa, Sri Lanka.

Toward the end of his *Asian Journal*, Merton says something quite extraordinary: "I believe that by openness to ... these great Asian traditions, we stand a wonderful chance of learning more about the potentiality of our own traditions, because they have gone, from the natural point of view, so much deeper into this than we have."[3] He is speaking of course about meditation, which is the theme of Chapter Two, 'The Well-Trained Mind.' The first article in this chapter is an interview with the inimitable Zen Master, Kobori Roshi, of Daitoku-ji temple in Kyoto. Referring to Buddhist practitioners as "ripening persimmons," Kobori says there is no more effective ripener than soaking the mind in samadhi (deep concentration) through the practice of zazen (sitting meditation). The second article, "On Practicing Tranquility," comes to us from K. G. von Dürckheim, who has been called the most influential Zen teacher in Europe. His theme, the "inexhaustible power that arises simply from sitting still," recalls the old Zen saying, "Sitting, only sitting, and the grass grows green by itself." Robert Aitken, an illustrious member of the first generation of American Zen masters, follows with "The Body of the Buddha," which discusses the practice of meditation against the background of the traditional doctrine of the Buddha's three bodies (*Trikaya*). Mary Stein writes on the martial art of Aikido ("the way of harmoniously blended energy") whose attentional practices appear cognate with those of Buddhism. Stein finds herself wondering whether the long-term practice of such disciplines might actually reconfigure our neural pathways. The final article, "The Practice of Attention" is a review of meditation practices from a number of spiritual traditions and a synthetic psychological sketch of how such practices may be understood to erode the 'false self' and contribute to the progress of awakening.

Chapter Three, 'Nonduality and Freedom,' is mostly the preserve of frequent *Parabola* contributor Frederick Franck. "Beyond Duality" is Franck's appreciation of the wisdom of the great medieval Japanese Zen Master, Dogen, by way of a review of K. Tanahashi's *Moon in a Dewdrop*. "Dürckheim's Zen," is his review of that author's penetrating psychological study, *Zen and Us*. Franck uses "Notes on the Koan" to comment not only on the most well-known approaches to Zen practice — Soto and Rinzai — but to introduce us to the originality of "Bankei's Zen," whose eponym he nominates as the greatest of all Japanese masters. His fourth and final piece in this chapter is nothing less than a mini-anthology of non-dualist poetry from Buddhism and Christianity. His Buddhist sources are Chinese and Japanese Zen masters, while his sole Christian source is Angelus Silesius, a little-known 17th century German Christian mystic whose simple rhymed verses strike us as remarkably edifying. The chapter culminates with Conrad Hyers' "The Smile of Truth," a delightful analysis of Zen's comic spirit which reminds us that silence is not the only way to slip the trap of words. There is also laughter.

One of this book's proudest moments is Chapter Four's reprise of E. F. Schumacher's "Buddhist Economics" from his widely influential *Small is Beautiful*. In the spheres of economics and social well-being, says Schumacher, the Buddha's Middle Way lies between a society of materialist heedlessness and one of traditionalist immobility. Because Buddhism sees the essence of civilization not as the multiplication of wants but as the purification of character, Buddhist economics is the art and science of attaining deeply satisfactory results from materially modest means.

Chapter Five explores the Teacher/Student relationship with two articles each from the Zen and Tibetan traditions. K. G. von Dürckheim's "The Call for the Master," examines the three senses of "master" — outer master, inner master, eternal master — and reveals how "student" "master," and "Way" co-create one another. William Segal guides us through the 10 Oxherding Pictures, an allegorical exposition of the path to Enlightenment that has been used as a teaching device in Ch'an and Zen monasteries for over 800 years. "Taming the Wild Horse" is an interview with Lobsang Lhalungpa that probes the challenges Tibetan Dharma-teachers face in the West. And in "The Transmission of Blessings," Deshung Rinpoche memorably describes his sense of how, in a well-evolved relationship between a qualified teacher and an apt student, the awakened qualities of the former actually extend into the latter. Rinpoche's closing remarks on the endlessness of the *bodhisattva* path set the stage for J. van de Wetering's whimsical closing piece, "Now What?"

In Chapter Six, 'Pulling Weeds,' two teachers respond to errors on the path. In "The Middle Way," Robert Aitken addresses the lure of spiritual materialism and the problem of becoming attached to nonattachment. In "The Real and the Mirage," an interviewer receives surprising responses from Mu Soeng, director of the Barre Center for Buddhist Studies, regarding the commodification of the *bodhisattva* ideal, the inaptness of the word "spiritual" in Buddhist contexts, and misconceptions of both *dukkha* and Buddha-nature.

The articles of Chapter Seven, On Buddhist Ethics, address the moral dimensions of awakening. Jesus' yardstick for spiritual maturity — "by their fruits shall ye know them" — is beloved by Buddhists. Tibetan teachers regularly remind us that wisdom lacking compassion is no wisdom at all. Or, as His Holiness the Dalai Lama has memorably put it, "My religion is kindness." The epigraphs to the chapter recall two of the Buddha's key qualities — the compassion that sparked his decision to abandon ordinary life and his abiding conviction that nobility was a matter of moral character, not heredity or outward piety. The interview with Tara Tulku Rinpoche, "High Resolve," is a magisterial discussion of the skills required on the *bodhisattva* path. Especially poignant here are Rinpoche's remarks on the cultivation of gratitude through an awareness of the myriad ways in which countless beings, unknown to us, are kind to us. In "The Excellence of Bodhichitta," Pema Chödrön, probably the best known Buddhist nun of our times, writes movingly of the compassionate element in this "intention toward Enlightenment." In an interview called "Changing the Impossible," His Holiness the Dalai Lama addresses the challenge of overcoming of life's obstacles. The chapter closes with an anecdote on compassion from the writings of Alexandra David-Neel and a few cryptic lessons from "Zen Master Raven" provided by Robert Aitken.

Chapter Eight's 'Tibetan Blessings' begin with Robert Thurman's "Tibet, Mystic Nation in Exile," a richly informed tribute to the global historical significance of Tibet and its Buddhist culture. "The Fullness of Emptiness" is an interview with the Dalai Lama that seeks his counsel on the meanings of freedom and wholeness and on the challenge of living in two worlds. Miranda Shaw's "Delight in This World," reveals and revels in the ecstatic sensibility of the Tantric path and its affirmation of sexuality as a way of awakening. Apropos Shaw, the chapter's epilogue, "The Real Is in You," belongs to the 8th century yogini, Yeshe Tsogyel, who is said to have helped Padmasambhava bring Buddhist teachings to Tibet.

The "Buddha-Fields" of Chapter Nine express the Buddhist belief that every awakening human location generates a field of positive influence in the world. In "Building the Buddha-Field," J. L. Walker reflects on the process of creating a Tibetan sand mandala to explain how each of us, by moving through our days intentionally, mindfully, generously and patiently, fashion Buddha-Fields of attractive, healing energy. In "This Quiet Place that Buddhas Love," Walker, taking a cue from the great Tibetan yogi, Milarepa, contemplates the ways in which Nature teaches Dharma. And in "Of the Same Root," another great voice of the first generation of American Zen Masters, Philip Kapleau, asks us carefully to consider our relationship to the speechless creatures with whom we share this rare existence.

The epigraph to Chapter Ten, 'On Pilgrimage,' commemorates the Buddha's suggestion that one visit the places where he was born, reached enlightenment, set the wheel of Dharma rolling across the earth (i.e., gave his first sermon) and died — Lumbini, Bodh-Gaya, Sarnath and Kushinagara, respectively. Having made this circuit, I hope the reader will not mind if I add one item to the itinerary that should not be missed: Shravasti, where lie ruins of the Jetavana monastery built on land donated by the grateful disciple, Anathapindika, and where the Buddha spent many a rainy season in quiet retreat. In this chapter's sole item, "A New Dwelling," Tara Tulku Rinpoche responds to questions about the nature of Buddhist pilgrimage.

Among all of the reminders that the Buddha could have chosen to impart in the moments before his death, he chose these: "Impermanent are all formations. Strive diligently for freedom." The two thoughts are closely connected.

It is *because* formations are impermanent, because there is finally nothing that can be clung to nor any self-same person who can do the clinging, that final freedom is possible. Therefore to 'study' Buddhism is largely to 'study' impermanence — in every moment and mood and season and stage of life — so as to comprehend the constantly changing constellation of evanescent events that one is. Chapter 11, 'This Too Shall Pass,' begins with Paul Jordan-Smith's retelling of a story long-used to convey the Buddha's "no-self" doctrine. In it, King Menander challenges a Buddhist monk, Nagasena, to make a coherent case for this counterintuitive teaching. Conrad Hyers follows with "Swimming in the Ocean of Becoming," a Zen perspective on death. Gomang Khen Rinpoche offers Tibetan Buddhist teachings on death and rebirth with reference to the *Tibetan Book of the Dead*. Finally, in "The Experience of Change," in a conversation with Daniel Goleman, the Dalai Lama grapples with the subject of time.

A final word needs to be said about the mix of articles in this book. The Buddhist schools best known to Western converts (as distinct from those of Asian immigrant communities) are Japan's Zen, Tibet's Vajrayana, and the Vipassana (i.e., "penetrative seeing") Meditation movement of southeast Asia's Theravada tradition. Compared with the former two, the latter receives comparatively little attention here. Accidents of time and place explain why. Zen and Vajrayana have institutional presences in America that predate those of the Vipassana movement by several decades. Both Zen and Vajrayana have vibrant hubs in New York where *Parabola* is published. And both of them are schools of the Mahayana form of Buddhism that has dominated the interest of Western academics in the late twentieth century. By contrast, the Vipassana movement in the West started to gather steam only in the mid-seventies and did not grow prolifically until the last 15 years. Cultural lag accounted for, we can therefore be confident that the voices of the Theravada and Vipassana traditions will speak more frequently in *Parabola*'s future issues. Yet it is also well to remember that at the time the Buddha taught there existed neither Zen, nor Vajrayana, nor Theravada, nor any other of the world's myriad Buddhisms. Once asked to encapsulate his entire teaching in a few words, the Buddha did so in terms that outflank all divisions of school, lineage, or sect:

Sabbapapassa akaranam
kusalassa upasampada
Sacittapariyodapanam
etam buddhana sasanam.

Avoid evil,
Cultivate the good,
Purify your mind —
This is the teaching of all awakened ones. [4]

1   Roger Corless, *The Vision of Buddhism* (New York: Paragon, 1989) 19.

2   Thomas Merton, *The Asian Journal of Thomas Merton* (New York: New Directions, 1968) 4-5.

3   Thomas Merton 343.

4   *Dhammapada* 183.

•

CHAPTER ONE

TURNING POINTS

I, Buddha, who wept with all my brother's tears,

Whose heart was broken by a whole world's woe,

Laugh and am glad, for there is liberty!

Ho! ye who suffer! know

Ye suffer from yourselves. None else compels

None other holds you that ye live and die,

And whirl upon the wheel, and hug and kiss

Its spokes of agony.

—Edwin Arnold, *Light of Asia*

Parabola
Volume: 17.4
Power and Energy

Discovering the Silence

Thomas Merton

Polonnaruwa with its vast area under trees. Fences. Few people. No beggars. A dirt road. Lost. Then we find Gal Vihara and the other monastic complex stupas. Cells. Distant mountains, like Yucatan.

The path dips down to Gal Vihara: a wide, quiet hollow, surrounded with trees. A low outcrop of rock with a cave cut into it, and beside the cave a big seated Buddha on the left, a reclining Buddha on the right, and Ananda, I guess, standing by the head of the reclining Buddha. In the cave, another seated Buddha. The vicar general, shying away from "paganism," hangs back and sits under a tree reading the guidebook. I am able to approach the Buddhas barefoot and undisturbed, my feet in wet grass, wet sand. Then the silence of the extraordinary faces. The great smiles. Huge and yet subtle. Filled with every possibility, questioning nothing, knowing everything, rejecting nothing, the peace not of emotional resignation but of Madhyamika, of sunyata, that has seen through every question without trying to discredit anyone or anything—*without refutation*—without establishing some other argument. For the doctrinaire, the mind that needs well-established positions, such peace, such silence, can be frightening. I was knocked over with a rush of relief and thankfulness at the *obvious* clarity of the figures, the clarity and fluidity of shape and line, the design of the monumental bodies composed into the rock shape and landscape, figure, rock, and tree. And the sweep of bare rock sloping away on the other side of the hollow, where you can go back and see different aspects of the figures.

Looking at these figures I was suddenly, almost forcibly, jerked clean out of the habitual, half-tied vision of things, and an inner clearness, clarity, as if exploding from the rocks themselves, became evident and obvious. The queer *evidence* of the reclining figure, the smile, the sad smile of Ananda standing with arms folded (much more "imperative" than Da Vinci's Mona Lisa because completely simple and straightforward). The thing about all this is that there is no puzzle, no problem, and really no "mystery." All problems are resolved and everything is clear, simply because what matters is clear. The rock, all matter, all life, is charged with dharmakaya … everything is emptiness and everything is compassion. I don't know when in my life I have ever had such a sense of beauty and spiritual validity running together in one aesthetic illumination. Surely, with Mahabalipuram and Polonnaruwa my Asian pilgrimage has come clear and purified itself. I mean, I know and have seen what I was obscurely looking for. I don't know what else remains but I have now seen and have pierced through the surface and have got beyond the shadow and the disguise. This is Asia in its purity, not covered over with garbage, Asian or European or American, and it is clear, pure, complete. It says everything; it needs nothing. And because it needs nothing it can afford to be silent, unnoticed, undiscovered. It does not need to be discovered. It is we, Asians included, who need to discover it.

Parabola
Volume: 25.3
The Teacher

NO OTHER TEACHINGS

From a new translation of *Siddhartha*

Hermann Hesse

At first light, a follower of the Buddha's, one of his oldest monks, went through the garden, calling everyone to him who had newly taken refuge in the teaching, so he could invest them with the yellow robe and instruct them in the initial precepts and duties of their new condition. Govinda pulled himself away from his childhood friend, embracing him one more time, and joined the procession of neophytes.

But Siddhartha wandered through the grove, thinking.

There Gotama, the Exalted One, encountered him. Siddhartha greeted him respectfully, and as the Buddha's gaze was so full of kindness and quietude, the youth took courage and asked the Venerable One's permission to address him. Without speaking, the Exalted One nodded his assent.

Siddhartha said: "Yesterday, O Exalted One, it was granted to me to hear your wondrous teaching. Together with my friend, I came from afar to hear the teaching. And now my friend is going to remain with you; he has taken refuge in you. I, however, am about to resume my wanderings."

"As you please," said the Venerable One politely.

"I speak far too boldly," Siddhartha continued, "but I would not like to leave the Exalted One without having straightforwardly communicated my thoughts to him. Would the Venerable One grant me a further moment's hearing?"

Silently the Buddha nodded assent.

Siddhartha said: "There is one thing in your teaching, most venerable sir, that I admire above everything else. Everything in your teaching is perfectly clear and irrefutable. You show the world as a never-broken, perfect chain, an eternal chain consisting of causes and their effects. Never has this been so clearly perceived and so incontrovertibly presented. Truly every brahmin's heart must beat faster in his breast when, through your teaching, he glimpses the world as a perfectly linked whole, without a break, clear as a crystal, not dependent on anything random, not dependent on the gods. ... But now, according to your own doctrine, this unity and consistency of all things is nevertheless broken at one point; through one small gap, there flows into this world of unity something alien, new, something that did not exist before, that cannot be demonstrated and proven. This is your own teaching of the overcoming of the world, of liberation. But by this small gap, this small break, the unified and eternal cosmic lawfulness, is again quashed and invalidated. Please pardon me for bringing up this objection."

Gotama had listened to him quietly, unmoved. Now in his kindly, polite, and clear voice, the Perfect One spoke: "You have heard the teaching, brahmin's son. Good for you for having pondered it so deeply. You have found a gap in it, a flaw. May you continue to ponder that. But beware, you who are greedy for knowledge, of the jungle of opinions and the battle of words. Opinions are worth little. They can be beautiful or ugly, anyone can espouse or reject them. But the teaching that you heard from me is not my opinion, and its aim is not to explain the world to those who are greedy for knowledge. It has a different aim—liberation from suffering. This is what Gotama teaches, nothing else."

"Please do not be angry with me, Exalted One," the youth said. "It was not to contend with you, not to fight with you over words, that I spoke the way I did. You are indeed right; opinions are worth little. But allow me to say one thing more: Not for a moment have I doubted you. I have not doubted for a moment that you are a buddha, that you have attained the goal, the supreme goal, toward which so many thousands of brahmins and brahmins' sons strive. You have found liberation from death. This came to you as a result of your own seeking on your own path, through thought, through meditation, through realization, through enlightenment. It did not come to you through a teaching! And that is my idea, O Exalted One—nobody attains enlightenment through a teaching. O Venerable One, you will not be able to express to anyone through words and doctrine what happened to you in the moment of your enlightenment! Much is contained in the doctrine of the enlightened Buddha, much is taught in it—to live in an honest and upright way, to avoid evil. But there is one thing that this so clear and so venerable teaching does not contain; it does not contain the mystery of what the Exalted One himself experienced, he alone among hundreds of thousands. This is what I understood and realized when I listened to the teaching. This is the reason I am going to continue my wandering—not to find another or a better teaching, for I know that one does not exist, but in order to leave behind all teachings and all teachers and to attain my goal on my own or die. But many a time will I recall this day, O Exalted One, and this moment when my eyes have beheld a holy man."

The Buddha gazed at the ground in stillness; his inscrutable countenance remained still in perfect equanimity.

"May your thoughts," the Venerable One said slowly, "not be false ones. May you reach the goal! But tell me: Have you seen the host of my shramanas, my many brothers who have taken refuge in the teaching? And do you believe, unknown shramana, that it would be better for all of them to abandon the teaching and return to the life of the world and its pleasures?"

"Such an idea is far from my mind," exclaimed Siddhartha. "May they all remain with the teaching, may they all reach their goal! It is not for me to judge the life of another! It

is only for myself that I must judge, that I must choose and refuse. Liberation from ego is what we shramanas are seeking, O Exalted One. If I were your disciple, O Venerable One, I am afraid it might befall me that my ego would be pacified and liberated only seemingly, only illusorily, that in reality it would survive and grow great, for then I would make the teaching, my discipleship, my love of you, and the community of monks into my ego!"

With a half smile, with an unshakable brightness and kindliness, Gotama looked the stranger in the eye and dismissed him with a scarcely visible gesture.

"You are clever, shramana," said the Venerable One. "You know how to speak cleverly, my friend. Beware of excessive cleverness!"

The Buddha moved on, and his gaze and his half smile remained engraved in Siddhartha's memory forever.

I have never seen anyone with such a gaze, I have never seen anyone smile, sit, and walk in such a way, he thought. In truth that is just the way I would like to be able to gaze, smile, sit, and walk—so free, so worthy, so hidden, so open, so childlike, and so mysterious. Truly only a person who has penetrated to the inmost part of his self gazes and walks like that. I, too, shall surely try to penetrate to the inmost part of my self.

I have seen a man, one and only one, Siddhartha thought, before whom I had to lower my gaze. Before no other will I ever lower my gaze, no other. No other teaching will seduce me, since this teaching has not seduced me.

The Buddha robbed me, thought Siddhartha, he robbed me, yet he gave me even more. He robbed me of my friend, who believed in me and now believes in him, who was my shadow and is now Gotama's shadow. But he gave me Siddhartha, he gave me myself.

From Hesse, Herman. *Siddhartha*. Trans. Sherab Chödzin Kohn. Boston: Shambhala Publications, Inc., 2000: 26-29.

•

CHAPTER TWO

"A Well-Trained Mind..."

More than those who hate you,
More than all your enemies,
An ill-trained mind does greater harm.
More than your mother or father,
More than all who love you,
A well-trained mind does greater good.

—*Dhammapada*

As irrigators guide water,
As archers straighten an arrow's shaft,
As carpenters carve wood,
So the wise shape their minds.

—*Dhammapada*

The [Path-farer] is always mindful and purposeful whether in going
forward or back, in looking before or behind, in drawing in or stretching out
his limbs, in conduct of cloak bowl and robes, in eating and drinking,
in chewing and tasting, in attending to the needs of nature, in walking or standing
still, in sitting or in lying down, asleep or awake, speaking or silent. As he
dwells thus unflagging, ardent, and purged of self, all worldly thoughts that idly
come and go are abandoned, and with their abandonment his heart
within grows established and planted fast, settled and concentrated.—
In this way, a [Path-farer] develops mindfulness of body.

—*Kayagata-Sati-Sutta*

Parabola
Volume: 10.1
Wholeness

THE RIPENING PERSIMMON

Interview with Kobori Nanrei Roshi

*Of the great Eastern traditions, perhaps the one to receive
the most publicity and to be most distorted in the West is Zen
Buddhism. The word "Zen" has entered our vocabulary and has
come to mean, in the inevitable devaluation of common coin-
age, anything from "indirect" to "eccentric." In order to catch
a glimpse of the authentic nature of Zen Buddhism and its
teachings about wholeness,* Parabola *asked Milhoko Okamura-
Bekku, secretary-companion for fourteen years to the great
Buddhist scholar Daisetz Suzuki, and currently on the Editorial Board of Kyoto's* The Eastern Buddhist, *to interview her
friend of twenty-eight years, Kobori Nanrei Roshi.*

*Born in 1918 in Kyoto, Kobori Roshi graduated in 1949
from Otani University and then began Zen training under
the guidance of Master Shimada Kikusen of Kokei Sodo of
the Gifu Prefecture. Twenty-one years later he became Head
Priest of the Ryōkō-in Sub-Temple of the Daitokuji Monastery in Kyoto, where he continues to reside while attending to
his many duties, including acting as the Honorary President of
the First Zen Institute of America in Japan, and while pursuing the crafts of pottery, painting, calligraphy, and poetry.*

Equipped with questions formulated by Parabola,

Ms. Okamura-Bekku met with Kobori Roshi on a warm late-summer's day in a room at the Sub-Temple. We wish to thank her for her willingness to conduct the interview for us, and for her care in translating and editing Kobori Roshi's responses. (Interviewed by Milhoko Okamura-Bekku.)

—Parabola *Editors*

Parabola: *I have heard the term "true man" used in the Zen tradition. I suppose that means the whole human being, the whole that is possible for a human being. Does it mean that this person lives simultaneously in two worlds?*

Kobori Nanrei Roshi: I suppose by "two worlds" you mean the worlds of the finite and the infinite, the form and the formless, the mortal and the immortal, the physical and the metaphysical, and so on. For the "true man," the two worlds work as one. Finite is infinite, infinite finite; the finite working in the infinite, the infinite working in the finite.

Actually, Buddhists do not like to talk about "two" or "one"; for "two" may remain "two" and yet be one; to speak of "one" already presupposes "two," "three," "four," and so on, and therefore can never be simply "one." So the finite and infinite are two and yet not-two.

As regards my own view of the experience: When the "true man" is realized in the state of so-called identity, the finite and the infinite, nothing "religious" can come from it. This is why Zen, which emphasizes the identity aspect, often appears irreligious or totally anti-religious at times. On the other hand, when one sees this same experience in the light of the infinity aspect, or when one can move away and look upon infinity objectively, so to speak, one is filled with a heightened sense of thankfulness, which develops into a deeper and fuller understanding of *karuna* (love, compassion) and *pranidhana* (prayer). This is the finite seen working in the infinite, and I would say that religious life in its truest sense begins here.

A recent trip I made to China brought home to me again how very much Zen stems from the Taoist traditions of Lao Tzu and Chuang Tzu. Even the term "true man," which the Chinese Zen Master Rinzai first used so effectively in the Zen tradition, was a borrowing from Taoism. This was natural. Buddhist thought was a latecomer that had to plant itself in native Taoist soil. Zen is, so to speak, a strange dragon with a Taoist torso, Confucian feet, and the Buddhist enlightenment-experience for its eyes. The ideal for the Taoists was to experience immortality in the literal sense; they conceived of three types of Immortals, the second of which was called the "true man."

Parabola: *Are human beings, then, in any way unfinished, incomplete?*

KNR: I would say that the "true man" is constantly in the process of ripening. It is often said that *prajna* (enlightenment, wisdom) has another face called *karuna* (love, compassion), that the two are different sides of a coin; or that they are one and the same thing, *prajna* is *karuna*, *karuna* is *prajna*. But in actual practice, I have found that the two are not immediately identified. Before *prajna* can begin to develop into the *karuna* aspect, one must go through considerable maturing. It is like a persimmon, sharp and astringent at first, but warmed by the autumn sun it begins to sweeten. Even its coloring gradually mellows. When still high on a branch, hard and green, in can benefit no one. But once it falls to the ground and disintegrates, other lives can partake of it, while its seeds go on to take new life.

But it takes a long time for a human being to mature in such a way. It may very well be an eternal task. From the Buddhist point of view, the human task of self-perfecting will never be completed until all beings have become *prajna-karuna* existences.

Parabola: *How would you describe the "realization" of the "fully-developed" person?*

KNR: The "realization" in Zen would be the awakening of the "true man" in oneself. This is the self that experiences a complete and thorough baptism of *samadhi*, or *ku* (emptiness). It lies in the nature of *samadhi* to dissolve or melt away the ego and any or all conceptual and obstructive elements. Once this happens a fresh ego replaces the old. This fresh ego opens out a whole new dimension known as *karuna* (love, compassion).

This is the start of a complete new outlook in which, "I am the other, and the other is myself." The barriers—which were really not there from the start—fall away. It is a world in which exclusivism is rendered meaningless, and wars unthinkable. A general feeling of affirmation and support, of acceptance of differences becomes second nature—a natural and effortless attitude. It is a spirit of "If you don't have, let me give you mine." One puts one's own interest aside and considers the other's benefit first. This is the "true man" in action. He is not an immortal, which is what the term "true man" would signify in Taoism, for example, or a god. He is a *bodhisattva*, an enlightened being. He is not a buddha yet. You don't want to become a buddha—then you just sit back and do nothing all day!

Parabola: *Does the experience of* samadhi *open a person, free him once for all from the ego?*

KNR: As I said before, it is essential in Buddhism for one's whole being to be totally immersed in *samadhi* or *ku*.

In Buddhism the ego is the main culprit. It insists on setting itself up against others, creating barriers and obstacles, oppositions and contradictions. Conflict and strife are all rooted in the ego. It is therefore all important that this ego undergo the most radical immersion in the sea of *samadhi* where obstructive, contradictory concepts are washed away. Yet to stop at this point would be to dwell in *nirvana*. Out of this *samadhi* a fresh and new self emerges. Compassion is born from here. Such a self can be described as "free and open."

Parabola: *Does "openness" mean the non-obstruction of life forces in oneself?*

KNR: I'm not sure I understand this question correctly, but if I can speak of a "life force" in the context of what I have been talking about so far, it would be the force of the ego dashing itself against other egos or obstacles in an attempt to overcome and conquer. Strangely enough, this very same force or energy is also what enables the ego to steer itself towards the "true man" as it aspires to be purified. Without the ego there would be no life force or movement; there would only be stillness.

If we must give this force a name we might call it "compassion-*prajna*." Like the power of Buddha's Will or Prayer, this vital impulse presses us forward in the direction of purity, and will not cease to do its work until all things have been thoroughly purified.

We may wonder why *prajna* (enlightenment, wisdom) takes *karuna* (compassion) as an indispensable partner. This is because *prajna* in itself is not a force. The *karuna* element must come into play in order for the two working together as one to be a living force. Once the ego is relieved of its dualistic nature it moves freely in an open and unobstructed field.

Parabola: *The expression often used in Zen of "effortless effort" is often misunderstood, at least by outsiders, to mean passivity. But surely, even if the "Buddha nature" is inherent in everyone, there must be an active inner effort necessary for this "true man" in oneself to be liberated and to manifest itself.*

KNR: The term "effortless effort" is another example of a Taoist expression appropriated by Zen. Originally in ancient China, the term meant simply naturalism. In the Zen context, this would be a mistake.

You know the wonderful story about a little boy who went outdoors to play. At the end of the day his mother, noticing his soiled clothes, asked, "Where did you go?" "Out," said the boy. "And what did you do?" "Nothing," he replied. Here is a delightful example of "effortless effort" at work. The little boy's day was obviously quite filled with many interesting activities. Yet as far as he was concerned it was all nothing.

As to the inner effort necessary, I would say, first of all, that you must have a firm faith or trust in your original self, or Buddha nature, or "true man." From this beginning you can work out your own development towards the awakening experience. A factor of utmost importance in this quest, however, is what is called in Zen "the great doubt." This is a persistent and a most urgent desire on the part of the seeker to come in direct contact with his original self, or the "true man." He would not rest until emancipation had been achieved. The "great doubt" is like a "thorn sticking in the heart," crying out to be removed. Without this "inner effort" no amount of quiet sitting in *dhyana* or *samadhi* will be fruitful.

As I have repeatedly stated, it is a necessary part of this effort to immerse your total self in *samadhi*; without *samadhi*, Buddhism cannot be actualized. You do it in order to purify or wash away all traces of the so-called "colors" that you have hitherto dyed yourself in—a sort of spiritual bleaching. It must be done in a most thoroughgoing manner. You may think you have come as close to pure white as you possibly can. But "white" too is a color and must be done away with. Even the Buddha, white as he may be, is an obstacle here. When you have reached this point, with everything washed away in emptiness, there is no room left

to assert this or that about anything. Out of this your original, untainted self emerges, the Buddha nature in you which in itself has no form, no title, or color.

The chief obstacle in this pursuit is usually one's own mind; it refuses to acknowledge that the intellect is not omniscient or omnipotent. Since the intellect's function is to divide and to discriminate it is therefore a totally unsuitable instrument for perceiving the whole.

One's greatest support in this endeavor are the many patriarchs and enlightened beings, both past and present. They are living examples for us to emulate. Buddhists talk very much about having the good karma of encountering such beings, or even of hearing of them—it is the greatest blessing one can hope for—for how else can we hope to be delivered?

Parabola: *What then is the proper role of the mind? There must be some relationship of knowledge to feeling in one's search for wholeness. And what role does the body play in this search?*

KNR: I am not really concerned about dividing knowledge and feeling. The important thing is to take your whole being—feeling, knowledge, body, mind, all if it—immerse it totally in *samadhi*, and have it purified. This should bring the usual functions of your mind to a standstill, so to speak. It also works to disentangle and liberate the involuntary nervous system, which controls our breathing, heartbeat, and so on. Once the balance of the involuntary nervous system has been sufficiently restored, then we may think about being analytical.

Parabola: *Is part of the effort of development directed toward subduing the lower energies natural to the human being? Are they to be eliminated entirely, or can they be transformed and become part of a higher force?*

KNR: As to the question of "lower" or "higher" forces or energies, Buddhists refrain from making such distinctions. They are all one energy at work. I might add that in Buddhist training what may be considered man's "higher forces" are often more troublesome to deal with than his so-called lower ones. Usually speaking, the higher energies are imagined to belong to the realm of sophisticated thought, the realm in which man distinguishes himself above all the other living creatures. But it is just here, in the midst of his most characteristic activity, that the root cause of human disorder is best observable. The remedy often involves a painstaking process, as all "thinking" is structured on dualistic grounds. To extricate himself from the maze of contradictions arising out of his own thought world is no mean feat.

The lower forces are less complicated and serious as they are aspects inherent in man's instinctive nature. As to how lower forces can be of help, well, these energies are mostly needed to stay alive. We could not go, for instance, without filling our stomach when we are hungry.

As far as Buddhism is concerned, the main thing is the crushing of the ego; and one is to go about it with all one's forces—irrespective of higher or lower.

Parabola: *Yet there are things in myself, for instance, that I would like to change. What should my attitude be toward them? Should I hate them, study them, try to eliminate them, learn to accept them? Or can they be transformed into something of a higher nature?*

KNR: A right attitude to have is to believe in the possibility of the "true man" in yourself, and diligently apply yourself to the task of awakening to it.

Once more the question wishes to divide good from bad, love from hate, high from low. But no such divisions can be made. All such differentiations are artificially set up by the intellectual mind. It is in the nature of the intellect to divide things. The mind is a convenient but treacherous instrument. The pitfalls of intellectual activity are constant and many. Be sure that the "true man" does not carry a divided image.

Certainly, religious life is spent in regulating and moderating one's daily thoughts and behavior. Care is taken that cravings or desires be kept to a minimum. Long established rules teach that excess or overindulgence of any sort will upset the balance of a healthful mind and body which is requisite to awakening the "true man" in oneself. Desires are accepted as being life-sustaining instincts, but having made the affirmation, moderation is practiced. We are creatures of habit. It is not always easy to rid ourselves of undesirable habits. Sometimes we may find ourselves spending the rest of our days trying to improve our ways. An orderly and regulated life is important for one's inner development. A sporadic attempt will not do. If you live in a temple, as I do, you rise early in the morning. You attend to your garden and do other menial tasks. These moments provide an excellent opportunity for gaining a deeper insight into yourself.

As for "transforming into something higher," if by this you mean some spiritual realm as opposed to a physical and material realm, the two aspects are inseparable; they are in fact one and the same reality.

Parabola: *What is the major difference between one who has begun the journey towards realization and one who ignores this possibility?*

KNR: I supposed the real difference lies in the quality of life as it is lived from moment to moment. The difference may not be apparent. One may appear healthy and cheerful, secure in one's job and surrounded by material comfort. But all worldly things being relative, we must assume that the opposite conditions of life are equally immanent. Frequently, behind the happy face lurks the shadow of deep fears and anxiety. One can choose, on the other hand, to set oneself free of such fears by resolving the dualistic situation and living in greater contentment. Qualitatively, I might say, it is the difference between pure gold and gold plate.

Parabola
Volume: 21.3
Peace

ON PRACTICING TRANQUILITY

Karlfried Graf von Dürckheim

There is a story that tells of Meister Eckhart's meeting with a poor man:

"You may be holy," says Eckhart, "but what made you holy, brother?" And the answer comes: "My sitting still, my elevated thoughts, and my union with God." It is useful for our present theme to note that the practice of sitting still is given pride of place.

In the Middle Ages people were well aware of the inexhaustible power that arises simply from sitting still. After that time, knowledge of the purifying power of stillness and its practice was, in the West, largely lost. The tradition of preparing man for the breakthrough of transcendence by means of inner quiet and motionless sitting has been preserved in the East to the present day. Even in cases where practice is apparently directed not to immobility but towards activity—as in archery, sword fighting, wrestling, painting, flower arrangement—it is always the inner attitude of quiet and not the successful performance of the ways which is regarded as of fundamental importance.

Once a technique has been mastered, any inadequate performance is mirrored in wrong attitudes. The traditional knowledge of the fact that it is possible for a man to be inwardly cleansed solely through the practice of right posture has kept alive the significance of correct sitting. The inner quiet which arises when the body is motionless and in its best possible form can become the source of transcendental experience. By emptying ourselves of all those matters that normally occupy us we become receptive to Greater Being.

It should be understood that the transformation which is brought about by means of meditation is not merely a change in man's inner life, but a renewal of his whole person. It is a mistake to imagine that enlightenment is no more than an experience which suddenly brings fresh inward understanding, as a brilliant physicist may have a sudden inspiration which throws new light on his work and causes a re-ordering of his whole system of thought. Such an experience leaves the person himself unchanged. True enlightenment has nothing to do with this kind of sudden insight. When it occurs, it has the effect of so fundamentally affecting and shaking the whole person that he himself, as well as his total physical existence in the world, is completely transformed.

To what extent the habit of sitting still can impress and change us becomes clear only when we have taken pains to practice it. After a short time we find ourselves asking: how is it possible that such a simple exercise can have such far-reaching effects on body and soul? Sitting still, we begin to realize, is not what we had imagined physical or spiritual practice to be. We are faced, therefore, with the question: "What is it we are really practicing if, although both are affected, it is neither body nor spirit?" The answer to this is that the person who practices is himself *being practiced.* The one who is worked upon is the Person in his original totality, who is present beneath and beyond all possible differentiation into the many and various physical, spiritual, and mental aspects. In so far as we regard and value ourselves as incarnate persons, certain manifestations in our life move from their accustomed shadow into the light of understanding. Thus our moods and postures take on new meaning. So long as we think of body and soul as two separate entities, we regard moods simply as "feelings," and look upon bodily attitudes and breathing as merely physical manifestations. When, however, the whole person is recognized as a "thou," it is no longer possible to separate the body from the soul. Once it becomes a question of transformation, our basic inner moods, together with all the gestures and postures that express them, acquire new significance. They are the means through which we grow aware of, manifest ourselves, and become physically present in the world. ...

The so-called "peace" of the world-ego, illustrated by the bourgeois aim of a "quiet life," comes about when all inner movement and growth have stopped. Of quite a different quality is the peace of inner being and the life which strives to manifest itself through it. This kind of peace can only prevail where nothing further interrupts the movement towards becoming. To achieve such an attitude to life is the aim of all practice and meditation; it can never represent a state of "having arrived" but is always a process of "being on the way." Such practice, therefore, is by no means acceptable to all. There are many who throng to the so-called prophets who promise a cheap kind of peace to troubled mankind. But such "masters" simply betray man by hiding from him the real cause of his anxiety, which lies in the desire for transformation inherent in his inner-most being.

From Karlfried Graf von Dürckheim, *Daily Life as Spiritual Exercise: The Way of Transformation*, translated by Ruth Lewinnek and P. L. Travers (London: Allen & Unwin, 1971), pp. 51–54, 58.

Parabola
Volume: 10.3
The Body

THE BODY OF THE BUDDHA

Robert Aitken

The body of the Buddha is my body and yours. "Yours" includes human and nonhuman, sentient and non-sentient—individually and collectively. "All beings by nature are Buddha," Hakuin Zenji says in his "Song of Zazen." "This very body is the Buddha."[1]

There is nothing that is not the Buddha body. In the Mahāyāna tradition, it is said that the historical Buddha, Śākyamuni, resolved his questions about suffering in the world and exclaimed, "Wonderful, wonderful! Now I see that all beings have the wisdom and virtue of Buddha. They cannot testify to that fact because of their delusions and preoccupations."

With this statement we have definition. All beings are the Buddha, but they cannot say so. They cannot acknowledge what is called Buddhahood: the emptiness, oneness, and uniqueness of their perceptions and all they perceive. They cannot acknowledge that delusions and preoccupations create suffering, yet have no substance.

The two elements of Śākyamuni's statement, the nature of beings, and their inability to formulate that nature, are the foundation of Buddhist experience, practice, and philosophy. Experience is the realization, by each according to individual capacity, of the truth Śākyamuni expressed. Practice is the way of realization, and philosophy is its post hoc formulation. I begin with the philosophy:

The three elements of Buddhahood, emptiness, oneness, and uniqueness, are the so-called "Three Bodies of the Buddha," the Dharmakāya, the Sambhogakāya, and the Nirmānakāya. All beings have these three qualities, as do all communities of beings, even the largest community, the universe itself.

The Dharmakāya is the "Pure and Clear Law Body." "Law," the etymological meaning of "Dharma" in Sanskrit, refers to the nature of things, animate and inanimate. In this context, the term refers to the infinite, fathomless void, charged with possibilities, that produces, infuses, and indeed is the "material" of all bodies. According to some Buddhists, one's body is only momentarily substantial. In the Zen view, and in the view of the Mahāyāna School generally, it has no substance, even for a moment.

Complementary to this emptiness, the Sambhogakāya is the body of fullness, or oneness, exemplified by the "Net of Indra" in Hua-yen philosophy. The whole universe is a vast, multidimensional net, with each point of the net a jewel that perfectly reflects and in fact contains all other jewels. "Your body is not your body, but is a constituent of all bodies."[2] The Sambhogakāya is known as the "Body of Bliss," a name that expresses the delight of freedom from the "small self" and oneness with all beings.

Finally, uniqueness, The Nirmānakāya is exemplified by Śākyamuni Buddha in the archetypal pantheon of the Three Bodies (the other two Bodies have their Buddhas too). Śākyamuni is surely a prime example of uniqueness,

but so am I. So is each "I." The earthworm and the nettle are individual; no other being will ever appear like this particular earthworm, this particular nettle.

Each of the Three Bodies is qualified and made possible by the other two. The potent void is the source and essence of being in its fullness and oneness. Uniqueness gives interpenetration its dynamism—without it, there would be no Chinese, as distinguished from the Norwegian, to be one with the Norwegian. And if in essence all things were not empty, then skins would be barriers, and unity would not be possible.

The Three Bodies of the Buddha are implicit in Śākyamuni's teaching, but it was his successors who formulated them, sometimes without being clear that work is necessary to realize them, and work is necessary to maintain and deepen that realization. Without practice philosophy is superstition. When he was very young, Dōgen Kigen looked at just one side of Śākyamuni's statement about all beings, and asked why he should train at all, since he was already intrinsically Buddha. This is like suggesting that one can harvest without first preparing the ground, and then planting and cultivating.

All forms of Buddhism that teach practice are designed to bring one to Śākyamuni's realization—though sometimes not until the next life, as in the Pure Land schools.

Practice in the Zen mode is a program of realization in this life, involving coordination of body, brain, and will, in directed meditation.

This is zazen. You sit, facing the wall, and place your legs in the half-lotus or full-lotus position. Lower your eyes, but do not completely close them. Breathe naturally, and count your inhalation and exhalation up to "ten," then up to "ten" again, and repeat. Try to settle yourself as you exhale. Keep your back straight, with your backbone bent slightly forward at your waist. Let your thoughts and feelings come and go, and pay no particular attention to them. Your practice of breath-counting is your home base, and your thoughts and feelings are your environment. When this environment entices you into some plan or memory, and you notice that you have drifted from your counting, then return home to "one" and begin again.

At first this is a practice of learning to concentrate. Then one discovers that each point in the breath-counting sequence is the only point in the whole universe, each point is the universe, and the body that counts and the universe are not separate. This experience is called makyō, "mysterious vision," a melting of the usual configurations of perception. Distinctions become blurred, or they disappear altogether. "Inside and outside become one,"[3] as do past, present, and future; tiny and huge;

life and no life. This is not realization, but it is a milestone on the path.

Kōan study follows breath-counting for the student who is interested in experiencing the Buddha's realization for himself or herself. This involves examination of the salient points in old Zen stories and making them clear. This act of making clear is called realization, and the first such experience is the most important. It is grace, if that word can be used by a Buddhist, after which everything is seen differently. One understands, more or less vividly, that the configurations which were blurred in makyō are really complementary, each completely true in itself, each identical with the other: I and that; time and no time; tiny and huge; form and emptiness; life and no life—in present time and place. As to the depth or quality of this first insight—it is likely to be rather superficial in nature, just a peep perhaps, something that will need further clarification in further practice.

I remember that when I first tried zazen many years ago, I could verify Śākyamuni's words a little. There was a tranquil tone in my breath-counting, reminiscent of the inner and outer calm I found as a child, listening to the silence of the house when I awoke in the night. This was an important hint for me. I also found that it was very difficult to attend to the simple act of counting my breaths, and I learned how readily I followed up on the least distraction. My mind turned out to be quite unsettled. This encounter with my delusions and preoccupations, my own suffering, pointed up my need to practice.

Zen practice is the work of the Zen student in the dōjō, the meditation hall, but that is only the beginning or foundation of one's life work in following the way of the Buddha. Dōgen Kigen said, "Zazen is itself realization,"[4] but realization is not limited to meditation on one's cushions. Singing and dancing are forms of profound truth, as Hakuin Ekaku said.

Unlike the way of zazen, the way of singing and dancing, and of eating and drinking, talking on the telephone, changing a diaper—this way of everyday life is not always so clearly set forth in the literature. Yet Zen Buddhism is not just a cult of people who sit around on cushions. As a Zen teacher, it is my responsibility to clarify what the essence of things has to do with the workaday world.

First of all, though the *Heart Sūtra* says that all perceptions and things perceived are empty, and there is "no eye, ear, nose, tongue, body, mind," we do see, hear, taste, and so on, as any child can testify. When the priest Tung-shan Liang-chieh was a child and his teacher instructed him in the doctrine of emptiness, he protested, "Well, I exist!"[5] The child of a physicist, hearing an exposition of the relatively vast reaches of space that lie between bits of matter, and

the weightless, yet not weightless nature of those bits, would probably object in a similar way. There is a certain experience of emptiness that comes with maturity, just as there is an experience of sex and an experience of death that appears when the time is ripe. Until one passes through such experiences, they are difficult to appreciate. The intellect alone cannot understand them.

Almost all Zen students understand that the way of the intellect is a byroad. They know that Śākyamuni's exclamation, "All beings have the wisdom and virtue of Buddha," was not just a simple deduction. At the same time, there is a widespread tendency to direct zazen toward analyzing the "delusions and preoccupations" which keep one from realizing one's own wisdom and virtue. The priority thus becomes therapy, rather than realization, and realization is postponed.

It is important to put one's priorities in order. Zazen has therapeutic results, but it is not useful to make therapy the primary target. Śākyamuni did not practice in order to emancipate himself and the world, but rather to understand the nature of suffering, and with this understanding came emancipation. I have an idea that therapy cannot be attained if it is the goal even in psychological practice. I suspect that good psychologists attain positive results with their clients by making the process interesting, and holding forth understanding as the mutual intention of their work. (One of my students, a psychologist, comments, "There is an esthetically satisfying quality to good therapy, which is to say that therapy is more art than science, and like all art, therapy is made narrow by our intentions and our goals, especially our virtuous ones.")

When I meet inquirers who have the conscious or unconscious purpose of correcting themselves, I try to encourage them, but I tell them that Zen is gnostic, a pursuit of knowledge. The process works when the motive is curiosity. If the motive is better human relations, then zazen can help bring improvement, but underlying questions about birth and death remain unanswered, and one's heart is not really put at ease.

The Buddha is the "King of Doctors," treating and curing all beings. When I asked the abbot of a large monastery in Kyoto about Zen practice for people with uncertain mental health, he replied, "Zen practice is for people who are exceptionally healthy." With the movement of Zen Buddhism to the West, the monastic walls came down, and anybody can enter.

When I speak of the Buddha as the King of Doctors, I am quoting Yung-chia, an early eighth-century Zen master, in his long poem in praise of realization, the *Cheng-tao ko*:

The sick meet the King of Doctors;
Why don't they recover?[6]

"They don't recover" because they—or we (Yung-chia includes us all)—expect the teaching to be medicine. It is not. The teaching is the prescription. Many people are content just to display the bottle.

Once the attendant of Bankei Yōtaku asked him, "How can one arrive at complete attainment?"

The master said, "On the whole, Zen students can reach seven or eight parts out of ten."

The attendant asked, "How does one get past them?"

The master said, "There is no way."

"They haven't reached complete attainment and there is no way that they can … Where does the fault lie?"

The master was silent for a moment. Then he said, "It's because, after all, their aspiration in the great Dharma is not strong enough."[7]

Two things should be said about this passage. The first is that some people have more capacity than others, as Dante makes clear in the *Paradiso*. Seven or eight parts for one person may be ten for another. All beings may be Buddha, but not everyone is Śākyamuni. It is appropriate to work toward deeper and clearer understanding, whatever one's insight may be, using great teachers like Sigmund Freud and his successors as well as those in the Zen lineage. At the same time, it is good to accept one's limitations, and enjoy one's own configurations.

The second point that should be made in connection with Bankei's observation relates to the quality of will or aspiration that is necessary. Concentration of mind is not a matter of tensing the muscles, as Simone Weil says.[8] Aspiration that is grim tends to be self-centered. Friends and family members are neglected or exploited. In my view, correct aspiration is a means that partakes of the end, a light, inclusive condition.

Will in Zen practice is not only light, it is delight. This is not an idea that is easy for the new student, struggling to bend into the half-lotus position, and enduring the pain of that unaccustomed position without moving for twenty-five minutes or longer, but even at such a time, one can find humor. Yamada Kōun Rōshi says, "Pain in the legs is the taste of Zen." Then looking around at his students, he says with a smile, "I wonder if you know what I mean!"

Thich Nhat Hanh says, "Sit with a half-smile."[9] When I look about the dōjō at the people sitting quietly and firmly, sometimes I will see someone wearing a broad smile. "Ah," I think, "a student with a strong will."

This kind of delight is different from ordinary, casual pleasure. It is an enjoyment of the emptiness of the self, of unity with all beings, and of the uniqueness of oneself and of birds and clouds and other people. Understanding the light nature of this enjoyment, quite short of any realization, one can stay light in the practice. However, if faith in the possibility of realization is faint, then the practice becomes difficult.

With realization the practice continues, even for Śākyamuni. This is a matter of maintaining a daily schedule of zazen, and of keeping aware of empty unity in the busiest times, when eating or cooking, talking or listening. Nyogen Senzaki used to say, "When you are at a party, and feel distracted by all the chatter, just close your eyes for a moment and you'll find your treasure right there." I would say that you don't even have to close your eyes.

One renews awareness of this treasure in the delight of ceremonies at the Zen center, as well as in daily zazen. See, for example, the Refuge Gāthā which Zen students recite regularly, as do all Buddhists:

I return to the Buddha;

I return to the Dharma;

I return to the Sangha.

Buddha, or realization; Dharma, the law; and Sangha, fellowship or harmony, are the Three Bodies of the Buddha, Dharmakāya, Sambhogakāya, and Nirmānakāya, set forth in different order. "I return to" is a translation of the original Sanskrit and Chinese words that also mean "I find my home in." To say, "I find my home in the Buddha," is to affirm that my home is already the Buddha. "I return to the Buddha," is to take Hakuin's words personally, "This very body is the Buddha." Likewise I find the Dharma, infinite emptiness, is none other than myself. I am the full and complete Body of Oneness, and I vow to realize that fact more and more clearly.

The Sambhogakāya, the Body of Oneness and Fullness, harmonizes self with its counterpart, the void. It joins all the relative counterparts, life and no life, time and no time, I and that. Sexual play and intercourse at their most loving are poignant models of the Sambhogakāya, bringing delight in mingling with the other. Sung-yüan Ch'ung-yüeh asked his disciples, "How is it that all the completely accomplished sages remain attached to the vermillion thread?"[10] The vermillion thread is the line of illusions and discriminations, according to Zenkei Shibayama, but the association of the color with women's undergarments and with sexual relations should not be glossed over. Sung-yüan's question points up the Buddha-nature of desires. If it is true that "This very body is the Buddha," then our practice must be directed toward its appropriate use, not toward its denial.

Vajrayāna people are fond of criticizing Zen students for their black robes, black cushions, and solemn faces, implying that we tend to shut ourselves from our natural being. They are right in some respects.

Dark, unpatterned clothing and black cushions help to minimize distractions in the dōjō, and encourage the deep-dream dimension of makyō, but solemn faces and the overemphasis on "great determination" and endurance reflect our samurai inheritance, an accretion on the Buddha Dharma that should be wiped away. For "samurai" read "male." In Far Eastern culture, the female virtues in women and in men tend to be covered over. In wiping the samurai from Zen practice, we expose gentle human nature that nurtures our own aspirations and those of all beings.

The highest and best kind of endurance, in the classification of the ten kinds of endurance, is *kūnin*, the endurance of one who knows that afflictions are empty.[11] Realization of this *kū*, this *śūnyatá*, this emptiness, is endurance transformed to delight. Lightly and joyfully, I return to the Buddha, Dharma, and Sangha. With each recitation of the Refuge Vows, I set forth my aspiration for more clarity, more understanding.

And more compassion. That is the upshot. When there is a selfless spirit, a sense of unity with other beings, and an acknowledgement that each person, animal, plant, stone, is unique—then the personal, human mind is the mind of the universe.

Notes:

1 Hakuin Ekaku, *Zazen Wasen.* "Hakuin Zenji's 'Song of Zazen,'" trans. Robert Aitken, *Taking the Path of Zen* (San Francisco: North Point Press, 1982).

2 Shaku Sōen, "The First Step in Meditation." First translated in a typescript broadside by Nyogen Senzaki.

3 Wu-men Hui-k'ai, *Wu-men kuan*, Case 1.

4 Hee-jin Kim, *Dogen Kigen—Mystical Realist* (Tucson: University of Arizona Press, 1975).

5 Norman Waddell, "Hakuin's Poison Words for the Heart," *The Eastern Buddhist*, Kyoto, Vol. XIII, No. 2, Autumn, 1980.

6 Yung-chia (Hsuan-chueh), Cheng-tao ko. Cf. "Song of Enlightenment," trans. D.T. Suzuki, *Manual of Zen Buddhism* (New York: Grove Press, 1960).

7 *The Unborn: The Life and Teaching of Zen Master Bankei*, 1622-1693, trans. Norman Waddell (San Francisco: North Point Press, 1984).

8 Simone Weil, "Reflections on the Right Use of School Studies with a View to the Love of God," *Waiting for God* (New York: Harper & Row, 1973).

9 Nhat Hanh, *The Miracle of Mindfullness!* (Boston: Beacon Press, 1976).

10 "Miscellaneous Kōans," mimeo, Diamond Sangha, Honolulu and Haiku, Hawaii.

11 William Edward Soothill and Lewis Hodous, *A Dictionary of Chinese Buddhist Terms* (London: Kegan Paul, Trench & Trubner, 1937).

Parabola
Volume: 27.1
The Ego and I

Sensing the Center
Secrets of a martial art

Mary Stein

The first time I watched the practice of Aikido, I was impressed with its vigor and fluidity. Picture two people, dressed in white *gi* and full-skirted black *ha-kama*, lifting their arms and coming together in a motion that sends them swirling about the mat. One of them arcs into a fall so light that she somersaults backward out of it, her arm rising like a wand as she leaps up for the next encounter. The two partners are then swept into another round of movement. Multiply this by several more pairs, moving in interweaving waves and circles of energy.

As I began to practice Aikido, however, it was soon clear that I had entered the challenging arena of a martial art, and that there were obstacles in me to its full expression. When someone offered a strike or a wrist-grab, my chest and shoulders tightened in reaction. Or my body collapsed, passively offering the resistance of no resistance. To get my partner to move, my arms pulled at him. To make sure he fell, they pushed as I tilted forward on stiffened legs, my neck (and head) literally sticking out. When it was time for me to fall, I tensed, unwilling to give up a spurious stability, fearful I'd be forced to. I was also uncertain of the techniques—where to put my foot?—and muscled through (or froze at) a confusion I was unwilling to accept. Call it ego, habit, conditioning—something else in me took over.

At the same time, another possibility was accessible at every moment. When I became aware that my legs were rigid (for a long time the teacher had to point that out), my knees knew how to bend, simply and quietly. When I sensed the tenseness of my shoulders, they could drop. Then relaxation could spread through my body, and I moved more effectively. The price was always the same—my willingness to see these habitual bodily tensions.

"That's Aikido," my teacher might say, when the more relaxed way of moving appeared. Or he might say, "That's not Aikido," referring to a movement resulting from ingrained muscular tensions and habits that had taken me through much of my life. If I wanted "Aikido"—and my body did, despite its attraction to habit—I had to sense what was "not Aikido."

Gradually I learned that within every Aikido technique there were bodily attitudes to be affirmed: bent knees, relaxed shoulders and an open chest, a spine that is upright yet flexible, arms that can strike or take hold without unbalancing the whole upper body, a head that rides calmly on top of the spine, breathing that is natural and unobstructed. Within these outer forms lay the mysteries of *ki*: the ancient sense that the body's center of gravity, direction, and intelligence lies in a point just below the navel, and that the universal energy ki flows into this point, coursing freely through the body of a normal human being. The physical attitudes of relaxation and openness that Aikido

taught were the means by which ki could flow normally, and the circular movements of Aikido were expressions of this cosmic energy, found everywhere in natural processes.

This paradoxical art, rooted in conflict yet transforming it, was developed by Morihei Ueshiba (1883–1969). As a young man, Ueshiba, descendant of samurai, mastered a number of the martial arts of Japan and earned a reputation as Japan's most formidable martial artist. At the same time he was drawn to mystical teachings, derived from Shinto and shamanism, that portrayed a cosmos of interlinked, ultimately harmonious forces. Through these teachings he came to question the emphasis on destruction in the martial arts. The samurai tradition had developed enormously sensitive individuals, totally alert and inwardly calm. That the aim of such development should be to kill other human beings seemed incongruous and painful to Ueshiba, as it must have seemed to many samurai.

Eventually Ueshiba received visions of a radiantly interconnected universe in which everything played its part. These visions, along with a revulsion toward Japan's role in World War II, led him to transform techniques designed to injure or kill into moves that protected the attacker as well as the defender. (Ueshiba had helped train military officers before the war but in 1942 withdrew from all participation in national affairs and spent the wartime years farming in the country.)[1]

The new art, which he called Aikido ("the way of harmoniously blended energy"), preserved swift movements, firmness, and efficient technique. Strikes of various kinds were still offered, and the attacker still fell at the end of the techniques. But Ueshiba's innovations created partners rather than opponents. The attacker was no longer struck down or harshly "thrown" but extended into a fall from which he might rebound lightly. Nor was his energy used against him. Rather, his energetic strike or grab was joined with and redirected into a new, circular configuration that brought peaceful resolution to the conflict. People who practiced with Ueshiba reported an almost magical encounter with lightning-like energy that tossed them exactly and refreshingly out of harm's way.

Ueshiba also transformed the social setting for Aikido. He forbade contests and tournaments within and between training halls (dōjōs), believing that competition arouses the very egoistic impulses that Aikido was meant to dispel. Ueshiba also reformed the dōjō caste system. In the old days, higher-ranking students let newer students take all the falls for months or years. Ueshiba insisted on a regular alternation of roles. In Aikido studios today, even the newest student takes her turn at giving and receiving falls, and much of the

ego's investment in winning and losing is removed by this simple rule of equality.

This does not mean that the competitive urge vanishes. My body still tenses with its desire to win and tightens with fear of defeat. These tensions are "not Aikido." But they are my indispensable material, what I need to see each time I practice. They're necessary pointers toward the way I want to go, and if I don't sense them, it means I'm swallowed by them to some degree.

Seeing my physical tensions can be welcomed as the way to a more sensitive response. Often, though, the seeing is followed by more tensions—of analysis, judgment, self-criticism. These reactions can be dangerously distracting, for the next moment in Aikido is already here, and I need to be alert. Without the interruption of talk, either inner or outer—and our daily practices are mainly silent—the wordless lessons of the seeing can soak into the body's memory, as practice continues.

My teacher, David O'Neill, who studied with Ueshiba during the last year of the master's life, has conveyed the idea of searching for a nonhabitual "middle way" of the body, neither too rigid nor too lax but somewhere in between: "firm-soft," as he puts it. When I take hold of a partner's wrist, what is the exact amount of energy needed in my grip and his response for a delicate, shifting stability within and between our bodies? It's a search that leads away from automatic responses toward a growing sense of a center that is relaxed yet deeply firm.

After a while one develops a vocabulary of movements in Aikido, so the grand moments of stark, ignorant confusion don't come so often. But every time we change partners, this new person, whose body may be much larger or smaller than my own, presents an unfamiliar situation to which the old responses won't quite apply. And then there's the sudden grab from behind, or the unfamiliar technique, that still sends my nervous system, if only momentarily, along primitive tracks of "fight, freeze, or flight."

Perhaps a free and sensitive practice of Aikido could open previously unexplored neural pathways. One thinks of the tremendous variety of responses in the play of children. Fred Donaldson, a social scientist and student of Aikido who has studied the play of wolves and also that of children, reports that the play of both is similar to Aikido in its characteristically circular forms—bodies leaping, joining, rolling, and falling in intuitive and joyful interaction. In both children and wolves, when play deteriorates into competition it loses its roundness, becoming tense, anxious, and more linear.[2]

The ego, as represented by my body, is far from free and playful. Rather, it's a bundle of limited responses and postures. These programmed responses like to anticipate what's going to happen and to charge ahead or lag behind. "Knowing" what's coming, I take a fall too soon, in a kind of false yielding, before falling becomes physically inevitable. Or I wait too long, till the optimal moment has passed and the fall turns bumpy. In either case, my tensions increase and my sensitivity decreases. What I insist I already know can be dangerous, because it's never quite what's going on. On the other hand, when I've surrendered to being in the present moment, where the ego doesn't rule, my partner and I can share the weightless grace of a well-timed joining. Aikido teaches me that my true safety—and delight—lies in the unknown, as it unfolds in our movement together, momentarily free of the separating ego. Such moments bring one closer to the mystery of "I," to a sense that perhaps the "I" appears only in such shared awareness.

It's helpful that this "art of peace," as it has been called, retains a strong sense of martial urgency. "Think of each moment as a life-and-death situation," we're told. A "life-and-death" premise means that there's a continuing need for inner and outer alertness. In our practice together we try to support this sense of urgency, watchful for any slackening in ourselves or our partners, maintaining a light but necessary "surface tension" between our bodies as they connect.

When attention lapses, it's often sensed by both partners. Sometimes I realize that the same quality of precise movement that I need with a partner would be needed to rescue a child who's falling into the fire. Protection of the other, as well as myself, can be a matter of life and death.

To Ueshiba, the aim of life was to develop the spirit. "The power of the body," he said, "is always limited." If one had to choose between meditating and practicing Aikido, one should meditate. But spiritual development was also the aim of Aikido, and he urged his students to practice Aikido constantly and steadfastly. Studying Aikido with their friends would assist them to an attentive way of life. "Crystal clear, sharp and bright," he wrote, the awareness nurtured by Aikido "allows no opening for evil to roost." Instead of "evil," we might say "ego," but the image is suggestive. Each time the birds of ego fly up and are seen, it's a good sign.

Notes:

1   For a biography of Ueshiba, see John Stevens, *Abundant Peace* (Boston: Shambhala Publications, 1987).

2   "Interview: Fred Donaldson," *Aikido Today Magazine* February–March 1994: 7–13.

Parabola
Volume: 15.2
Attention

THE PRACTICE OF ATTENTION

Philip Novak

Practices that strengthen the capacity for concentration or attention play a role in most great religious traditions. The importance of developing attention is most readily seen in the great traditions that arose in India, namely Hinduism and Buddhism. From the Upanisadic seers down to the present day, there is in India an unbroken tradition of man's attempt to yoke his self (body and mind) to ultimate reality. Yoga takes many forms, but its essential psychological form is the practice of one-pointed attention or concentration (*citta-ekāgratā*). Whether by fixing the attention on a mantra or on the flow of the breath or on some other object, the attempt to quiet the automatized activities of the mind through concentrated attention is the first step and continuing theme of Hindu psycho-spiritual yoga.

It could hardly be otherwise for the traditions that stemmed from Gautama Buddha. The *samatha* and *vipassanā* forms of meditation in the Theravāda tradition require as their root and anchor an ever increasing ability to attend, to hold one's attention fast without relinquishing it to the various psychological forces that tend to scatter it. *Samatha* is the cultivation of one-pointed attention and is the common starting point for all major types of Buddhist meditation. *Vipassanā* meditation consists in the deployment of the concentrated attention developed in *samatha* from point to point within the organism, with the intent of understanding certain Buddhist doctrines at subtle experiential levels. Though the attention sought in *vipassanā* meditation is not one-pointed in the sense of being fixed on a single object, it remains a highly concentrated and directed form of attention, the very antithesis of dispersed mental wandering. Likewise, the Tibetan practice of visualization, which is attempted only after preparatory training in *samatha*, is a way of developing the mind's ability to remain steadfastly attentive by requiring it to construct elaborate sacred images upon the screen of consciousness. The two practices central to the Zen tradition, *kōan* and *zazen*, have as their common denominator the practice of sustained, vigilant attention. Moreover, the major contemplative schools of Buddhism stress the virtue of mindfulness, the quality of being present, aware, and, in a word, attentive.

Arthur Waley tells us in *The Way and Its Power* (New York: Random House, 1958) that by the fourth century B.C. the Taoists had already developed methods of meditation and trance induction which were probably only indirectly influenced by Indian methods. They were called *tso-wang* and *tso-ch'an* and were fundamentally a training of concentration by the fixation of attention on breath. Buddhism would likely have had a far more difficult time developing in China had it not been for such indigenous Chinese parallelisms.

When we turn to the three great Western monotheisms, the phenomenon of attention is not as starkly visible. Nevertheless it is there. Broadly

speaking, spiritual disciplines in the monotheisms are not as fully developed as those of their cousins in the East. Often forced underground by hostile theological or theopolitical currents, many spiritual practices of the monotheisms appear to have succumbed to a process leading from esotericism, to obscurity and corruption, and eventually to forgetfulness. Still, these monotheisms contain profound mystical dimensions, and it is there we must look for the practice of attention.

The actual practices and methods of Jewish mystical prayer are difficult to determine, but references to method can be found intermittently in the ancient Talmudic texts, quite frequently in the words of Abraham Abulafia and some of his contemporaries, in the Safed Kabbalists of the sixteenth century, in the works of Isaac Luria, and in the Hasidic texts. The key terms are *hitbodedut* (meditation), *hitboded* (to meditate), and *kavanah* (concentration, attention, and intention). The first two come from a root meaning "to be secluded." They often point beyond mere physical seclusion, however, to the seclusion beyond the discursive activity of the mind attained through concentration. *Kavanah* likewise refers to a concentrative or attentive form of prayer capable of inducing an altered, "higher" state of consciousness. For the Jewish mystical tradition as a whole, *mantram*-like repetitions of sacred liturgical words seem to be the central vehicles for the training of attention, but references to concentration upon mental images, letter designs, and color and light visualizations can also be found in the texts. Concentrative exercises are also linked with bodily movements and the movement of the breath. Some of the exercises prescribed by the thirteenth-century Abulafia involve long, complex series of instructions and would seem to require massive attentive capability to perform without distraction. In this they seem akin to the Tibetan Buddhist practice of elaborate visualization.

In the Christian world we find, in Eastern Orthodoxy, the prayer of the heart, or Jesus prayer, a Christian *mantram* which the contemplative uses to recollect the self, to unify attention and thereby to open the heart to the Divine Presence. The bulk of contemplative texts in the Roman Catholic tradition, like those of the Judaic tradition, are concerned with theory and doctrine rather than specifics of method. In the early Middle Ages, one can find references to contemplation as a seeking for God in stillness, repose, and tranquility, but the specificity ends here. The late Middle Ages witnessed among contemplatives the growth of a prayer form called *lectio divina*, or meditative reading of the scriptures. Cistercian monk Thomas Keating describes *lectio divina* as the cultivation of a

"capacity to listen at ever deepening levels of inward attention."[1]

Practical mysticism comes more fully into bloom with the arrival of Teresa of Avila and John of the Cross in the sixteenth century. John's way was the way of inner silence, of non-discursive prayer, of states of mind brought about by what he called "peaceful loving attention unto God." Lately an attempt has been made to popularize this kind of contemplative attention in the "centering prayer," again a *mantram*-like technique for the focusing of attention and the quieting of the mind similar to the Jesus prayer of Eastern Orthodoxy.

In the world of Islam we have the contemplative practices of both silent and vocal *dhikr*, again a *mantram*-like repetition, usually of the names of Allah, aimed at harnessing the will and its power of attention. A more generic term for the kind of meditative attention achieved in *dhikr* is *moraqebeh*, described as "a concentration of one's attention upon God," as the "presence of heart with God," "the involvement of the [human] spirit (*ruh*) in God's breath," and the "concentrating of one's whole being upon God."[2] *Moraqebeh*, the Sufis say, is not only a human activity but a divine one as well: it is because God is constantly attentive to us that we should be attentive to him.

Two men who have drawn on the traditions listed above and whose eclectic writings have had a significant impact among those interested in self-transformation are G. I. Gurdjieff and J. Krishnamurti. Crucial to the Gurdjieff work is the exercise of "self-remembering," fundamentally an attempt to develop sustained, undistracted, observational attention both outwardly toward experience and simultaneously, inwardly toward the experiencer. This particular aspect of Gurdjieff's work is similar to the "bare attention" exercises of Buddhist *vipassanā* meditation. Krishnamurti teaches that the practice fundamental to psychological transformation is "choiceless awareness." It is, again, the cultivation of sustained, observational, nonreactive attention to inner and outer experience. Looked at in isolation from the rest of Krishnamurti's teachings, this gesture of attention is not significantly different from either that of the Gurdjieff work or Buddhist "bare attention."

Attention is, of course, a concept that occurs outside that domain of religious praxis as well. It is part of the vocabulary of everyday mental functioning, and even there it seems to be overworked, a single, blunt term for a wide variety of mental states. The temptation to think of it as one thing should be resisted. It is better to think of it as a spectrum that reaches from the virtual absence of attention, as in sheer daydreaming and mechanically determined mental flux, to acutely active alertness. Though contemplative practices themselves vary widely,

the quality of attention that they require and at which they aim resides at the upper end of the spectrum. The varieties of contemplative attention, in other words, resemble each other more than any one of them resembles that uneven and intermittent phenomenon of ordinary mental functioning we usually call attention. Some further notion of the relative difference between ordinary kinds of attention and the kinds of attention at which contemplative practices aim must be developed if we are to avoid confusion later on.

Ordinary attention may be described as discursive, intermittent, and passive. It moves incessantly from object to object, its intensity "flickers," often succumbing to mental wandering, and it is reactive, or "passive," in relation to some sequence of external objects or to the autonomous stream of consciousness. Let us take, for example, the act in which the reader is currently engaged. You are following this exposition closely, attempting to understand it. Surely this is attention rather than inattention. The contemplative would agree. But he would suggest that this attention is discursive, and largely passive. In this particular case, my words are doing the discursing for your attention, leading it from place to place. Moreover, it is highly likely that, while reading, your attention will have wandered a surprising number of times, pulled down one associational path or another by autonomous psychic fluctuations. Even if you now turned away from this article and turned inward to work out a chain of reasoning, it is likely that you would do so in a state of predominantly passive attention, for such creative activity largely involves a sorting out of what the automatic activity of the psyche presents.

In ordinary meditation, attention is not a quality of mind that we bring to experience, but something that occurs, rather haphazardly, as our organism becomes momentarily more interested in some inner or outer sequence of phenomena. Ordinary attention comes and goes without our consent; it is not something we do, but something that happens to us. For most of us most of the time, "attention" is stimulated, conditioned, and led by mobilizations of energy along the habit-pathways within our organism so that when it confronts its object it is always faced, as it were, by a *fait accompli*.

The attention at which contemplative exercises aim, then, may be distinguished not only from sheer inattention but from ordinary discursive attention as well. It is, instead, sustained, non-discursive, active attention which is, in fact, quite extraordinary. For there are many of us who in all our uncountable billions of mental moments and in all their variety, have never known a moment of truly active attention. Such a moment curtails the autonomous activities of ordinary psychological

activity. If the reader doubts this, he may perform a simple experiment. Take up a "speak-I-am-listening" attitude of acute attention toward the screen of consciousness, standing close guard, as it were, at the place where the contents of consciousness are born. For as long as one is able to hold this posture of intense active attention, the inner dialogue and the flow of images will be stopped. As Hubert Benoit proposes:

> *Our attention, when it functions in the active mode, is pure attention without manifested object. My mobilized energy is not perceptible in itself, but only in the effects of its disintegration, the images. But this disintegration occurs only when my attention operates in the passive mode; active attention forestalls this disintegration.*[3]

Anyone who has ever attempted active attention as we have just described it finds, however, that it is difficult to maintain for any extended duration. The ubiquitous admonition in contemplative texts to somehow go beyond images, ideas, and all discursive thought involves one in the seemingly self-defeating task of trying to stop the mind with the mind. And so we find under the guidance of a teacher that this admonition against discursive thought is but a cavalry charge subsequently balanced by a far more subtle strategy, a second movement as it were.

Given the fact that the deep-seated habit patterns of the psyche will repeatedly overpower an inchoate concentrative ability and assuming that the practitioner will repeatedly attempt to establish active, concentrative attention, his constant companions in all of this are impartiality, equanimity, and nonreactive acceptance. When concentrated attention falters, one is to be a non-reactive witness to what has arisen. Whatever emerges in the mind is observed and allowed to pass without being elaborated upon or reacted to. Images, thoughts, and feelings arise because of the automatism of deeply embedded psychological structures, but their lure is not taken. They are not allowed to steal attention and send it floundering down a stream of associations. One establishes and reestablishes concentrated attention, but when it is interrupted one learns to disidentify with the contents of consciousness, to maintain a choiceless, nonreactive awareness, and to quiet the ego with its preferences.

Should this description appear distinctly Asian and raise doubts regarding its relevance to contemplative prayer practices in the monotheisms, consider, by way of balance, this passage from *Your Word Is Fire*, a work on Hasidic prayer:

> Any teaching that places such great emphasis on total concentration in prayer must ... deal with the question of distraction. What is a person to do when alien thoughts enter his mind and lead him away from prayer? ... The Baal Shem Tov ... spoke against the attempts of his contemporaries to ... do battle with distracting thoughts ... He taught that each distraction may become a ladder by which one may ascend to a new level of devotion ... God [is] present in that moment of distraction! And only he who truly knows that God is present in all *things, including those thoughts he seeks to flee, can be a leader of prayer.*[4]

Though some scholars have drawn a mutually exclusive distinction between "concentrative" and "receptive" forms of attentional practice, the foregoing suggests that this distinction must not be pressed too far.

In any case, this scholarly quibble need not detain us any longer from looking at the more important issue. The question is: How does the regular and long-term practice of attention, in the context of a spiritual tradition, enable the self to extricate itself from compulsive ego-centeredness and from the blindness to subtler and more inclusive realities which result therefrom?

More spiritual traditions contain some notion or other of the false consciousness, or false self, which when overcome, rendered transparent, or otherwise transcended, allows the self-manifesting quality of truth to disclose itself. Let us say, therefore, that the central significance of attentional exercises is to release the human being from bondage to the machinations of that false self.

To better grasp this concept, let us consider that human beings experience a persistent need to preserve and expand their being, and thus each of us, from birth, undertakes what may be called a self-project. Everyone longs to be special, to be a center of importance and value, to possess life's fullness even unto immortality, and everyone spends energy in pursuit of those things that, according to his level of understanding, will fulfill these longings. According to many contemplative traditions, such longing is grounded in a profound truth: ultimately, we share in the undying life of the ultimately real. Unfortunately, however, the ego transcendence that contemplative traditions prescribe is usually rejected in favor of endless vain attempts to expand the ego in the external world through possession, projection, and gratification.

The false self, then, can be understood as a metaphor for psychic automatism, that is, automatic, egocentric, habit-determined patterns of thought, emotive reaction and assessment, and imaginary activity that filter and distort reality and skew behavior, according to the needs of the self-project. Having hardened into relatively permanent psychological "structures," these predispositional patterns may be conceived as constantly feeding on available psychic energy, dissolving it into the endless associational flotsam in the stream of consciousness. Energy that would otherwise be manifested as the delight of open and present-centered awareness is inexorably drawn to these structures and there disintegrates into the image-films and commentaries—the "noise"—that suffuse ordinary consciousness.

What allows the self-aggravating automatism of the false self to function unchecked is, in a word, *identification*. As long as we are unconsciously and automatically identifying with the changing contents of consciousness, we never suspect that our true nature remains hidden from us. If spiritual freedom means anything, however, it means first and foremost a freedom from such automatic identification.

Once automatism and identification are understood to be the sustainers of the false self, we are in a position to understand the psychotransformative power of concentrated, nonreactive attention. For whether a human being is a Muslim repeating the names of God or a Theravāda Buddhist practicing bare attention, he or she is, to one degree or another, cultivating the disidentification that leads to the de-automatization[5] of the false self.

The mere act of trying to hold the mind to a single point, an act with which higher forms of meditation begin, teaches the beginner in a radically concrete and experiential way that he or she has little or no control over the mental flow. All attentional training starts with this failure. This is the first great step in the work of objectifying the mental flow, that is, of seeing it not as something that "I" am doing but something that is simply happening. Without this realization no progress can be made, for one must first know one is in prison in order to work intelligently to escape. Thus, when the Christian is asked to concentrate his attention solely upon God, when the Muslim attempts to link his attention solely to the names of God, when the Tibetan Buddhist attempts with massive attention to construct elaborate images of Tārā on the screen of consciousness, the first lesson these practitioners learn is that they *cannot* do it. Ordinary mentation is freshly understood to be foreign to the deepest reality of one's being. The more regularly this is seen the clearer it becomes that one is *not* one's thoughts, and the more profoundly one understands the distinction between consciousness as such and the contents of consciousness. Objectification of the contents of consciousness and disidentification with them are natural outcomes.

Contemplative attentional exercises are strategies of starvation. Every moment that available energy is consolidated in concentrative and nonreactive attention is a moment when automatized processes cannot replenish themselves. In the dynamic world of the psyche, there is no stasis: if automatisms do not grow more strongly solidified, they begin to weaken and dissolve. When deprived of the nutriment formerly afforded to them by distracted states of mind, the automatized processes of the mind begin to disintegrate. Contemplative attention practiced over a long period of time may dissolve and uproot even the most recalcitrant pockets of psychological automatism, allowing consciousness to re-collect the ontic freedom and clarity that are its birthright.

De-automatization, then, describes an essential aspect of the process of spiritual liberation, the freeing of oneself from bondage to the false self. It names, furthermore, a gradual, long-term process of transformation, a process within which discrete mystical experiences reach fruition and without which they are destined to fade into ineffectual memories.

However, it should be clear that the function of contemplative work is largely destructive. The accoutrements of a spiritual tradition provide a protective and constructive framework within which this destructive work can proceed. The more seriously the foundations of the false self are undermined by the practice of attention, the fiercer become the storms of protest from within. The "dying" that occurs during contemplative work can cause internal shocks and reactions so profound that only the deep contours of a tradition can absorb them and turn them to creative effect. The support of a tradition hundreds of years old—rich in symbolism, metaphysical and psychological maps, and the accumulated experience of thousands of past wayfarers—and the guidance of an experienced teacher are indispensable. A "new age" movement that wishes to champion contemplative technique but jettison the traditional context in which it was originally lodged seems likely to be either very superficial or very dangerous or both.

Moreover, tradition stresses and a spiritual community supports, in a way that a mere technique cannot, the importance of morality as a *sine qua non* foundation and necessary ongoing accompaniment to the inner work. Without the rectification of external conduct, inner work cannot proceed far. One would be hard pressed to find a single exception to this rule in the great traditions.

Finally, human transformation is effected not solely by isolated bouts of intense attentional training; such training must be linked to ordinary life by an intentionality that makes every aspect of life a part of the spiritual work. The contemplative opus, in other words, is hardly limited to formal periods of attentional practice. Ordinary activity and formal contemplative practice must reinforce each other and between them sustain the continuity of practice that alone can awaken the mind and help it realize the *telos* adumbrated for it in the images and concepts of the tradition to which it belongs.

Attentional exercises are hardly meant to be practiced in isolation. Their effectiveness requires not only long practice but also the support of a community, the guidance of tradition, the tranquility effected by moral purification, and, finally, the continuity of practice that allows the power of will, indispensable to the transformative work, to be fully born.

Notes:

1   "Contemplative Prayer in the Christian Tradition," *America* (1978): 278 ff.

2   Javad Nurbakhsh, *In the Paradise of the Sufis* (New York: Khaniqahi-Nimatullahi Publications, 1979) 72.

3   *The Supreme Doctrine* (New York: Viking Press, 1959) 40.

4   1977, 15-16.

5   A concept for which we are indebted to Arthur I. Deikman, "Deautomatization and the Mystic Experience," *Psychiatry* 29 (1966): 324-338.

Abridged with the permission of Philip Novak from two of his previously written articles: "Attention," *The Encyclopedia of Religion*, ed. Mircea Eliade, vol. I (New York: Macmillan, 1987), and "Dynamics of Attention: Core of the Contemplative Way," *Journal of Studies in Formative Spirituality* 5.1 (1984).

•

CHAPTER THREE

Nonduality and Freedom

*One disciple said: "My master stands on one side of the river. I stand on the other
holding a piece of paper. He draws a picture in the air and the
picture appears on the paper. He works miracles."
The other disciple said:
"My master works greater miracles than that.
When he sleeps, he sleeps.
When he eats, he eats.
When he works, he works.
When he meditates, he meditates."*

—Zen Buddhist Story

*Joshu asked the teacher Nansen, "What is the true Way?"
Nansen answered, "Everyday way is the true Way."
Joshu asked, "Can I study it?"
Nansen answered, "The more you study, the further from the Way."
Joshu asked, "If I don't study it, how can I know it?"
Nansen answered, "The Way does not belong to things seen: nor to things unseen.
It does not belong to things known: nor to things unknown. Do not seek it, study it,
or name it. To find yourself on it, open yourself wide as the sky."*

—Zen Story

Parabola
Volume: 12.1
The Knight and the
Hermit

Beyond Duality

Frederick Franck

Buddhism took root in Japan in the sixth century. During the centuries that followed, cruel wars, devastating epidemics, and famines plagued medieval Japan. Buddhism held the promise of salvation, and the Pure Land sect with its unquestioning faith in Amida (the Buddha of Infinite Light and Compassion) together with the aggressively proselytizing Nichiren sect (for which recitation of praise to the Lotus Sutra guaranteed salvation) became mass movements.

Zen Buddhism, which as *Chan* flourished in China and inspired the brilliant Sung Dynasty culture in art, philosophy, and poetry (960-1279), was introduced into Japan by missionaries, who accompanied trade missions. However, it became only firmly established on Japanese soil by two great pioneers of whom Esai (1141-1215) was the first. He traveled to China and eventually returned to his homeland as a fully qualified Zen master of the Rinzai School. Somewhat later, Dogen, an unusually forceful figure of aristocratic birth, went to China in search of the essence of Buddhism, which he had failed to find in Japan. He was on the point of returning home, disabused and empty handed, when he happened on a master, Ju Ching (Jpn., Nyogo), who transmitted to him the authentic Dharma of the Buddha and Patriarchs. It happened when Ju-Ching spoke of the essence of Zen as "dropping off of body and mind" that Dogen experienced the sudden and full awakening that transcended all dualism of body and spirit.

Returning to Kyoto in 1227, Dogen started his phenomenal career. He fought the commonly held belief that Buddhism had entered its stage of final decay (*mappo*). Every person, he taught, is empowered to attain the Way, regardless of the period in which he is born. In 1233 he started to write his life work, the *Shobogenzo* (Treasure of the True Dharma Eye). His disciple Ejo transcribed his informal sermons in the *Record of Things Heard*. In his early forties Dogen, harassed by the Tendai hierarchy of Mount Hiei, moved his monastery to Echizen Province on the Japan Sea. The discipline was strict. Dogen became known as the founder of the Soto School of Zen, although he himself frowned on the use of the label Zen ("He who speaks of Zen as a Buddhist sect is a devil") and rejected also the epithet *Soto*. He merely taught what ŚŚŚ had preached under the Tree of Enlightenment, and that was all! "Buddhahood cannot be obtained at will, and not for oneself's sake but only for its own sake," he said. Further: "If you want to obtain a certain thing, you must first become a certain person. Once you have become that certain person, you will not care anymore about obtaining that certain thing."

Dogen sees the Dharma (Truth/Reality) entirely present in each person, but without "practice" it fails to manifest itself. For him practice is *shikantaza*, "just sitting" in meditation. This way of doing zazen he declares to be "as beginningless as enlightenment is endless." It is the "casting off of body and mind" to which Ju-Ching had opened his heart. The concept of practice as a means to enlightenment is therefore thrown overboard: Buddha Nature is not the outcome, but the very basis of doing zazen. He himself spent his whole life in the most rigorous monastic discipline. He was so uncompromising that when, after he had given a sermon at the seat of government in Kamakura, the regent sent one of Dogen's disciples with a land grant for his monastery, he not only refused it, but threw out the disciple, had the chair he had occupied burned and the earth under it dug out and thrown away.

Dogen's writings were forgotten until some sixty years ago when the philosopher Tetsuro Watsuji drew attention to them, followed by the attention of another distinguished thinker, Hajime Tanabe, in 1939. The first English translation appeared only in 1958, and in the 1960s the late Shunryu Suzuki Roshi at the San Francisco Zen Center began to teach zazen strictly according to Dogen's principles. Since then, this practice became firmly established in this country and in Europe. "The *Shobogenzo*," says Masao Abe, whose brilliant *Zen and Western Thought* was recently reviewed in these pages, "is perhaps unsurpassed in its philosophical speculation, one of the monumental documents of Japanese intellectual history."

Moon in a Dewdrop contains the essential writings and poetry of Dogen, edited by Kazuaki Tanahashi, translated by a distinguished team of translators including Robert Aitken Roshi, and most attractively published by Northpoint Press. Tanahashi's introduction is elegant and useful. Nevertheless, the work is far from easily accessible to the general reader. Dogen's style, highly personal, is grounded in his profound realization. Moreover, the *Shobogenzo* was written eight centuries ago in a cultural context very few Westerners are familiar with. To make it more difficult, Dogen's highly original mind uses traditional Buddhist terminology but endows it with radically new meanings. Meditation, speculation, and poetry are here inextricably interwoven.

Characteristic of Dogen's reinterpretation of Buddhist terms, in accordance with his awesome insights, is his interpretation of the Nirvana Sutra's "All sentient beings without exception have the Buddha Nature" and "The Buddha Nature is permanent and changeless." Dogen translates these sayings as: "All beings are the Buddha Nature" and "Buddha Nature is permanent, nonbeing, being and change." Although the same Chinese character stands for both "to be" and "to have" this translation has been criticized as grammatically inaccurate. Still, it expresses precisely and radically what was for this enlightened mind the very essence of Mahayana. He is not concerned with "having" or "not having." For Dogen, not only all human beings, not only even all living beings, but literally *all* beings are indeed the Buddha Nature.

Dogen therefore sees the traditional reading as incorrect or even heretical. For him the Buddha Nature is not a seed of a potential awakening at some point in the future; on the contrary, all beings, whether living or not, are originally Buddha Nature. All duality of subject and object, of potentiality and actuality, present and future, *samsara* and nirvana, are obliterated.

The basic dimension, which humans and all living beings share, is birth-and-death, or more generally speaking, generation-and-extinction. Where inanimate beings are included (mountains, for instance), the shared dimension is appearance-and-disappearance. The basic human predicament of birth as opposed to death is not viewed anthropocentrically, but cosmically. Birth-and-death (*samsara*) and the emancipation from it (nirvana) can be realized only on the basis of generation-and-extinction, which takes place at every moment, a realization that constitutes awakening without implying the independent existence of a spirit, soul, or *atman*.

In this view, human beings do not have a position superior to that of other living beings. They are not the carriers of an *imago Dei* as in Judaism, Christianity, and Islam, which are strictly anthropocentric and in which salvation is closely bound to a view of personhood in which God discloses Himself as a Person with whom we human persons have a dialogic I-Thou relationship. What in the Buddhist view distinguishes us from other living beings is that the realization of the nature of generation-and-extinction can constitute our liberation. To be born human, in the Buddhist view, is the windfall that endows us with the capacity to be a "thinking reed," able to awaken to the Dharma that governs the universe, to Reality/Truth. Thus, the ground for salvation differs radically in Buddhism and Western monotheistic traditions.

For Dogen, Buddha Nature is far from being a "something." It is not only unnamable, it is *the* Unnamable, the Unobjectifiable, that is neither immanent nor transcendent. To touch Buddha Nature all forms of egocentrism must be overcome in favor of what all beings (whether living or inanimate) share ... impermanence. For Dogen, as Masao Abe puts it, all beings, impermanence, and Buddha Nature are identical, with the realization of impermanence as the dynamic axis. (This is as far removed from Spinoza's God as the Infinite Cause as it is from Heidegger's distinction between *Sein* and *Seiendes*. Spinoza looked at reality *sub specie*

aeternitatis, under the aspect of eternity; Dogen sees reality under the aspect of impermanence.)

Dogen was first of all a religious practitioner. His insights are derived directly from his discipline, in the Buddha Way, of zazen as "just sitting." His view of impermanence/Buddha Nature is not a philosophical thesis but the deeply experienced pain and suffering of all beings, the "groaning of creation." Buddha Nature, in his perspective, manifests itself as time in the sense of present time; for time is beyond continuity and discontinuity. Each moment contains all of time and has the aspect of timelessness. To realize time as time is realizing the Buddha Nature. Time is, for Dogen, inseparable from being: time is being, and being is time: "I am my existence time." In other words, the plum blossom does not announce spring; spring *is* the opening of the plum blossom.

He alone is detached from ego who has "cast off body and mind" to find out who he really is: selfless. This selflessness is, however, the True Self, the Original Face before the birth of one's parents. For the True Self, the total interdependence to the point of mutual interpenetration of all beings becomes pure experience.

In the "Genjokoan" chapter of *Shobogenzo*, he says: "To learn the Buddha Way is to learn oneself. To learn oneself is to become confirmed by all things. To be confirmed by all things is to effect the dropping off of one's own body and mind and simultaneously that of the other." Keiji Nishitani comments on this saying by laconically quoting another ancient master: "Hills and rivers, the earth, plants and trees, all these are the True Self's own original part." And he adds: "It is existence on a field where birth-and-death as such is the Life of the Buddha."

Moon in a Dewdrop is not a book to add to one's pile of books for the next few weeks' reading. It requires considerable patience, concentration, and perseverance. Even then, the profundity and idiosyncratic formulations of this thirteenth-century giant often remain enigmatic. The translators have attempted to be helpful by adding an exceptionally long and thorough glossary-cum-index of about a hundred pages after the over two hundred pages of translation. This, however, makes the book even more difficult to handle than if copious footnotes had been added. On certain pages, one has to interrupt one's reading half a dozen times to consult the glossary, so that continuity is severely interfered with. Still, this impressive, almost heroic, collective effort is an invaluable addition to the recent spate of Dogen literature and demands respect and gratitude.

Parabola
Volume: 12.4
The Sense of Humor

Dürckheim's Zen

Frederick Franck

*A slim, 130-page paperback, Zen and Us was published
in October 1987, as if to celebrate the ninety-first birthday of
its author, Count Dürckheim, undoubtedly the most influential
Zen teacher in Europe. He is still in charge—together with
Maria Hippius, whom he married quite recently after almost
half a century of close collaboration—of his "Existential-Psychological Training Center" at Todtmuss-Rütte in Germany's
Black Forest. Here Dürckheim and Hippius, assisted by a score
of therapists and assistants, practice their "Initiatory Therapy,"
which they have been developing since the foundation of their
Western ashram in the late forties. It embodies Dürckheim's
commitment to present a viable synthesis of Eastern and
Western spirituality.*

Karlfried Graf Dürckheim was born into high Bavarian
nobility in 1896. From his eighteenth to his twenty-second
year he served as a lieutenant in World War I. He managed
to survive even the hell of Verdun and returned to Munich,
only to be saved at the last minute from being shot as a
"traitor" during the bloody Spartacist Putsch of 1918. Having seen death face to face, and after revelatory experiences
while reading Lao Tzu, Eckhart and Rilke, he decided he
had to break with the centuries-old military tradition of

his family, and to renounce his rights to the inheritance of its estates. He enrolled as a student in philosophy and psychology at the University of Munich, and received his Ph.D. from the University of Kiel, where he was eventually appointed professor of psychology and lecturer in philosophy. He was one of the first academics to introduce the ideas of Freud, Adler, and Jung. Contacts with Heidegger and, at the Bauhaus, with artists of the stature of Kandinsky, Klee, and Mies van der Rohe widened his horizon considerably. He became connected with the Ministry of Foreign Affairs, but declined to join the Nazis. In 1937 he was sent to Japan to maintain contact with German scientists at work there and to supply teachers of German with libraries of German literature. In Japan he befriended Eugen Herrigel, author of *Zen in the Art of Archery*. He became a student of Zen and found in it confirmation of what he had gleaned from Eckhart, recognizing in the "Buddha Nature" of Zen an analogy of the "divine spark in the soul" of which Eckhart speaks as the core of human reality, the True Self. In *Zen and Us*, Dürckheim calls it "Being" (*Sein*), a Presence that can be realized by everyone born human, provided the shell of the empirical ego (which he calls the "defining ego" because of its compulsively objectifying function) is pierced. His "Initiatory Therapy" at Rütte has the breakthrough to this awareness of "Being" as its central

purpose. He recalls how, when he practiced archery in Japan, his teacher told him: "Now that you have mastered the form to which you aspired during this training period I can see the change in you in the very way you open a door. But having achieved this form that is yours, the form of your work, of your life, the greatest misfortune that could befall you would be to cling to it. It is my task as your teacher to wrench it from your hand before it hardens." All Zen practice has as its aim to pierce the surface, the liberation from the ambitions of the empirical, ever-defining ego, so that action, no longer flawed by ambition and will, may rise from the Ground of one's Being. This "Being" is not at all some pious point of faith, Dürckheim insists. It can be experienced within, so that the old Adam may die and the new Adam may be born. This resurrection experience is "the Great Experience," that satori which, especially for the Westerner, demands overcoming almost insurmountable obstacles; those of his culture-bound individualism and body/soul dualism.

Zen is not the business of "destroying" the ego, but of transforming it ... [of] changing the person determined solely by the puny, power-hungry, self-assertive, possessive ego into one who is determined by his true nature.[1]

Satori is not blissfully dissolving in All/One/Being; it means constantly seeing/creating and bearing witness to Being ... to the True Self in the ego, *to the absolute in the relative, to the divine in the world.[2]*

Soon after Japan's surrender Dürckheim, like all other German residents of Japan, was arrested. He was initially accused of having organized a Nazi propaganda center in Shanghai, where he had only gone for a few days' visit. He spent sixteen months in prison, was hardly ever questioned about his personal activities, and was suddenly set free. He never resented having been locked up in a cell. It gave him such an opportunity to practice his zazen without constant interruption that he said he would wish it on anyone seriously intent on advancing on the Way.

On his return to Germany he met by coincidence a former student at Kiel, Maria Hippius, who had written her doctoral thesis on the "Graphic Expression of Feeling" under his guidance. She had been married, but had lost her husband, Rudolf. At the end of the war he was rounded up with other Germans in Prague, where he taught philosophy. During the Communist coup he was sent to Siberia and never returned. Maria Hippius, penniless, succeeded in slipping across the border into Germany with her three small children. She was providentially offered the small house in the Black Forest that was to become the core of the present center with its large staff and its constant stream of patients and carefully screened trainees.

The center's "Initiatory Therapy," while rooted in Dürckheim's Zen experience, is strongly influenced by Jungian concepts of the "rejected, unadmitted and repressed contents of the psyche, the bipolarity of male and female, of animus and anima and of the shadow which becomes perceptible when all acquired role playing is broken through." It seems to be especially Frau Hippius who integrated therapeutic drawing and painting, clay modeling, musical expression and bodywork ("you do not have a body, you are a body") into Rütte's "Initiatory Therapy." She became the stern task-master of whom it has been said that "whoever does not arrive in Rütte in a state of crisis will have to confront one soon."

The compatibility of Jungian principles and Zen is far from uncontroversial. Masao Abe remarks that the Self which for Jung is the total personality, which cannot be fully known, contradicts the Zen view radically. At the conclusion of a dialogue between Sin'ichi Hisamatsu, the great authority on Zen, and Jung in 1958, Jung had to admit that indeed the collective unconscious could be overcome, as the very lives of the Buddha and the Christ clearly manifested.

Thomas Kapulis stresses that "in psychotherapy the doctor too is a patient," that his is a profession, whereas the Zen master's method is simply his entire way of life. "Indeed," Erich Fromm agrees, "the Zen master is not a teacher in the Western sense.

He is a master insofar as he has mastered his own mind and is capable of transmitting to his student the only thing that can be conveyed: his own quality of existence."

For the Zen master exploration of past experiences is of no interest whatsoever. Neither does he recognize the fragmentation of the psyche into parts. There is no id, ego, super-ego for the Roshi, no conscious and unconscious—whether personal or collective—no shadow, no problems of transference, no need to interpret childhood data and dreams. The true Master responds directly from his "non-thinking thinking" (the opposite of both thinking and not-thinking) existentially. It is the very quality of his being that responds pre-reflectively, that makes the blind see, the lame walk, the Gadarene swine tumble over the cliff.

It is, however, not Rütte's eclectic methodology that is being evaluated here, but *Zen and Us*, the book which embodies Dürckheim's Zen, necessarily as personal as Suzuki's or Nishitani's Zen. It shows his Zen as that which touches the reality within his students, which aims at opening their Inner Eye, to transform, to redeem, to transmit what can only be transmitted from heart to heart as that lifelong Way of becoming that must never be allowed to become petrified at any fixed point.

The Inner Eye, as Zen understands it, opens only when the experience of

Being reveals unity to us in and with the world, showing us that the world is both the barrier that divides us from Being and the medium through which Being, the world's hidden true nature, manifests itself and forces its way towards the light.[3]

When a person "wakes," Being not only becomes an inner presence, but the cause that obscured it, the "root of evil" is seen from within.[4]

The inner eye looks in two directions. It sees both the world-self and the true self, and once it opens, we see the world-self not only as a constant threat to Being's inner presence, but also as the medium through which Being reveals itself in the here-and-now existence.[5]

The opening of the inner eye is also—and chiefly—the unmasking of the ego. When the inner eye has been opened, a person continues to live normally in the here-and-now, but transcendence enters the here-and-now.[6]

Zen addresses itself to a basic, universally human dilemma beyond all cultural demarcation lines. As a Way it had to be imported from the East when we in the West became aware that half of our humanness had been repressed, rejected to the point of having atrophied. The other half had meanwhile become the dominant cerebral one, had developed a ruthless, naively "rational" mentality, increasingly ego-centered ever since Descartes surmised that he was because he cogitated instead of the other way around.

As men and women must fail to become fully human as long as they deny the respectively female and masculine components of their nature, Westerners cannot recover their atrophied Eastern half, from which they became so estranged that when they were confronted with it it looked utterly exotic.

Father Bede Griffith, the Benedictine monk, when interviewed by Renée Weber in his Indian ashram, "Shantivanam," said that in contrast to the modern West, everything in India is sacred. Earth, food, water are still seen as part of that "sacral" universe whose destruction was begun in the West in the sixteenth century in a deliberate effort to escape from centuries of clerical despotism. Gradually every aspect of life became secularized, rationalized, until only in the last fifty years are we beginning to retrieve the lost sense of the Sacred, the numinous.

The monk and the count would be in close agreement, while conversing either on the floor of Father Griffith's bare ashram or in Dürckheim's well-furnished study, on the reality of the sacred, the divine mystery manifest in all of nature, on a sacred universe mirroring God, in which everything is saturated with the divine, manifest in the world and at the same time beyond manifestation. They would be at one in their conviction that where the biblical is complemented by the

Oriental view, only deeper understanding can result. Both would affirm that in every human being there is the Imago Dei, hence that everyone born human is in some way open to the transcendent Mystery, and that the realization of this Mystery demands, in the East as in the West, the letting go of the empirical self. "When the body weeps for that which it has lost, the spirit laughs for what it has gained," says an ancient Sūfi sage.

"We simply practice meditation in Zen style," says Dürckheim, who considers himself a Christian and denies wishing to convert Christians to Buddhism, but who seems to feel with Carl Jung that "Christianity must begin all over again, must be humanized if it is to meet its high educational task, for the Western psyche, not even remotely touched by it, went on vegetating in its archaic barbarity." Dürckheim's Zen in *Zen and Us* appears as both strong and primal, firmly rooted in Dōgen's Sōtō Zen. It is based on his own "Great Experience" of almost half a century ago, and is not dated in the least.

If *Zen and Us* seems to neglect certain aspects of Zen, especially in its relation to Christianity, which have been clarified and deepened since World War II by the rigorous thoughts and insights of Kitaro Nishida, Keiji Nishitani, T. Izutsu, Masao Abe, and David Bohm's dialogues with the Dalai Lama on the "Implicate Order," it fulfills its

function. For, like the two other
books of Dürckheim's available in
English translation (*Hara* and *The
Way of Transformation*), *Zen and Us*
is a manifesto, a witness to the old
teacher's bodhisattvic vocation to
awaken hope and trust in the human
capacity to solve the Basic Dilemma.
As such it must be read. Moreover,
it reveals the proven impact of this
Germanic exponent of Zen on the
European spirit.

Notes

1 Karlfried Graf Dürckheim, *Zen and Us*
   (New York: E.P. Dutton, 1987), 89.

2 Dürckheim, 70.

3 Dürckheim, 67.

4 Dürckheim, 67.

5 Dürckheim, 68.

6 Dürckheim, 71.

Parabola
Volume: 13.3
Questions

Notes on the Koan

Frederick Franck

When Daisetz T. Suzuki was once asked, "What is Zen?" his answer was: "Zen is that which makes you ask the question, for the answer comes from where the question arises. ... When you ask what Zen is, you are asking who you are, what your Self is. Isn't it the height of stupidity to ask what your Self is, when it is this very Self that makes you ask the question?"

Our usual questionings do not come from the depth of our being, but from sheer curiosity, from the intellect. Only when the intellect becomes aware of its limitations, or of its being handicapped by that dichotomy between subject and object without which discursive reasoning is impossible, are we ready to ask the existential question. The self, this ultimate Self of which Suzuki speaks, is above the level of duality. It is neither a metaphysical nor a psychological concept. It is not a concept at all: it is experienced! Rinzai pointed at it as "the True Man without rank," Tillich called it Being, Eckhart spoke of the soul, Mahayana speaks of it as *Sunyata*, No-Thing, as "our Original Face before we even have been born."

The term koan originally referred to "a public document," an authoritative statement which may consist of a phrase from a sutra, a *mondo*—question and answer exchange between master and disciple—or a story, as for instance the one about the monk who questioned Master Joshu whether a dog has the Buddha nature and received as answer "*Mu!*": "Not!"

Joshu's dog is one of the basic koans of Rinzai Zen; to solve it may well take one a number of years.

The koan then is more than a mere riddle. It is the jolting question, theme, or problem, paradoxical, often even nonsensical in appearance, which—in Rinzai Zen—the master presents to his disciple to be solved. It serves to test the authenticity of the insight, perhaps the Enlightenment, the aspirant claims or imagines to have attained, and is at the same time the device to speed up, to intensify the process that leads to confrontation with the true self, "that Self that is infinitely 'other' yet in reality 'infinitely ourselves'" (Frithjof Schuon).

"The Koan is actually in ourselves," says D. T. Suzuki. "Each one of us brings it with him into the world and tries to decipher it before passing away. What the Zen master does is no more than point it out to us, so we may see it more plainly than before."

The koan is used as the tool that cuts through all the conceits and rationalizations of the intellect by making it impossible to sidestep the central, existential questions by the usual stratagems of discursive reasoning. It lets the intellect struggle until it has to give up. One after the other of its crutches are kicked away. *In extremis*, having given up all hope of "solving" the koan, but having become totally identified with it, one may break through the bottom

of the empirical ego and encounter the self, that self which is not a something that "I" am, nor a self contained within "me," but the self in which I am and have my being.

If this should sound all too enigmatic, Suzuki says that in Zen terms the Real is indeed unintelligible and can only be grasped as being ungraspable. Hence the self can be attained only in its quality of *being unattainable*. Long before Suzuki, the 9th century Master Butsugen told his disciples: "If you fail to understand Zen, your fault lies in not seeing that all is essentially beyond understanding, and somehow you persist in trying to find a way to understand it." Thomas Merton, one of those Westerners who was wide open to the essence of Zen, recognized in the koan a "paradigm of life itself."

When you start questing, in the Zen sense, it must be because you intuitively feel within yourself the presence of another "I" that is basically invulnerable to all your psychological quirks and quandaries. This invulnerable "I" may well be unattainable, but Zen, instead of abandoning the quest in resignation, eggs us on to grasp this self *in its ungraspability*. The koan is one of the methods to force this momentous feat that amounts to the "Great Death" that precedes a resurrection in which all at once "all things become new."

Oriental as the invention of the koan may be, the most august and pregnant dicta of Western scripture are as impenetrably resistant to the speculating intellect, which can only play hide and seek with riddles that are not a whit less baffling than Joshu's "*Mu!*"

If I may interpolate a personal note here: the koans with which the inner Zen master saddled me early in life were words like "I and my Father are one ..." "Who has seen Me, has seen the Father ..." and perhaps most poignantly: "Before Abraham was, I am."

Who is this "I," this "me," that is speaking here? No one could help me to solve the conundrum, neither book, nor priest, nor theologian. It is the koan that cannot be ignored by anyone born in this Western culture that is so inextricably interwoven with Christian vocabulary, even if that culture has as such failed to recognize the words as great koans and has only provided intellectual platitudes by way of answer.

Even earlier in life there were certain "koans," those primal religious questions we have all asked before entering grade school, before they were blocked: "Who am I? Why did my pet rooster and Uncle Henry die? Where are they now?"—questionings that come from the center of one's being and are forms of the koan "each one brings along into the world and must solve before passing away."

Looking back, I even remember a koan I fabricated on my own, or rather, one which something inside me must have concocted under pressure of circumstance. For I was born precisely at that point where Holland, Germany, and Belgium meet, the very point where both World Wars started, and we lived less than a mile from the Belgian border. During the first one Holland remained neutral; but as from a grandstand, I was from my fifth to my ninth year confronted with the incomprehensible horror of seeing living human flesh in the tatters of German, Belgian, and French uniforms coming across the border on pushcarts and other improvised ambulances. It sensitized me against all forms of physical violence for life.

Confrontation with the suffering of human flesh made it repulsive, almost impossible for me to eat animal flesh, as I was forced to do at home. One day we had sardines for supper; five of these were lying on my plate. The day after, mother served cod for dinner and I had to eat a thick slice. From then on I became obsessed with my home-grown koan: "What was more abhorrent, wicked, even evil: to eat those five whole, silvery sardines or one slice of cod?" The question remained with me for years. I found it silly, but couldn't solve it, until years later I broke through the impasse and my "koan" was solved. It happened in a restaurant when a fragrant *filet de sole amandine* was put in front of me. I took my fork, but it refused to touch the fish; I ate the *pommes duchesse* and never knowingly ate animal flesh again.

"Cornered one passes through, passing through one changes," says the 20th century Zen master Hisamatsu.

Yoko Daishi, in the eighth century—presumably an early fan of *tofu amandine*—said: "You cannot get hold of it, you cannot get rid of it, and while you do neither, it goes its own way."

"Why do Buddhas go around teaching, when the Buddha nature already is in us living beings?" is the home-made koan that arose in the mind of the young Dogen who later was to become the founder of Soto Zen.

It indeed may take many years before one can identify and resolve the point which has worried one all one's life. Daito, the founder of Daitoku-ji in Kyoto wrote when his moment of crystallization of the life problem had come: "Over thirty years I have lived in a fox hole, now I have changed to human status."

The solution of the life problem indeed is the reaching of our fully human status, whether with or without the help of a koan to "show the deaf man the moon by pointing at it, and let the blind man know where the gate is by knocking on it," as Buko put it in the days of Sung.

The koan came into fashion only around the 10th and 11th centuries as the tool *par excellence* towards enlightenment. The ancient Zen masters Hui Neng, Matsu, Huang Po, who had reached it on their own—or had been initiated by predecessors who did a great deal of pointing and, indeed, knocking—simply demonstrated That Which Matters by either raising a finger, opening and closing their eyes, by sipping tea, by the give and take of *mondo*, and often by raining blows on their baffled disciples.

The koan, especially propagated and systematized by Daie, intended to awaken artificially, systematically, sometimes mechanically, in the Zen disciple's consciousness what the early masters had often awakened in themselves intuitively and transmitted spontaneously. The koan served as a pole to help one leap over the stream of the relative to the other shore of the Absolute (which is nowhere else than here and now!)—a leap, energized by a keen and sustained spirit of inquiry and by the resolve to attain freedom from the bondage of karma. The koan lets the psyche become a spiritual battlefield, until all the mental resources of the disciple are exhausted. Then, suddenly, abruptly, at the end of this prolonged shock treatment, what is referred to as "the ball of doubt" may dissolve, and the true self, the self nature, be realized—in the double sense of having become conscious, and having become actualized.

This is the koan's crucial function in Rinzai's "abrupt school," of which Hakuin was the greatest Japanese exponent. In its highly dynamic form of training, Rinzai Zen stands in sharp contrast to Soto Zen's "gradual enlightenment," "silent illumination," "zazen only." Soto is colored by a certain quietism. On the surface level our waking consciousness is in a state of constant agitation with an uninterrupted film of images and a constant stream of concepts and purposeful thinking, forever chasing after objectives in the external world.

There is, however, a deeper level of the mind which remains serene, despite all the surface turmoil, as the deepest layers of the ocean are quiet below the agitation of the waves. The aim of the "zazen-only" of Soto Zen is to bring the mind to a one-pointed, concentrated state of unity in full awareness of this depth level. This "mere sitting" in equanimity and with the "stability of a rock," without focusing on a koan or any other tangible object of concentration, is regarded by the Soto masters as being by itself the manifestation of the original enlightenment, of that Buddha nature, which according to Dogen all beings not merely *have*, but which all beings *are*. Dogen demands "body and mind to be dropped off."

The conflicts between Rinzai and Soto Zen have been bitter. Daie, in his fierce fidelity to Hui Neng's teachings, was so strongly opposed to Soto's meditational methods that he accused its masters of being "false masters," for Rinzai's dynamic training confronts the existential dilemma hidden in the koan until mind and koan are no longer separable and the empirical ego has lost itself totally.

What might it be that launches us humans on our quest for a reality that transcends our ego-centered existence, a transcendence intuited and verbalized in models of the really Real?

Let me, (with unavoidable, hence inadequate brevity) hint at three such congruent models, of which the first is hoary with age: the Hua Yen, formulated by Fa T'sang in the seventh century. It posits an infinite continuum of interdependently related phenomena in the universe. In this continuum each phenomenon, each being, is at once totally itself, yet totally interwoven, equivalent—even "self-identical"—with every other phenomenon or being: "One in one, All in all, all in One, One in all."

Alfred North Whitehead—unfamiliar as he was with Hua Yen—came to the recognition of this "mutual immanence" of all phenomena. A very recent model confronts our reality situation like a hologram: in which each point contains all the information about the compounded object it represents, much as every cell in one's body carries the information of one's total organism. As in Hua Yen's radically "ecological" model, here too the Whole is seen in each part and vice versa. All of humankind, one might conclude, is present in each of its members in its entirety. "Pick up anything you like and see IT in everything so clearly manifested ..." (Wanshi, 11th century).

The contemporary Zen scholar Toshihiko Izutsu refers to the Undifferentiated Whole, with the modern term "field," which can only exist insofar as it articulates itself in myriads of beings, each of whom (as in the hologram) actualizing the field in its entirety. By way of example, he applies his model to two famous koans:

When a monk once asked Master Joshu about the fundamental meaning of Zen, Joshu kept silent but pointed at the cypress tree in the front yard. "Here," says Izutsu, "the field, the undifferentiated whole [Nagarjuna's Sunyata, Emptiness, No-Thingness], actualizes itself in its totality in the 'object,' the cypress tree, this *particular* cypress tree."

In the other great koan, Rinzai says to his disciples: "In this mass of reddish flesh [the body] there is a True Man without rank or label. He ceaselessly enters and exits through your sense organs. If you have not met him yet, catch him now!"

A monk asked, "What kind of fellow is this True Man?" Rinzai grabbed him and shouted, "Say it! Say it! Speak!!" The monk was taken aback. Rinzai released his grip and said, "What a good-for-nothing this True Man of yours is …"

Here the undifferentiated whole has concretized itself totally in the "subject," in the monk's still unrealized absolute subjectivity. "I and the field are not-two."

Izutsu is well aware that any intellectual analysis of a koan is doomed to miss the point, but the game he plays here is not precisely an intellectual game, rather it is that of the poetic imagination, and hence it can point in the right direction, make us glimpse the objective and subjective world from a new viewpoint, embracing tree, monk, Joshu, Rinzai, you, and me, as articulations of the field.

Apart from Rinzai Zen and Dogen's Soto Zen, and the eclectic mixtures of these two methodologies which many Zen masters have used, but quite possibly superseding all, there is Bankei's Zen. Bankei, probably the greatest Zen master of Japan, was strenuously opposed to the koan method as being artificial, but objected as much to Soto's "zazen-only" which he found equally spurious. His teaching is centered in "the Unborn" and he told his followers to live by "the Unborn Buddha mind with which everyone is endowed as he comes into this world." "The Unborn is our own being as we have it prior to the world itself." It is the Cosmic Unconsciousness somehow become conscious of itself.

According to Bankei, this Unborn Buddha mind at work in us and our everyday mind are not-two. What Bankei has to say is as simple as it is profound, as transculturally as it is timelessly valid. His sermons are not so much preaching as they are friendly person-to-person communications in which he does not hide the foibles, the obsession with austerities which he had to overcome in his own life: "My own struggle was undertaken mistakenly because I didn't happen to meet with a clear-eyed master. I am not different from any of you." He had freed himself from all that is superfluous, all that is mere convention, faithful and reverent as he was to the authentic tradition. About the teaching methods of the great Zen masters of the past he says: "All were different, because they all responded to particular cases at a particular time."

His own directness and simplicity may well make Bankei's Zen especially suitable for transmission to the Western psyche, a no-nonsense Zen, freed from exotic Oriental tinsel, that can dispense with kimonos and zabutons. "I don't preach on Buddhist teachings," he said, "I only point out the false notions you bring with you. I don't spend my time on old Zen words and stories, quoting this master and that one, feeding on their dregs. Here, from the start, I make people stand absolutely alone and independent, with their eyes fully open."

He says about the use of koans: "I don't let them waste their time on worthless old documents like that. If you don't know yet about your Unborn Buddha mind and it's illuminative wisdom, let me make it clear to you and the Unborn will take care of things."

Notwithstanding his gentleness, he leaves no one in doubt about the rigor of his discipline, but speaking of doubt, he has written critically of the highly praised "ball of doubt" of koan Zen: "People who don't have a doubt, are now saddled with one and have turned their Buddha mind into a 'ball of doubt'... absolutely wrong!"

To the pedantically fundamentalist priests of the Precept Sect, he smiles: "Oh, those Precepts, they were only given by the Buddha because of the evil priests." It is delightful to listen to Bankei defending the monk who fell asleep during zazen: "Don't hit him, do you think he leaves the Buddha mind behind when he sleeps? They can't be sleeping all the time, so they get up, they can't talk constantly, so they stop and do a little zazen. They are not bound here by rules."

"A Zen master," he says, "if he is to be worth anything, must have the Dharma eye. Each word he speaks must strike at the place of the disciple's affliction like a sharp gimlet, so as to usher him into a realm of wonderful freedom and joy."

It is precisely this joy one feels while listening to this utterly sane master telling a group of women—in 17th century Japan!—"Men are Buddha beings, but so are women. Don't doubt it for a moment! Grasp the principle of the Unborn, whether man or woman. Women, unlike men, are very straight-forward about things … In their directness they are the ones who become Buddhas, rather than the men with all their shrewd intellectuality."

Bankei is astute in his psychological diagnosis of our worst foibles as being the result of conditioning and sheer imitation: "You fell into your deluded ways by picking them up gradually from the time you were a baby and watched and listened to people losing their temper. So you were schooled in anger until it became your own habit." His treatment of "thinking" versus "non-thinking" is of utmost clarity.

His single article of faith is the Unborn, and faith here denotes the unconditioned trust in its Presence in each one born human. He could not be more orthodox: had not the Buddha told his listeners about that Unborn, that Unconditioned in us, without which we would never be able to transcend what is born and conditioned? Could it be analogous to St. John's Light that lighteth every man come into the world? "You are all Buddhas sitting here in front of me, you just forgot the Unborn." Bankei's faith in the Unborn, his trust in what is specifically human in everyone born human, of which the Christ and the Buddha are the pioneers and perennial paradigms, might, in modern terminology, be expressed as faith in the mystery of our specifically human genetic code which differentiates us from all ani-mal species and which, if radically denied, condemns us to a sub-animal existence. It is universal, radically transcultural, and an antidote to all narcissistic pseudo-"spirituality."

The last words in these notes on the koan belong to Daisetz T. Suzuki (1870-1966) without whom American Zen is completely inconceivable: "The koan fulfills its purpose when the discipline is guided by an experienced master. Thus, properly guided, the imitator may some day become genuine. But there is one thing which requires full recognition on the part of every koan devotee: it is to remember that each koan is an expression of that Great Wisdom (*Mahaprajna*) and that every such expression gains significance only when associated with the Great Compassion (*Mahakaruna*)."

Parabola
Volume: 1.3
Initiation

Angelus Silesius: Western Zen Poet

Frederick Franck

This is essentially a translation of a little book I rediscovered while browsing in a secondhand bookshop in Copenhagen. I had first read it as a medical student in Holland, where I was born. It had made an impression on me then, this collection of deceptively naïve, mystical rhymes, which I remembered finding much too pious at the time. Some I still recalled vaguely.

That night in my Copenhagen hotel room they opened up in their full and rather awesome profundity, these little rhymes written by a man who died three hundred years ago. He had written them during four days and nights of illumination, satori—in direct confrontation with That which he addressed as God.

The eyes which reread Angelus Silesius, however, had been opened meanwhile by some twenty-five years of almost daily Zen study, and as I was reading, it was as if the ancient Zen masters, who had become my companions and friends, were bending over me, whispering their own—sometimes quite ironic—commentaries in my ear.

It was a fascinating spiritual entertainment, and I decided then and there to translate Angelus Silesius into English and let the Oriental echoes be the running commentary, leaving it to the reader in his meditation and free association to judge their relevancy, their contradictions and agreements.

Angelus Silesius was born Johannes Scheffler in 1624, in a Lutheran family in Breslau, the capital of Silesia. He is a Christian although an unconventional one—and in every breath he mentions God, love, sin, prayer, heavenly bliss. To the Zen man these words mean little or nothing. But when the poet talks about human fate and foibles and of his firsthand experience of what lies beyond, when he speaks about ego and what lies beyond ego, he is a radical for whom God is the unknown Mystery, Nothingness, Abyss. Here the Zen Master would understand him perfectly. Are they perhaps speaking in different words of a very similar experience?

To pretend that all religions are "the same" is as superficial as it is untrue. One might as well say that Madras curry and strawberry sundae are the same, since both are food. Religions were born in very different cultural climates. Each speaks in its own language of man's irrepressible concern with Ultimate Meaning, and each one points to the overcoming of ego as the precondition for the perception of this meaning. To make a hodgepodge of their vocabularies and concepts is confusing rather than helpful. On the other hand, to notice parallels and convergences has become unavoidable, for we are becoming less and less imprisoned within set cultural borders.

The world is fast becoming a single spiritual continent. Symbols and concepts (yes, even God versus no-God) may clash in the brain, yet fuse quite naturally in the much more clairvoyant heart. Our spiritual home is where the heart is. And the human heart has no plural.

Hui Han in the ninth century spoke the definitive word on this underlying unity. He was asked: "Do Confucianism, Taoism, and Buddhism really amount to three teachings or to one?" He answered: "As understood by men of great understanding they are the same. For men of mediocre understanding they differ. All of them spring from the functioning of the same Self-Nature. It is views involving differentiation that make them three. Whether a man gains Illumination or remains deluded depends on himself, not on differences and similarities in doctrine."

Only recently has modern psychology, after a century or more of concentration on mental abnormalities, started to study healthy, integrated human beings. And soon it discovered in the history of these quite normal people what became known as "peak experiences," moments which these ordinary mortals had felt Reality break through, and when, in a flash, life in its inexpressible fullness had opened up. This is the kind of revelation that had always been regarded as the monopoly of privileged mystics. It was found to be within the reach of normal human experience. It may well be the human experience par excellence.

Such experiences one remembers as long as one lives. They are the root experiences of art and of religion. They are the first manifestations of the True Man within. And all too often these first intimations of wonder are blotted out by years of schooling and conditioning instead of being encouraged. But to the extent that conditioning and indoctrination fail, the inner-artist may still blossom and the inner-mystic find scope to ripen that is, to find his treasure house within. Religious experience is the finding of the treasure house within.

Of time and eternity

There is that which precedes
heaven and earth.
It is formless, nameless.
The eye cannot perceive it.
To speak of it as mind or Buddha
is inexact,
then it becomes again
something in our imagination.
The Tao
cannot be expressed in words.
*   —Dai-o-Kokushi*

There is no here, no there.
Infinity lies before our eyes.
*   —Sengtsan*

A man who has seen into
his Self-Nature
sees it whenever questioned
about it.
*   —Hui Neng*

To what shall I compare
this life of ours? Even
before I can say it is
like a lightning flash or a dewdrop,
it is no more.
*   —Sengai*

Do not compute eternity
as light-year after year.
One step across
that line called Time:
Eternity is here.

The rose that
with my mortal eye I see
flowers in God
through all eternity.

Eternity is time,
Time, eternity.
To see the two as opposites
is mind's perversity.

Man has two eyes.
One only sees what moves in
fleeting time,
the other
what is eternal and divine.

Timelessness
is so much part of you,
of me,
We cannot hope to find
the Self
until aware of our eternity.

I am God's alter ego.
He is my counterpart.
In timelessness we merge—
in time we seem apart.

At the end of that
which we call history
God is who IS:
for Him there is no past
nor future yet to be.
*   —Angelus Silesius*

Of the one and the many

The Tao can be shared,
it cannot be divided.
        —Chuang Tzu

The Supreme Wisdom (Prajna)
is the Oneness of things;
the Supreme Compassion (Karuna)
is the Manyness of things.
        —D. T. Suzuki

In the world of Reality
there is no Self,
there is no other than Self.
        —Sengtsan

The mind, the Buddha and
living beings,
these are not
three different things.
        —Avatamsaka Sutra

When the Ten Thousand Things
are seen in their Oneness,
we return to the Origin
where we have always been.
        —Sengtsan

It is not that things are illusory
but their separateness in
the fabric of Reality
is illusory.
        —Anon.

The wise have one wish left:
to know the Whole, the Absolute.
The foolish lose themselves
        in fragments
and ignore the root.

To reflect God in all that is
both now and here,
my heart must be a mirror
empty, bright, and clear.

Do not malign
a single thing
for God
not only is its maker
but also its design.

Who is God? No one can tell.
He is not dark of night
nor light of day.
He is not One nor Many
nor a Father as some say.
Nor is he wisdom
intellect, or even mercy;
He is not Being—
nor non-Being
neither thing
nor no-thing.
Perhaps He is
what I and all
who ever did or will have being
could ever be capable of seeing
before becoming what He is.

God is the circle's center
for those who dare to embrace Him.
For those who merely stand in awe
He is the circle's rim.

> *A ruby*
> *is not lovelier*
> *than a rock,*
> *an angel*
> *not more glorious*
> *than a frog.*
>   *—Angelus Silesius*

Of ego and the makings of destiny

We are like those who,
immersed in water,
stretch out their hands
begging for a drink.
                —*Seppo*

We have one moon,
clear and unclouded,
yet we are lost
in the darkness of the world.
                —*Ikkyu*

Because of our accepting
and rejecting
the Suchness of things
escapes us.
The way is not
difficult, provided we stop
picking and choosing.
                —*Sengtsan*

If you want to do a certain thing
you first have to be a certain
person.
Once you have become
that certain person
you will not care any more
about doing that certain thing.
                —*Dogen*

There once was a one-legged dragon
called Hui—How on earth do you manage
all those legs, he asked
a centipede,
I can hardly manage one.
—Matter of fact,
said the centipede, I do not
manage my legs.
                —*Chuang Tzu*

By honors, medals, titles
no true man is elated.
To realize that which we are,
this is the honor
for which we are created.

All evils—
murder, war, and cruel oppression—
from what else do they spring
than from the Me's obsession?

Be sure as long as
worldly fancies you pursue
you are a hollow man—
a pauper lives in you.

Go out and God comes in;
die and in God withdraw—
not-being you will be,
not-doing you will live His Law.

Man the great glutton,
devours the whole cosmos
like a beast.
Then, hungry still,
claims yet another cosmos
for his feast.

She blooms because she blooms,
the rose …
Does not ask why,
nor does she preen herself
to catch my eye.
                —*Angelus Silesius*

Of life and death

Whence is my life?
Whither does it go?
I sit alone in my hut
and meditate quietly.
With all my thinking
I know nowhere
nor do I come to any whither:
such is my present.
Eternally changing—
all in Emptiness.

In this Emptiness the ego
rests for a while
with its yeas and nays.
I know not where to place them.
I follow my Karma as it moves
with perfect contentment.
            —Ryokwan

If you long to transcend life and death
coming and going, if you want
to attain liberation
you must recognize the man who
is now listening to the Dharma.
You who sit here listening to me
are not the elements that make
up your bodies. You are that which
makes use of these elements.
Be able to see into this truth and
you will be free, whether coming
or going.
            —Rinzai

I shall not die.
I shall not go anywhere.
I'll be here …
Just don't ask me anything.
            —Ikkyu

Of an early death
showing no signs
the cicada sang.
            —Basho

All you achieve
must perish
when this world ends.
Therefore become that which you are
and which the world transcends.

Christ is forever
rising from the grave—
the Spirit cannot be
held captive in a cave.

Death does not frighten me,
it only makes me see
how in the here-and-now
life conquers death in me.

You are not real, Death,
for I die every minute
and am reborn in the next
into life infinite.

The arrow always fails the mark—
will never enter—
if it is I who take the aim
instead of That which is my center.

The heart that grasps the point
of each contingency
sees the chaos that surrounds it
as pure transparency.

Saints do not die.
It is their lot
to die while on this earth
to all that God is not.
            —Angelus Silesius

Of heaven and hell

—*Do hell and heaven really exist?*
a samurai asked. Hakuin growled:
—*Who are you?*
—*I am a samurai.*
—*You a samurai? You look like a bum*
to me!
    Infuriated, the samurai grabbed for
    his sword.
—*So you do have a sword, huh?*
It is probably too dull
to cut off my head.
    As the sword came out of its
    sheath, Hakuin cried:
—*Here open the gates of hell!*
    The samurai, impressed with Hakuin's
calm, put his sword back and bowed.
—*Here open the gates of paradise,*
said Hakuin.

That which acts in all and meddles
in none, is Heaven (Tao).
    —*Chuang Tzu*

All sins committed
in the three worlds
will fade and disappear
together with myself.
    —*Ikkyu*

Your treasure house is within.
It contains all you will ever need.
Use it fully instead of
seeking vainly outside yourself.
    —*Hui Hai*

No thought for the hereafter
have the wise,
for on this very earth
they live in paradise.

All heaven's glory is within
and so is hell's fierce burning.
You must yourself decide
in which direction
you are turning.

Unless you find paradise
at your own center
there is not
the smallest chance
that you may enter.

What is it not to sin?
I did not ever know
until, one day,
my eye did really see
a flower grow.

He whose treasure house is God
his earth is paradise.
Why then call those
who make this earth a hell
the worldly wise?
    —*Angelus Silesius*

Of prayer and meditation

—*What is the Buddha? a monk asked.*
—*Will you believe me? Can I tell you?*
—*Of course, Master!*
—*Well, you are it!*
—*How can I remain it?*
—*Ah, if your eye is just the slightest*
bit blurred, all you see are hallucinations.

We pray for our life tomorrow.
Ephemeral as life may be,
this is the habit of our mind
that passed away yesterday.
            —*Ikkyu*

The mind remaining
just as it was born—
without any prayer
it becomes the Buddha.
            —*Ikkyu*

Zen practiced in the state of
activity is incomparably
superior to that practiced
in the state of withdrawal.
            —*Daie*

If you seek the Buddha outside of
the mind, the Buddha changes
into a devil.
            —*Dogen*

How often have I prayed
"Lord, do your will . . . "
But see: He does no willing—
motionless He is and still.

The deepest prayer
which I could ever say
is that which makes me One
with That to which I pray.

God is such as He is,
I am as I must be.
And yet no two-ness
do I see.

Give me all your bounty,
give me eternal bliss—
as long as You withhold Yourself
all things I miss.

Be still and empty:
He shall fill
you with far greater fullness
than you could ever
wish or will.

So far beyond all words is He,
I know no other way
than not to speak.
Thus without words
I pray.

In the depth of His Abyss
God is pure contemplation.
The deepest ground
of all that is
dwells in perpetual adoration.

Prayer is neither word nor gesture,
chant nor sound.
It is to be in still communication
with our Ground.
            —*Angelus Silesius*

Of the inner light
and enlightenment

—*What is the Buddha, Master?*
—*You have no Buddha Nature!*
—*Then what about the animals?*
—*They do have the Buddha Nature!*
—*And why should I be devoid of it?*
—*Because you have to ask and do not*
recognize it yourself.
        —*Chuang Tzu*

Walking is Zen, sitting is Zen;
whether we speak or are silent
move or are still,
it is unperturbed.
        —*Yungchia*

—*What happens when an enlightened*
Man slides back into delusion? a monk
asked.
—*A broken mirror does not reflect properly,*
fallen flowers do not jump back onto the
branch!
        —*Sengtsan*

I know the joy of a fish
in the river
through my own joy
walking along the river.
        —*Chuang Tzu*

Do not search for Truth.
Just stop having opinions.
        —*Sengtsan*

The longest way to God,
the indirect,
lies through the intellect.
The shortest way
lies through the heart.
Here is my journey's end
and here its start.

Unknowable, unnamable,
You seem the other pole.
And yet
my human heart
contains You whole.

The Clear Light
Cannot be attained
until both heart and mind
have deepest insight gained.

Desire returns
as soon as we ignore
the divine essence
at our core.

Mysterious Being
infinitely far from me,
who yet in every beating
of this heart must be.

I am not outside God,
He is not outside me.
I am His radiance;
my light is He.

No sweeter tone
from any lute could spring
than when this heart
and that of God
resound as with one string.
        —*Angelus Silesius*

Of God and the true Self

God is not nice. God is no uncle.
God is an earthquake!
　　　　—Hassidic saying

—I came here to find the Truth, Master.
—Why wander around? Why do you
neglect your precious treasure at home?
—What do you call my precious treasure?
—That which asks the question is the
treasure.

—All these mountains, rivers, this whole
great earth, where does it all come from?
—Where does your question come from?
　　　　—Cheng-Tao ke

—What is the deepest meaning of Bud-
dhism, Master?

The Master made a deep bow to his pupil.

Wherever I may be, I meet him—
　　He is no other than myself.
　　Yet I am not he.
　　　　—Dosan

All the Buddhas and Bodhisattvas are his
servants. Who is he?
Whoever sees him clearly, feels
as if he has met his own father
on the street corner—
　　he does not have to ask others
　　if he is right or wrong.
　　　　—Mumonkan

The figure of the True Man
standing there—
One glimpse
of him and we are in love.
　　　　—Ikkyu

Gautama and Amida too were
originally human beings.
Have I not also the face of a man?
　　　　—Ikkyu

Within our impure mind
the pure one is to be found.
　　　　—Hui Neng

I am as rich as God.
Each dust mote
more or less
do I in common
with my God possess.

See what no eye can see,
go where no foot can go
choose that which is no choice—
then you may hear
what makes no sound—
God's voice.

Do not cry out to God.
Your own heart is the source
from which He flows unceasingly
unless you stop its course.

God is a phantom
drifting by—
until you see Him all around you
and stop asking
who? what? why?

The saint forgets
all about God's commands.
He acts spontaneously
as love of man—and God—demands.

God is abundance,
His gifts beyond all measure.
My heart is bewildered—
afraid to hold such treasure.

As great as God I am,
as small as I is He.
How could I below Him
or He above me be?

Do not seek God
in outer space—
Your heart's the only place
in which to meet Him
face to face.
　　　　—Angelus Silesius

Of bondage and freedom

Whether you are bound by a gold
chain or an iron one,
you are in captivity.
Your virtuous activities are the
gold chain, your evil ones the
iron one. He who shakes off both
the chains of good and evil
that imprison him,
him I call a Brahman—
he has attained the Supreme Truth.
                    —Buddhist Scripture

One of his disciples asked the
Buddha: —If I should be questioned about
my Master's opinion, what shall I say?

—You shall say: The Venerable One
holds no opinions.
He is freed of all opinions.
                    —Buddhist Scripture

When one no longer believes
* in the "I,"*
When one has rejected
all beliefs, the time has come
* to bestow gifts.*
                    —Buddhist Scripture

A monk asked:
—Please help me: Show me how to attain
liberation.
—Who has bound you? the Master
questioned him.
—No one has bound me.
—Then why ask me to be released?
The monk had a profound realization.
                    —Sengtsan

Nothing keeps you bound
except your Me—
until you break
its chains, its handcuffs,
and are free.

To see the light at all
I must first leap across
all barriers,
destroy the Me's defenses,
tear down its wall.

The emptier I do become
the more delivered from the Me,
the better shall I understand
God's liberty.

I was God inside God
before I became Me
and shall be God again
when from my Me set free.

You who did create
and can unmake this earth,
You cannot force
against my will
my second birth.

Who freedom loves
loves God
and only he is free
who freed from all desire
in God finds liberty.
                    —Angelus Silesius

Of the central mystery

Form is the Void, and the Void is Form.
The Void is nothing else but Form
and the Form is nothing else but the Void.
Outside the Void there is no Form,
and outside the Form there is no Void.
                    —Nagarjuna

The infinitely small is as large as the
infinitely big. Limits are nonexistent. The
infinitely large is as small as the infinitely
minute.
No eye can see their boundaries.
                    —Sengtsan

Outside the Buddha
there is no mind,
outside the mind
there is no Buddha.
                    —Baso

—I come to you with nothing, said the
monk.
—All right, just drop it! Joshu
answered.
—But I just said that I have
nothing; what is there to be
dropped?
—Then just carry it away with you!

If you break open the cherry tree
where are the blossoms?
But in springtime
how they bloom!
                    —Ikkyu

It is spring
In this hut
*   there is nothing*
*   there is everything.*
                    —Ryoto

How this heart
no larger than my hand
can enfold heaven, hell, and
*   this wide earth*
this is the Mystery
no man will ever understand.

All the unfolding, growth
and evolution we are seeing,
all this changing and becoming
God sees as timeless Being.

I know, but don't know why,
that without me
God cannot live
nor without Him
can I.

When I am neither you nor me,
When there is no more
here nor there—
then I begin to be
of God as Nothingness aware.
Nothingness You are,
fathomless Abyss.
To see Abyss in all
is seeing
that which Is.

He is pure Nothingness.
He is not now, not here.
I reach for Him
and see Him disappear.

De profundis,
my heart cries out
to the divine Abyss.
Which of the two
the deeper is?

Now I must end.
Beloved,
if you would read more,
look deep into your heart
all Scripture's
root and core.
                    —Angelus Silesius

Material reprinted with the cooperation and permission of the author and publisher from *The Book of Angelus Silesius*, trans., drawn, and handwritten by Frederick Franck (New York: Alfred A. Knopf, Inc., 1976).

Parabola
Volume: 12.4
The Sense of Humor

THE SMILE OF TRUTH

Conrad Hyers

> *When one has understanding, one should laugh;*
> *One should not weep.*
>
> —*Hsüeh-t'ou*

The smile of Asian peoples has often been represented, usually in the caricatures of politically inspired cartooning and the stereotypes of popular Caucasian imagination to which both the Chinese and Japanese have been subjected. But that smile, insofar as it corresponds to reality at all, has a profound basis in the unusual stress in both Chinese and Japanese culture upon the human sphere and the natural graces, and indeed upon the most practical, earthen, everyday phenomena of life. It is a smile that is grounded in the peculiarly Oriental aversion to the more abstract flights and ethereal delights of Indian and Western peoples, and a preference for the concrete, this-worldly, ordinary-human, even "trivial" moments of day-to-day existence. In fact, if one may speak of a special, and seldom appreciated, contribution of Asian peoples to world civilization, it is to be found here: in this smile and what it symbolizes.

A smile, of course, can mean many things. Here it may be said to represent a special sensitivity to the comic-mundane, a tender affection for even the commonplace things of life. Or—relative to the spiritual other-worldliness and mythological fantasy and philosophical grandeur of so many other cultures—it may be seen as a collapse of the sublime, an affirmation of unaffected naturalness and simplicity. As in the Tao of Lao-tzu, it is the smile of the child, and the smile of the sage.

It is in this soil, simple, earthy, pragmatic and humanistic in its most sophisticated forms, that the comic spirit of Zen is rooted, like the lotus flower that radiates from the lowliness of the mud at the bottom of the pond, and whose leaf-pads provide seats for all those little bullfrog Buddhas that are favored in Zen art and poetry. In both its Chinese origins and its later Japanese elaborations, the development of Buddhism known as Ch'an and later Zen owes much of its particularity to the distinctiveness of this Chinese and Japanese worldview. Out of the collision of the lofty spiritualism of Indian Buddhism and the earthiness of Oriental humanism and naturalism come both Zen and the comic spirit of Zen. For all of the austerities and rigors of Zen, and the serenity of its religious vision, in it the Chinese dragon smiles and the Indian Buddha roars with laughter.

Out from the hollow

Of the Great Buddha's nose

A swallow comes.

— *Issa[1]*

The Zen tradition, in fact, according to legend, begins with a smile. This in itself, however apocryphal its basis, is a remarkable distinction in the history of religion, and profoundly suggestive of the character of Zen. Insofar as Zen has concerned itself with the question of its lineage, and of its relationship to the historical Buddha and his teachings, it has traced its ancestry not only to the awesome meditation master Bodhidharma, or to the philosophically formidable figure of Nāgārjuna, but to one of the Buddha's disciples, Kāśyapa, whose principal distinction is that, at a critical moment, he smiled. According to the tale, when once the Buddha was gathered with his disciples, a Brahma-raja came to him with an offering of a beautiful golden flower, and requested that he preach a sermon. When the Buddha ascended to his customary seat of instruction, however, he spoke no words to the expectant audience, but simply held up the sandalwood flower before the assembly. None of those present understood the Buddha's meaning, except for Kāśyapa who received the teaching instantly and acknowledged it with a smile.

This is the peculiar and profoundly symbolic origin attributed to Zen. And it is this smile, this sudden intuition of Truth, and this wordless transmission of the Dharma, that is said to have been handed down through twenty-eight Indian Patriarchs, the last of which was Bodhidharma who brought the doctrineless "teaching" to China in the sixth century A.D. The Buddha's silent gaze on Vulture Peak is the commencement of that propositionless communication of the innermost nature of things that is pivotal in Zen, that first and last word which cannot be spoken and which cannot be heard. This is the emphasis customarily and not incorrectly given to the Zen use of the legend. But the other aspect of the story is also important, and that is Kāśyapa's smile of understanding—a smile that is carried through in the subtlest to the most raucous forms throughout the later developments of Zen. This smile is the signature of the sudden realization of the "point," and the joyful approval of its significance. It is the smile of Truth, or the Truth smiling. It is the glad reception of that moment of insight which has taken the whole world by surprise, a moment of seeing with the freshness and immediacy of the little child, full of amazement and wonder—a "holy yea" which is capable of transforming even specks of dust into stars and frogs into Buddhas. And it is this smile, historically authentic or not, which is the beginning and end of Zen.

Insofar as one can speak of fundamental images in a tradition that is so strongly non-symbolic and iconoclastic, there may be said to be two basic types of images in Zen, most noticeable at first in Zen paintings where they are constantly recurring, as if each calls forth and counterbalances the other. The one is the epitome of resolute seriousness; the other of buoyant laughter. The one is seated in the placid stillness of meditation; the other is airily dancing a folkdance.

The one suggests the extremities of earnestness and commitment; the other the carefreeness of gaiety, if not frivolity. The one presents the visage of the master or sage; the other of the child or clown or fool.

The first set of images in Zen is typified by the figure of Bodhidharma, determinedly facing the wall of a cave for nine years in intense meditation until, according to legend, his legs rotted off. Or Bodhidharma, accepting Hui-k'o as a disciple after the latter had cut off his arm in demonstration of his absolute sincerity and utter seriousness. Or Bodhidharma, confronting all would-be seekers of enlightenment like some fierce and formidable giant whose sheer presence overwhelms the staunchest defenses of the ego. Or Bodhidharma, whose piercing eyes shoot forth like daggers from beneath shaggy brows set in a great craggy forehead, seeing through all the schemes of desire and the fortresses of ignorance.

The other set of images in Zen is typified by the figure of Pu-tai (Hotei, d. A.D. 916) who is even larger in bulk than Bodhidharma, yet more like an overgrown child, and no more awesome and fearsome than the pot-bellied "laughing Buddha" which he becomes. Pu-tai, who refuses to enter a monastery on any basis suggestive of permanence, and instead wanders freely without attachment even to the securities of cloistered walls and the forms of monkish discipline. Pu-tai who, like a carefree vagabond, carries a large linen sack from place to place as his only home. Pu-tai, whose jolly, roly-poly figure is to be seen dancing merrily, as if (as in Liang-k'ai's sketch, thirteenth century) floating gracefully in the air in spite of his size, seeming barely to touch the earth without leaving a trace. Pu-tai, whose religious life consists of playing with village children, as if life had now come full circle, as if the end were in some way a return to the beginning, as if even children and fools knew what priests and monks did not.

In consort with the herculean image of Bodhidharma is an impressive train of like figures, such as Lin-chi (Rinzai) with his lion's roar, snarling face and clenched fist, shouting and frightening monks directly into Nirvana, as it were. Or Tē-shan (Tokusan) sitting almost menacingly, with his oak-stick poised in his lap, intently awaiting the precise moment when it will be needed for the collapsing of all categories (e.g., the Bodhidharma triptych by Soga Shōhaku, fifteenth century). Similarly, one may point to the two favorite Zen creatures, the tiger (or lion) and the dragon, which seem to have reincarnated themselves in so many Zen masters, and which, sharing in this same symbolism, serve as powerful animal emblems of the Zen sect.

Yet Pu-tai also has his retinue of attendant "Bodhisattvas" and "totems." And a strange retinue it is. There are the two poet-recluses and

monastery fools, Han-shan (Kanzan) and Shih-tē (Jitto-ku), with their boisterous, almost mad, and seemingly near-demonic laughter. And there are the three laughing sages of Hu-hsi, overcome with mirth in every painting, as if a Zen trinity were enjoying some eternal joke. Or there is Ryōkwan (1758-1831), the "Great Fool," as he called himself, of the Japanese Sōtō tradition who, like his Chinese predecessor and counterpart, delighted in playing games with children, or folk-dancing in the village. In fact, so absorbed would Ryōkwan become in this kind of "*zazen*" that in one game of hide-and-seek he is reputed to have hid himself with such success under a haystack as not to be discovered until the next morning by a farmer!

Furthermore, this set of comic figures also has its favorite animals with which it, too, is associated, like the animal vehicles (*vāhanas*) of the Hindu gods. But instead of the tiger and dragon, in this case it is the monkey, or the frog, or the chicken, or even the louse! Liang-k'ai depicts Pu-tai in one painting as deeply and delightedly engrossed in a cockfight, like a little boy hovering over a crucial game of marbles. Mu-ch'i, in addition to tigers and dragons, favored monkeys, cranes, and swallows. Sengai was fond of frogs. Indeed, one of his frog sketches carries the heterodox inscription: "If by sitting in meditation (*zazen*) one becomes a Buddha ... [then all frogs are Buddhas!]."

Ryōkwan, among his many peculiarities, devoted special attention to lice, not only giving them a place of honor in his poetry, but sheltering them in his robe. And *haiku* verse—a literary oddity in itself—under Zen inspiration came to add a motley garden variety of lowly creatures to the sublime objects of aesthetic and religious representation: dogs, geese, and carp; the thrush, the cuckoo, the sparrow, and the crow; yes, and butterflies, fireflies, caterpillars, locusts, ants, bees, and common flies.

Sitting like the Buddha,

But bitten by mosquitoes

In my Nirvana.

—*Demaru*[2]

The tiger is now reduced to a house cat, grinning from the veranda. The dragon is gone, and in his place— a dragonfly.

He who appears

Before you now—is the toad

Of this thicket.

—*Issa*[3]

The set of images and symbols that cluster about the figure of Bodhidharma have been dealt with extensively in the literature on Zen. But what is one to do with this other set of images and symbols, especially when they, and their lowly animal "vehicles," are given such prominence in Zen legend, literature, poetry and art? What is their function and meaning in this curiously unfolding dialectic? What is it that they reveal? What mysteries do they open up? To what level of being and knowing do they point?

Most of what has been written about Zen, to phrase it as boldly as possible, is Bodhidharma Zen to the virtual exclusion of Pu-tai Zen; or dragon and tiger Zen apart from frog and flea Zen. Only occasionally in some writings, and never at all in others, does this dimension make its appearance and suggest its significance—as if it were only accidentally related to Zen, or perhaps not related at all. And in some cases, no doubt, this fairly accurately reflects the character of the Zen of a certain period, or school, or master, or interpreter; and especially when Zen is reduced to an orthodoxy or orthopraxy. Yet the images of Pu-tai, and his strange brethren, and his stranger menagerie of fellow-creatures, right down to the despicable louse, have persisted with the persistence of exuberant children, chirping crickets and croaking frogs. And in their earthiness and unorthodoxy, their lowliness and commonplaceness, and in their playfulness and laughter and freedom, they continue to call attention to something very important, perhaps even supremely important, about both Zen and life.

In these terms, a basic Zen question—a *kōan* in its own right—is: What does Pu-tai symbolize?

Toward what level of existence, into what kind of spirit, unto what insight and realization, does he, and the odd train of figures that accompany him, like the Pied Pipers of an Oriental carnival, lead?

It is to be expected that some objection, perhaps even offense, will be taken because of the association suggested here, and frequently made hereafter, between Zen and the clown-figure and the comic-mundane, as if this were making light of, or ridiculing, or debasing Zen. Quite the contrary. This is not to detract or subtract from Zen in the slightest, but rather to add to it that dimension apart from which one is left with only "half-a-person" Zen. Of course, if one understands Zen as simply a "serious business" and therefore sees clown-figures like Pu-tai or Ryōkwan or Han-Shan and Shih-tē as threatening to a Zen so conceived, or if one understands the clown as being a peripheral, shadowy, base, or corrupting figure in relation to the priest or master or seer or sage, then this is correct. But there is far more depth and significance, yes, and spirituality, in the clown than has commonly been recognized. He, too, belongs to a venerable tradition, and has an ancient history, and is no more intrinsically superficial or childish or base than the sacred personages which he often stands over against, parodies and counterbalances. If his function and meaning has suffered many biases and misunderstandings,

so has theirs. If his historical record and actual performance has often been coarse or dehumanizing or even demonic, they are no exception either. But at his best and profoundest he, too, is a religious figure and a religious symbol. And in this role he stands at least on a par with all other religious *personae*, and, in some respects, even above them. For, as in the case of Pu-tai, he represents a larger spirit and a fuller, more embracing truth. The roundness of Pu-tai is the full circle of existence and the complete vision of life.

It is one of the peculiar distinctions of Zen in the history of religion to have appreciated this possibility, indeed necessity, and to have made it an integral part of the Zen experience and Zen perspective. Among the many unusual—though from the Zen standpoint perfectly normal—features of Zen is precisely that there is a singular and delightful at-homeness of the comic in Zen, and of Zen in the comic, an at-homeness which is surely remarkable and significant enough to be worthy of more extended treatment than it has heretofore been granted. And if this appears to be a way into Zen, and a way of Zen, which is strange and uncommon, it must be remembered that Zen masters themselves, as evidenced from the earliest anecdotal records, have often had some strange and uncommon ways of coming into Zen, and of pointing others to it: ways frequently eccentric and unorthodox, nonsensical and clownish, absurd and humorous. A tile falling off the roof and cracking the skull, the ping of a stone striking a stalk of bamboo, a slap in the face or a kick in the chest, a deafening roar or a rollicking guffaw, a single finger held up in silence or an enigmatic barrage of doubletalk; this is but a small sampling of the bizarre techniques and curious occasions for spiritual realization that form the patchwork of Zen history.

What is being alluded to here, then, is not the clown as some inferior species, approaching the infantile or subhuman or chaotic, but the clown who in all his lowliness and simplicity and childlikeness, as well as in his iconoclasm and redemptive profanity, is truly great, truly profound, truly free. In this sense Pu-tai is a larger image of the Zen-man than Bodhidharma. For he is Bodhidharma having transcended the cave and returned to the light—and, as legend would have it, the very incarnation, in this lowliest of forms, of the Future Buddha, Maitreya.

Like all mysticisms, Zen is concerned to overcome certain dualities which are seen as splitting up existence, delimiting experience, and hiding true reality. But in overcoming such dualities, it is very easy to become caught up, perhaps quite unwittingly, in certain other dualities, in particular those in which the dialectic of Bodhidharma and Pu-tai are involved: seriousness and laugh-

ter, sobriety and gaiety, holiness and humor, the dramatic and the comic, commitment and detachment, zealousness and frivolity, earnestness and disinterestedness, sense and nonsense, purpose and purposelessness, work and play. If the "resolution" of Zen does not resolve this, then everything has only been resolved into yet another duality. And one is still left with only "half-a-person" Zen.

Defeating the ego, desire, attachment and discrimination is one thing. Defeating the mentality of seriousness, labor and the dramatic alone is another—especially when the latter is seen as fundamental not only to the defeat, but also to the marking and maintenance of the victory over the former. If this is all that Zen achieves, then even the little child knows more than Bodhidharma. If this is the terminus of Zen, then even the fool is wiser than the supreme wisdom of the *Prājnāpāramitā*. For if Bodhidharma cannot laugh, it is because he has not seen through his meditation wall. If he cannot play, it is because he is still imprisoned in his cave. If he cannot dance, it is because his legs have indeed rotted off.

Among the 1700 *kōans* which are said to be suitable for precipitating or deepening an inner spiritual illumination, and also for providing a test of its genuineness as an "awakening," is the following question attributed to Hsiang-yen (Kyōgen, 819-914) and furnished with commentary by

Wu-mēn (Mumon, 1184-1260) in his *"Gateless Gate" to Zen Experience:*

(Zen) is like a man up a tree who hangs on a branch by his teeth with his hands and feet in the air. A man at the foot of the tree asks him, "What is the point of Bodhidharma's coming from the West [i.e., from India to China]?" If he does not answer he would seem to evade the question. If he answers he would fall to his death. In such a predicament what response should he given?

[Wu-mēn's commentary and verse] It is as useless to be gifted with a flowing stream of eloquence as to discourse on the teaching in the great Tripitaka. *Whoever answers this question correctly can give life to the dead and take life from the living. Whoever cannot must wait for the coming of Maitreya and ask him.*

Hsiang-yen (Kyōgen) is really outrageous. The poison he brewed spreads everywhere. It closes the mouths of Zen monks, And makes their eyes goggle.[4]

According to the later *Imperial Collection of Ch'an (Zen) Sayings* (1723-35), when Hsiang-yen first posed this *kōan* a leading monk, Chao, of another monastery who was present commented: "I do not ask this question when the man is on the tree, but I ask it before he climbs up! Will the Venerable Master speak to this?" Whereupon Hsiang-yen gave a loud roar of laughter.[5]

In the elements of humor and laughter visible in such enigmatic *kōans* and *mondōs* (dialogues) and

their witty commentaries and versified parodies is to be found but one of many examples of the important place granted to the whole spectrum of the comic in Zen. In Zen, too, in fact especially, there is a time to laugh and a time to dance, as well as a time to weep and to mourn (Eccl 3:4). D. T. Suzuki has argued that "Zen is the only religion or teaching that finds room for laughter."[6] Though in relation to other religions this is, no doubt, an overstatement, in relation to Zen it is more of an understatement. For Zen does more than find room for laughter—which might, after all, mean only a very small and rarely occupied room at the back of the house. In a unique sense, the house of Zen is the house of laughter.

R. H. Blyth, with his penchant for dashing comment and characterization, has defined the essence of Zen as humor.[7] Whether or not one might be satisfied to state the matter so bluntly, such an equation of Zen and humor nevertheless points to the possibility of interpreting Zen as that point in the movement of Buddhism from India to China and Japan in which humor comes to be most fully developed and self-consciously employed as an integral part of both a pedagogical method and an enlightened outlook—that is, both as one of the stratagems for realizing enlightenment and as one of the consequences of enlightenment. Indeed, no more fitting token of this could be found than that of the "loud roaring laughter" for which so many Zen masters have been noted, and which very early in the tradition becomes a favorite motif in both Zen literature and painting.

A standard phrase in Zen training, applied to a monk who is so ultra-serious about his disciplines and his "Zennishness" that his very zeal and fanaticism are self-defeating, is that "he stinks (or reeks) of Zen." Over against what is seen here as bondage to earnestness, striving and sincerity, if not a bit of that old demon Pride, stands the commonly repeated phrase in the extensive corpus of Zen anecdotes, and the catharsis and wisdom which it brings: "And the monk (or master) clapped his hands and gave a loud roar of laughter." At the same time, as has already been intimated, three of the most frequently represented themes in Zen art are the gleefully dancing Pu-tai, the rotund embodiment of playfulness and mirth, the monastery fools, Han-shan and Shih-tē, bending over and laughing with hilarious abandon, and the "Three Laughing Sages of Hu-hsi," beside themselves in merriment.

This is particularly striking when one recalls that the Indian Buddhist scholastics, following the dramatic classifications of Bharata (fourth century A.D.), carefully distinguished among six classes of laughter arranged in hierarchical fashion from the most sublime to the most sensuous and unrefined,

only the most restrained forms of which were considered appropriate to the comportment of gentlemen and monks, and to the theatrical representation of such. The descending scale of categories in itself suggests that the fullest and most pronounced and enjoyable forms of laughter are *per se* at the furthest remove from both piety and propriety: *sita*, a faint, almost imperceptible smile manifest in the subtleties of facial expression and countenance alone; *hasita*, a smile involving a slight movement of the lips, and barely revealing the tips of the teeth; *vihasita*, a broad smile accompanied by a modicum of laughter; *upahasita*, accentuated laughter, louder in volume, associated with movements of the head, shoulders and arms; *apahasita*, loud laughter that brings tears; and *atihasita*, the most boisterous, uproarious laughter attended by movements of the entire body (e.g., doubling over in raucous guffawing, convulsions, hysterics, "rolling in the aisles," etc.).

Given this classification, obviously influenced by the ideals of aristocratic sophistication, it was understood that the first two types represented the restrained, polite laughter of the highly cultured and refined individual, the middle categories the moderate laughter of the average man, while the last two characterized the intemperate and vulgar laughter of the uncouth lower classes. The religious interpretation of this dramatic scheme followed suit, if it did not to some extent influence it. The first two forms approach the spiritual and the sublime; the last two descend into the crassness of the physical and the sensual, lowering and degrading the spirit. And, as might be expected from the logic of the system, and the presumed threat of laughter with respect to holy things, the Buddha was supposed to have indulged only in *sita*, the most serene, subtle and refined form of laughter.[8] It is almost as if to say that the Buddha was only "guilty" of the first form of laughter!

To the puritanism of the pious imagination, and the humorlessness of the scholastic *lack* of imagination, it has always seemed unthinkable that the Buddha should have stooped to the "barbarous" level of openly displaying the teeth in a jovial grin, or of emitting even modest chuckles of amusement, let alone the more "immodest" forms of hilarity. Yet what is commonly found in Zen, so much so as not only to characterize Zen but to be symbolic of it, is none other than *apahasita* and *atihasita*, the loud, uproarious, unrestrained laughter that is presumably at the furthest remove from the delicate and scarcely detectable smile of the Buddha, and from the placidity that Nirvāna represents. As Christmas Humphreys has commented: "There is more honest 'belly laughter' in a Zen monastery than surely in any other religious institution on earth. To laugh is a sign of sanity; and the comic is deliberately used to break

up concepts, to release tensions and to teach what cannot be taught in words. Nonsense is used to point to the beyond of rational sense."[9]

While it may be true at a preliminary level that, as one Japanese *senryu* puts it, "the man who giggles is omitted from the selection for the ambush,"[10] it is also true at another level that the man who is incapable of laughter, and of seeing the humor in his situation, is both trapped by his own ambush and omitted from the celebration that follows the ambush. Zen is a kind of ambush undertaking against the traditional Buddhist "devils" of ego, ignorance, desire, attachment, and bondage. But what a strange ambush it is! The peculiarity of the Zen onslaught and surprise is that it is often undertaken in the spirit and with the weapons of the comic rather than the dramatic, in laughter as well as seriousness, and therefore stands from beginning to end within the comic parenthesis. As Yüan-wu (Engo, 1063-1135) commented with respect to a Zen episode which culminated, like so many Zen episodes, in the master's hearty laugh: "His laughter is like a cool, refreshing breeze passing through the source of all things."[11]

Thus, while one many be accustomed to seeking for signs of enlightened attainment in the sober features of deep meditation and intense absorption, in Zen one may like as not be presented with images of gaiety, lightheartedness, and mirth.

Where we expect a representation of determined resolution and grave demeanor, we are often given instead a picture that seems to suggest profanity more than piety, and frivolity rather than zealousness. When intimations of sublime serenity and unperturbable tranquility are anticipated, we may in fact be confronted with the raucousness of a laughter that seems to shake the very foundation of the world—which, indeed, is exactly what it does! For Zen is not only the tradition of the overwhelming ferocity of Bodhidharma, who seems to pounce like a great Bengal tiger out of every ink-sketch to break the arms and legs of unsuspecting monks, or like a celebrated Chinese dragon summarily to devour all traces of ego, desire and attachment. It is also the tradition of the jolly Putai, spurning cloistered confinement, dancing with innocent abandon, and playing with children in the streets, or of the clamorous laughter and mad buffoonery of the monastery fools, Han-shan and Shih-tē. And here, too, one discovers that ego, desire and attachment have a way of getting themselves broken and devoured in the realization of some great Cosmic Joke, and in the greatness of a Cosmic Laughter, which reveals itself in the strange holiness and wisdom of these Holy Fools.

This is, as it were, something of the little comedy that Zen presents in relation to the whole of the Buddhist drama. In fact, the initial impression when confronted with the classical literature and artistic representation of Zen is that one has searched diligently for a spiritual master only to find a figure more akin to a court jester of Mahāyāna, or has taught himself to have entered the peaceful repose of the Monastery of Eternal Rest, only to be greeted by shouts and roars seemingly having more affinity with insane or drunken laughter and the blows of a tavern brawl. Bharata's aristocratic and spiritualistic schema seems abruptly to have been stood on its head! Yet it is precisely this entire range of laughter, and the many related categories of clownishness, nonsense, absurdity, foolishness, playfulness, joking, and humor, that have come to be endowed by Zen with important religious functions and significance, and woven into a remarkable way of perceiving and experiencing life.

> *There are things that even the wise fail to do,*
> *While the fool hits the point*
> *Unexpectedly discovering the way to life in the midst of death,*
> *he bursts out in hearty laughter.*
>
> *—Sengai[12]*

Notes:

1 Harold G. Henderson, *An Introduction to Haiku* (Garden City: Doubleday, 1958) 147.

2 R. H. Blyth, *Haiku*, 4 vols. (Tokyo: Hokuseido, 1949-52) 4:49.

3 Henderson 142.

4 *Wu-mēn-kuan (Mumonkan*, 1229 A.D.), trans. Sohaku Ogata, *Zen for the West* (London: Rider, 1960-2) 1:131.

5 Charles Luk, *Ch'an and Zen Teaching*, 3 vols. (London: Rider, 1960-2) 1:131.

6 Daisetz T. *Suzuki, Sengai, the Zen Master* (New York: New York Graphic Society, 1971) 147.

7 R. H. Blyth, *Oriental Humor* (Tokyo: Hokuseido, 1959) 87.

8 Bharata, Nātya Shāstra, 6:vv. 61-2. Cf. Shwe Zan Aung, *The Compendium of Philosophy*, a translation of the *Abhid-hammattah-Sangaha*, rev. and ed. Mrs. Rhys Davids (London: Luzac, 1910) 22-5.

9 *The Middle Way*, XLV (August, 1970) 91.

10 Blyth, *Oriental Humor* 331.

11 Suzuki 10.

12 Suzuki 134.

From Hyers, M. Conrad. *Zen and the Comic Spirit*. Philadelphia: The Westminster Press, 1973

•

CHAPTER FOUR

On the Middle Way: Buddhist Economics

The Tathagata [Perfect One] does not seek salvation in austerities,
but neither does he for that reason indulge in worldly pleasures, nor live in
abundance. He has found the middle path.

Neither abstinence from fish and flesh, nor going naked,
nor shaving the head, nor wearing matted hair, nor dressing in a
rough garment, nor covering oneself with dirt, nor sacrificing to Agni, will
cleanse a man who is not free from delusions. Anger, drunkenness,
obstinacy, bigotry, deception, envy, self-praise, disparagement, superciliousness
and evil intentions constitute uncleanness; not verily the eating of flesh.

And sensuality is enervating. The self-indulgent man is a slave
to his passions, and pleasure-seeking is degrading and vulgar. But to satisfy
the necessities of life is not evil. To keep the body in good health is a duty,
for otherwise we shall not be able to trim the lamp of wisdom, and keep
our minds strong and clear. Water surrounds the lotus, but does
not wet its petals. This is the middle path that keeps
aloof from both extremes.

—The Buddha

Parabola
Volume: 16.1
Money

Buddhist Economics

E. F. Schumacher

"Right livelihood" is one of the requirements of the Buddha's Noble Eightfold Path. It is clear, therefore, that there must be such a thing as Buddhist economics.

Buddhist countries have often stated that they wish to remain faithful to their heritage. So Burma: "The New Burma sees no conflict between religious values and economic progress. Spiritual health and material well-being are not enemies: they are natural allies."[1] Or: "We can blend successfully the religious and spiritual values of our heritage with the benefits of modern technology."[2] Or: "We Burmans have a sacred duty to conform both our dreams and our acts to our faith. This we shall ever do."[3]

All the same, such countries invariably assume that they can model their economic development plans in accordance with modern economics, and they call upon modern economists from so-called advanced countries to advise them, to formulate the policies to be pursued, and to construct the grand design for development, the Five-Year Plan or whatever it may be called. No one seems to think that a Buddhist way of life would call for Buddhist economics, just as the modern materialist way of life has brought forth modern economics.

Economists themselves, like most specialists, normally suffer from a kind of metaphysical blindness, assuming that there is a science of absolute and invariable truths, without any presuppositions. Some go as far as to claim that economic laws are as free from "metaphysics" or "values" as the law of gravitation. We need not, however, get involved in arguments of methodology. Instead, let us take some fundamentals and see what they look like when viewed by a modern economist and a Buddhist economist.

There is universal agreement that a fundamental source of wealth is human labor. Now, the modern economist has been brought up to consider "labor" or work as little more than a necessary evil. From the point of view of the employer, it is in any case simply an item of cost, to be reduced to a minimum if it cannot be eliminated altogether, say, by automation. From the point of view of the workman, it is a "disutility"; to work is to make a sacrifice of one's leisure and comfort, and wages are a kind of compensation for the sacrifice. Hence the ideal from the point of view of the employer is to have output without employees, and the ideal from the point of view of the employee is to have income without employment.

The consequences of these attitudes both in theory and in practice are, of course, extremely far-reaching. If the ideal with regard to work is to get rid of it, every method that "reduces the work load" is a good thing. The most potent method, short of automation, is the so-called "division of labor" and the classical example is the pin factory eulogized in Adam Smith's *Wealth of Nations*.

Here it is not a matter of ordinary specialization, which mankind has practiced from time immemorial, but of dividing up every complete process of production into minute parts, so that the final product can be produced at great speed without anyone having had to contribute more than a totally insignificant and, in most cases, unskilled movement of his limbs.

The Buddhist point of view takes the function of work to be at least threefold: to give man a chance to utilize and develop his faculties; to enable him to overcome his ego-centeredness by joining with other people in a common task; and to bring forth the goods and services needed for a becoming existence. Again, the consequences that flow from this view are endless. To organize work in such a manner that it becomes meaningless, boring, stultifying, or nerve-racking for the worker would be little short of criminal; it would indicate a greater concern with goods than with people, an evil lack of compassion and a soul-destroying degree of attachment to the most primitive side of this worldly existence. Equally, to strive for leisure as an alternative to work would be considered a complete misunderstanding of one of the basic truths of human existence, namely that work and leisure are complementary parts of the same living process and cannot be separated without destroying the joy of work and the bliss of leisure.

From the Buddhist point of view, there are therefore two types of mechanization which must be clearly distinguished: one that enhances a man's skill and power and one that turns the work of man over to a mechanical slave, leaving man in a position of having to serve the slave. How to tell the one from the other? "The craftsman himself," says Ananda Coomaraswamy, a man equally competent to talk about the modern West as the ancient East, "can always, if allowed to, draw the delicate distinction between the machine and the tool. The carpet loom is a tool, a contrivance for holding warp threads at a stretch for the pile to be woven round them by the craftmen's fingers; but the power loom is a machine, and its significance as a destroyer of culture lies in the fact that it does the essentially human part of the work."[4] It is clear, therefore, that Buddhist economics must be very different from the economics of modern materialism, since the Buddhist sees the essence of civilization not in a multiplication of wants but in the purification of human character. Character, at the same time, is formed primarily by a man's work. And work, properly conducted in conditions of human dignity and freedom, blesses those who do it and equally their products. The Indian philosopher and economist J. C. Kumarappa sums the matter up as follows:

If the nature of the work is properly appreciated and applied, it will stand in the same relation to the higher faculties as food is to the physical body. It nourishes and enlivens the higher man and urges him to produce the best he is capable of. It directs his free will along the proper course and disciplines the animal in him into progressive channels. It furnishes an excellent background for man to display his scale of values and develop his personality.[5]

If a man has no chance of obtaining work he is in a desperate position, not simply because he lacks an income but because he lacks this nourishing and enlivening factor of disciplined work which nothing can replace. A modern economist may engage in highly sophisticated calculations on whether full employment "pays" or whether it might be more "economic" to run an economy at less than full employment so as to ensure a greater mobility of labor, a better stability of wages, and so forth. His fundamental criterion of success is simply the total quantity of goods produced during a given period of time. "If the marginal urgency of goods is low," says Professor Galbraith in *The Affluent Society*, "then so is the urgency of employing the last man or the last million men in the labor force."[6] And again:

If ... we can afford some unemployment in the interest of stability—a proposition, incidentally, of impeccably conservative antecedents—then we can afford to give those who are unemployed the goods that enable them to sustain their accustomed standard of living.

From a Buddhist point of view, this is standing the truth on its head by considering goods as more important than people and consumption as more important than creative activity. It means shifting the emphasis from the worker to the product of work, that is, from the human to the subhuman, a surrender to the forces of evil. The very start of Buddhist economic planning would be a planning for full employment, and the primary purpose of this would in fact be employment for everyone who needs an "outside" job: it would not be the maximization of employment nor the maximization of production. Women, on the whole, do not need an "outside" job, and the large-scale employment of women in offices or factories would be considered a sign of serious economic failure. In particular, to let mothers of young children work in factories while the children run wild would be as uneconomic in the eyes of a Buddhist economist as the employment of a skilled worker as a soldier in the eyes of a modern economist.

While the materialist is mainly interested in goods, the Buddhist is mainly interested in liberation. But Buddhism is "The Middle Way" and therefore in no way antagonistic to physical well-being. It is not wealth that stands in the way of liberation but the attachment to wealth; not the enjoyment of pleasurable things but the craving for them. The keynote of Buddhist economics, therefore, is simplicity and non-violence. From an economist's point of view, the marvel of the Buddhist way of life is the utter rationality of its pattern—amazingly small means leading to extraordinarily satisfactory results.

For the modern economist this is very difficult to understand. He is used to measuring the "standard of living" by the amount of annual consumption, assuming all the time that a man who consumes more is "better off" than a man who consumes less. A Buddhist economist would consider this approach excessively irrational: since consumption is merely a means to human well-being, the aim should be to obtain the maximum of well-being with the minimum of consumption. Thus, if the purpose of clothing is a certain amount of temperature comfort and an attractive appearance, the task is to attain this purpose with the smallest possible effort, that is, with the smallest annual destruction of cloth and with the help of designs that involve the smallest possible input of toil. The less toil there is, the more time and strength is left for artistic creativity. It would be highly uneconomic, for instance, to go in for complicated tailoring, like the modern West, when a much more beautiful effect can be achieved by the skillful draping of uncut material. It would be the height of folly to make material so that it should wear out quickly and the height of barbarity to make anything ugly, shabby, or mean. What has just been said about clothing applies equally to all other human requirements. The ownership and the consumption of goods is a means to an end, and Buddhist economics is the systematic study of how to attain given ends with the minimum means.

Modern economics, on the other hand, considers consumption to be the sole end and purpose of all economic activity, taking the factors of production—land, labor, and capital—as the means. The former, in short, tries to maximize human satisfactions by the optimal pattern of consumption, while the latter tries to maximize consumption by the optimal pattern of productive effort. It is easy to see that the effort needed to sustain a way of life which seeks to attain the optimal pattern of consumption is likely to be much smaller than the effort needed to sustain a drive for maximum consumption. We need not be surprised, therefore, that the pressure and strain of living is very much less in, say, Burma than it is in the United States, in spite of the fact that the amount of labor-saving machinery used in the former country is only a minute fraction of the amount used in the latter.

Simplicity and non-violence are obviously closely related. The optimal pattern of consumption, producing a high degree of human satisfaction by means of a relatively low rate of consumption, allows people to live without great pressure and strain and to fulfill the primary injunction of Buddhist teaching: "Cease to do evil; try to do good." As physical resources are everywhere limited, people satisfying their needs by means of a modest use of resources are obviously less likely to be at each other's throats than people depending upon a high rate of use. Equally, people who live in highly self-sufficient local communities are less likely to get involved in large-scale violence than people whose existence depends on worldwide systems of trade.

From the point of view of Buddhist economics, therefore, production from local resources for local needs is the most rational way of economic life, while dependence on imports from afar and the consequent need to produce for export to unknown and distant peoples is highly uneconomic and justifiable only in exceptional cases and on a small scale. Just as the modern economist would admit that a high rate of consumption of transport services between a man's home and his place of work signifies a misfortune and not a high standard of life, so the Buddhist economist would hold that to satisfy human wants from faraway sources rather than from sources nearby signifies failure rather than success. The former tends to take statistics showing an increase in the number of ton/miles per head of the population carried by a country's transport system as proof of economic progress, while to the latter—the Buddhist economist—the same statistics would indicate a highly undesirable deterioration in the *pattern* of consumption.

Another striking difference between modern economics and Buddhist economics arises over the use of natural resources. Bertrand de Jouvenel, the eminent French political philosopher, has characterized "Western man" in words which may be taken as a fair description of the modern economist:

He tends to count nothing as an expenditure, other than human effort; he does not seem to mind how much mineral matter he wastes and, far worse, how much living matter he destroys. He does not seem to realize at all that human life is a dependent part of an ecosystem of many different forms of life. As the world is ruled from towns where men are cut off from any form of life other than human, the feeling of belonging to an ecosystem is not revived. This results in a harsh and improvident treatment of things upon which we ultimately depend, such as water and trees.[7]

The teaching of the Buddha, on the other hand, enjoins a reverent and non-violent attitude not only to all sentient beings but also, with great emphasis, to trees. Every follower of the Buddha ought to plant a tree every few years and look after it until it is safely established, and the Buddhist economist can demonstrate without difficulty that the universal observation of this rule would result in a high rate of genuine economic development independent of any foreign aid. Much of the economic decay of Southeast Asia (as of many other parts of the world) is undoubtedly due to a heedless and shameful neglect of trees.

Modern economics does not distinguish between renewable and non-renewable materials, as its very method is to equalize and quantify everything by means of a money price. Thus, taking various alternative fuels, like coal, oil, wood, or water-power: the only difference between them recognized by modern economics is relative cost per equivalent unit. The cheapest is automatically the one to be preferred, as to do otherwise would be irrational and "un-economic." From a Buddhist point of view, of course, this will not do; the essential difference between non-renewable fuels like coal and oil on the one hand and renewable fuels like wood and water-power on the other cannot be simply overlooked. Non-renewable goods must be used only if they are indispensable, and then only with the greatest care and the most meticulous concern for conservation. To use them heedlessly or extravagantly is an act of violence, and while complete non-violence may not be attainable on this earth, there is nonetheless an ineluctable duty on man to aim at the ideal of non-violence in all he does.

Just as a modern European economist would not consider it a great economic achievement if all European art treasures were sold to America at attractive prices, so the Buddhist economist would insist that a population basing its economic life on non-renewable fuels is living parasitically, on capital instead of income. Such a way of life could have no permanence and could therefore be justified only as a purely temporary expedient. As the world's resources of non-renewable fuels—coal, oil and natural gas—are exceedingly unevenly distributed over the globe and undoubtedly limited in quantity, it is clear that their exploitation at an ever-increasing rate is an act of violence against nature which must almost inevitably lead to violence between men.

This fact alone might give food for thought even to those people in Buddhist countries who care nothing for the religious and spiritual values of their heritage and ardently desire to embrace the materialism of modern economics at the fastest possible speed. Before they dismiss Buddhist economics as nothing better than a nostalgic dream, they might wish to consider whether the path of economic development outlined by modern economists is likely to lead them to places where they really want to be. Towards the end of his courageous book *The Challenge of Man's Future*, Professor Harrison Brown of the California Institute of Technology gives the following appraisal:

Thus we see that, just as industrial society is fundamentally unstable and subject to reversion to agrarian existence, so within it the conditions which offer individual freedom are unstable in their ability to avoid the conditions which impose rigid organization and totalitarian control. Indeed, when we examine all of the foreseeable difficulties which threaten the survival of industrial civilization, it is difficult to see how the achievement of stability and the maintenance of individual liberty can be made compatible.[8]

Even if this were dismissed as a long-term view there is the immediate question of whether "modernization," as currently practiced without regard to religious and spiritual values, is actually producing agreeable results. As far as the masses are concerned, the results appear to be disastrous—a collapse of the rural economy, a rising tide of unemployment in town and country, and the growth of a city proletariat without nourishment for either body or soul.

It is in the light of both immediate experience and long-term prospects that the study of Buddhist economics could be recommended even to those who believe that economic growth is more important than any spiritual or religious values. For it is not a question of choosing between "modern growth" and "traditional stagnation." It is a question of finding the right path of development, the Middle Way between materialist heedlessness and traditionalist immobility, in short, of finding "Right Livelihood."

1   *The New Burma* (Economic and Social Board, Government of the Union of Burma, 1954).

2   *The New Burma.*

3   *The New Burma.*

4   Ananda K. Coomaraswamy, *Art and Swadeshi* (Madras: Ganesh & Co., n.d.).

5   J. C. Kumarappa, *Economy of Permanence,* 4th ed. (Rajghat, Kashi: Sarva-Seva Sangh Publication, 1958).

6   John Kenneth Galbraith, *The Affluent Society* (N.p.: Penguin Books Ltd., 1962).

7   Richard B. Gregg, *A Philosophy of Indian Economic Development* (Ahmedabad, India: Navajivan Publishing House, 1958).

8   Harrison Brown, *The Challenge of Man's Future* (New York: The Viking Press, 1954).

From Schumacher, E. F. *Small is Beautiful.* (N.p.: HarperCollins Publishers, 1973).

Buddhist Imagery

The Buddha's peaceful face. A simple footprint. Hands held out in a gesture of blessing and peace. Images such as these have been a vital part of the Buddhist tradition for centuries.

Many followers find that images give them feelings of serenity, awareness, and purpose while providing an example they can follow as they pursue their own personal enlightenment.

•

Teacher and Student

*This is all I can explain here, for the master's task cannot go
beyond transmitting technique and illustrating the reason for it.
It is yourself who realizes the truth of it. The truth is self-attained, it is
transmitted from mind to mind, it is a special transmission
outside the scriptural teaching. There is here no willful deviation from traditional
teaching, for even the master is powerless in this respect.
Nor is this confined to the study of Zen. From the mind-training initiated
by the ancient sages down to various branches of art, self-realization
is the keynote of them all, and it is transmitted from mind to mind—
a special transmission outside the scriptural teaching.
What is performed by scriptural teaching is to point out for you what
you have within yourself. There is no transference of secrets from master
to disciple. Teaching is not difficult, listening is not difficult either,
but what is truly difficult is to become conscious of what you
have in yourself and be able to use it as your own.
This self-realization is known as "seeing into one's own being,"
which is satori. Satori is an awakening from a dream.
Awakening and self-realization and seeing into one's
own being—these are synonymous.*

—D. T. Suzuki

Parabola
Volume: 14.1
Disciples and
Discipline

THE CALL FOR THE MASTER

Karlfried Graf von Dürckheim

The word *master* means three things: the eternal master, the here-and-now master, the inner master.

The eternal master is a principle perceived in a primal image, an idea, an archetype. The here-and-now master is the living embodiment of that principle in a given time and place. The inner master is the possibility—individually sensed as promise, potential, and obligation—of giving the eternal master physical form and reality in one's own life.

As idea, person, or inner obligation, *the master* always signifies Life become human—otherworldly Life manifesting itself in the world in human form.

The master exists only in relation to a person who is totally absorbed in the quest for Life's Way to this form—the student. And so there can be no master without the Way and without a student.

The idea behind the word *master* is that of the *homo maximus*, the universal man or woman, in whom Being—Life in its totality, as fullness, order, and unity—manifests itself in human form and, changing and creating, works itself out in the world in a way that both transcends the world and masters it. For students, the true master realizes the idea that has woken in them as the inner master (as potential and obligation), the idea that they hope and intend to realize themselves on the way shown them by the master.

Like the master, the student and the Way also exist in three senses: as idea, actuality, and inner truth.

It is in the threefold unity of master, student, and Way that absolute, otherworldly Being overcomes all resistance and limitations and takes on form in our here-and-now world. Our duty and destiny as human beings is to prepare ourselves increasingly to play a part in this process; that is, to obey Life's urge to manifest itself in the world and cooperate with it. It is only at a certain stage in our development that we can achieve awareness of Life and recognize it in this sense, consciously accepting that our central obligation is to help it manifest itself and advancing on the "way" this realization reveals to us.

In the past, peoples and individuals have realized the ideas of master, student, and Way in many different forms, depending on their character, maturity, and spiritual traditions. Every one of these forms has expressed an archetypal triunity imprinted in human nature—eternal master, eternal student, and eternal way.

Our true nature is the mode in which otherworldly Life is individually present within us and seeking to manifest itself, in and through us, in the world. In this true nature, we always remain the children of Life—Life that reveals itself in everlasting change—and this is why the barriers raised against it, without our knowledge, by our defining consciousness, involve us in a typically human type of anguish. When it builds to a certain intensity, this anguish finally enables us to hear the voice of our disregarded true nature. We hear it in many different ways: in depression and sickness, unexpected turns in our own lives, windfalls and disasters, strange meetings and "coincidences" in which Life appears to be moving against the things that stop it from emerging. We also hear it, however, in a growing thirst for something new, in anxiety and optimism, in an unfocused longing for freedom, in a sense of the numinous, in fleeting contacts with Being, and at last, also in certain "mighty experiences" that shock us into consciousness and tell us that the time has come to change our lives completely. This is when we need the master.

Two things can take us over the threshold that leads to the master: suffering and promise. Suffering is always the result of standing still or going astray on the way we are meant to follow, of offending against the inner wholeness that seeks to realize its own totality and depends on constant change. The inner promise first comes home to us when the ultimate source of true selfhood, the life-stream from our true nature, swells until it threatens, in one liberating act, to sweep away the barriers of objective consciousness; suddenly we wake to the sense of a greater life within us that is merely waiting to be let in. It is at moments like this that the Absolute, present within us as a latent creative force, can defeat the contingent in an instant. When this happens, a new conscience is born—and the inner master, who embodies Life, awakes!

There are always two levels on which master and student cooperate in bringing Being into existence in human shape: one is the external, contingent world, where master and student meet as real human beings—and the other is within the seeker himself. The master here is not an outside figure but an authority directing the student from within. Deep inside ourselves, we are all masters and students in this sense, and this is due to the anguish and strength of true nature, forcing its way within us toward self-realization in worldly form. But we must bring this fact to consciousness. Seeking and finding the external master depend, like everything that the master does, on the inner master.

People who have matured to the Way and are looking for a master to guide them, but who cannot find the master they need near at hand, should know that they carry a master—the inner master—in themselves. Otherwise they could never find an outer master—would not recognize him even if they met him. As Goethe put it in *Venien*: "And were the eye not of the sun, it never could the sun descry." Nor, if they had no inner master, could an "outer" master do anything for them.

We can find and accept outside masters only if, deep down in our true natures, we are masters ourselves and are starting to realize this. This is what one master meant when he answered the question "How does one become a master?" by saying "Simply let him out." From the outset we are always ourselves, fundamentally the person we seek to become. The inner urge that sets us seeking is itself the thing we are looking for.

The outer and inner master come only when we need them, when we have reached a point in our development where separation from Being has become a source of suffering. A master is someone who has overcome this separation and reunited himself with his true nature. In our true nature we are at one with Being; in the worldly ego we are parted from it. The worldly ego separates us from animals, but when it claims to be absolute it also separates us from God. This is why we must bring worldly ego and true nature together and make them serve Being. We can find the strength to do this in our true nature, which is permanently at one with Being. The master's task is to let this strength become conscious and effective.

The anguish of looking for the master is the anguish of losing one's way—the Way we are now seeking. We have already seen that the master is an inner as well as an outer authority and that the way we are looking for is also within us to start with. True nature is Being present within us, and we must not see it as a static image but as the inborn way on which our task is gradually to achieve a form that fuses true nature with the ego and makes it effective in the world—that is, capable of transforming existence in and around us in a manner consonant with Being.

The inner master is primal knowledge, now active and transforming us from within, of the inborn way on which we can fulfill our destiny. He appears when this knowledge combines with an ethical imperative—a new conscience that has power to generate the way on which Life can reveal itself ever more fully and clearly in the world. And so the master is also the voice of absolute conscience, something very different from conscience as the voice of a given community's standards and expectations.

The inner master is awareness of our own potential, of the person we could and should be. We sense, recognize, and obey the inner master (this potential) only when we reach a certain stage in our development. We do not hear his summons until we are in some sense ready to follow it—and following it requires not just courage but a certain humility as well.

There is nothing arrogant about recognizing the master in ourselves. This recognition is at once inspiration, happiness, and burden. Following the way that now opens in front of us is a weighty task, and to shoulder that weight we need humility. To be truly humble is not just to avoid seeming more than one is—it is also to accept that one is, in some respects, more than one seems. There exists a false modesty, actually a disguised fear of greater responsibility, that prevents the inner master from emerging. We have independent power to find and follow the Way, but this power becomes effective only when we sense the inner master as an instinctive urge to "be like God" and accept that urge.

Whenever it is used of a specific person living in a specific place and time, the word *master* denotes someone in whom Life is fully, actively, and physically present in human shape.

Marked by and charged with this greater Life, the master has overcome many of the obstacles that prevent Life from emerging fully, and is thus human and superhuman at the same time. His ways of thinking and acting are no longer ruled by the world's social, moral, or theological systems and demands; for he is rooted in other-worldly freedom. He may respect the world's conventions, but is not obligated to conform to them. This is what makes him a troublemaker. Life's truth accepts the world's fixities only as long as they neither interfere with nor obstruct the process of becoming.

The master's broadened consciousness provides a sounding board on which the ground notes of Being can ring out in all their purity. He is also a perfect medium, and through him these ground notes can ring out and re-echo in others as well.

The master embodies unity refound—a unity preceded by death and dislocation of the original unity. Being's presence in his consciousness is the sequel to catastrophe—loss of union with Being, and the brutal tearing out of the primal roots. The master's light is born of the night through which he has passed, and his knowledge harks back to a time when everything he knew had been lost. He is strong because he knows all about weakness and death, and can love because he has known and endured the anguish of solitude.

It is not only because he embodies what the student is seeking and senses in him that the master can reach the student. Often, the reverberation of the master's past estrangement from Being goes even further toward bridging the gap, allowing him to draw close to the student in his or her anguish, as if they were still united by some fraternal bond. This is what makes the master's love a special kind of love.

The three essential qualities of Life are all combined and present in the master. Life's fullness is tangibly apparent in his primal potency and strength. Its laws and order are manifest in the special authority that allows him to generate form that accords with being, even when he "does" nothing. Its unity can be sensed in his primal connection with everything that lives, in the depth of

his humanity, and in a love that has largely left "feeling" behind. All of these are signs of his maturity. And so he also possesses the three primal qualities of true nature: power, status, and maturity.

The master stands in the radiance of Life, present within him and infusing his consciousness. And so he stands in the light of a higher insight and in strength that has power to act and transform.

The master is master only in relation to a world that is capable of changing and wants to change. The sage requires no students but a master without students is like music without listeners—nonexistent.[1]

The master is master only because he is linked to a higher authority, at whose command he acts and to which he is responsible. When he mediates between heaven and earth, he always acts at its bidding. He never claims to be the source himself, but refers to a higher reality, to an otherworldly authority, to God or to his own master. His submission to this authority and veneration for those who have served it before him are an intrinsic part of what he is and does. It's presence shapes and infuses all his "ceremonial" actions.

A master who lacks humility is no master, or is an inverted master—the satanic emanation and embodiment of transcendence usurped by the ego.

The master is neither a schoolmaster nor a reading master, but—as Meister Eckhart, the fourteenth-century mystic, put it—a life-master. He is the embodiment and mediator, the guardian and champion of Life, perpetually renewing itself in everlasting movement and change. And so nothing we are, nothing we become, can satisfy him. For the student, listening to a master means handing himself over to everlasting uproar. He can only do this in the long run if he starts to hear primal silence in this tumult and also to sense it in the master, behind all his sudden changes of direction.

The stillness of Life lies beyond peace and uproar, beyond silence and noise. It expresses the peace that enters once we start seeing our own and the world's restlessness as the background and active source of ultimate tranquility.

The master's entrance is like the lion's roar—it heralds a life-and-death struggle, the struggle that no one destined for a higher level is spared, that no one called to the Way can escape. It is a struggle that holds the ultimate promise but demands the ultimate effort: "dying and becoming" in the fullest sense, and not once, but as the Way's everlasting rule and principle.

The master is not a conventionally perfect human being. He does not embody the traditional values and virtues of beauty, truth, and goodness in any obvious sense. He says and does things that horrify the normal, decent citizen—and repeatedly aims his sharpest arrows at precisely that normal, decent citizen. He does not shore things up, but turns them upside-down. No one can say what he will do next. He is as unpredictable and contradictory as life itself, for he embodies Life, and is himself life and death, Yin *and* Yang in never-ending alternation. He is both a creative and a redeeming force. He is living *and* dying—perilous, incomprehensible, and hard. Peace, security, and harmony are our normal human goals, but the master tears up the roots we have barely put down, knocks over the things we thought secure, sunders the bonds we have contracted, and pulls away the ground on which we stand; for the point is walking and not standing still, traveling and not arriving, change and not completion. Life exists only as transition—and the master keeps it alive by making transition a never-ending process.

The master overturns the neat and ordered. But no sooner has he done so—shattered the existing structure, created what looks like total chaos, and left his student floored and gasping—than that student suddenly senses that something new is taking shape, a new order being born and a new form emerging. And he starts to see the love behind the master's harshness and the meaning of the darkness into which the master plunged him, for a new and unexpected light is dawning.

The master knows all about being a student, for being a master means having the eye that recognizes the students, the heart that loves men from true nature to true nature, and the hand that guides them both gently and sternly. The master knows about the Way—and about the things in people that prevent them from following it. He knows about the conditions that allow them to act as mediums, or stop them from doing so. He knows about the steps that mark the way written into the student's true nature, and helps the student to take them. He knows about the laws of becoming, and the various levels on the path. He knows about the guiding lights on the Way—and also about will-o'-the-wisps that lead the student astray. He knows about the kind of dying we must do before we can wake to new life.

The eternal master is Life on the way to worldly manifestation of itself in human shape. The here-and-now master appears only in a person who is recognized as bearing witness to Life by another person who summons and needs him.

Whenever people previously content with ego-world consciousness come to see that they are in fact the prisoners of contingency, the moment of total change has come. When they then unmistakably hear the voice of the Absolute in their true nature, hear the summons to conversion, and wake to the possibility of obeying it, the student wakes within them. But they become students in the full sense only when they *decide* to accept

the "great service" and call for a master to guide them.

People can be said to have woken and become students only when the other dimension calls them in a way that casts doubt on the whole direction in which they were previously heading—in other words, when they receive the certainty, or at least the commanding intuition, of a Life that is no longer worldly but remains transcendent through every aspect of worldly life and action. When the student wakes, the inner master wakes with him—and the instant, urgent search for a real-life, here-and-now master itself guarantees that such a master will shortly make his appearance.

Students and masters are parts of the same process. They are twin aspects of Life, breaking through to self-manifestation in the world, both in the consciousness of one individual and in the encounter of two. Fundamentally, we are all students—if only dormant students—of the everlasting master, potential disciples of Being, which is present in our true nature and calling us to follow it.

The only way in which we can fulfill our destiny is by attending to the inner master. This means that every one of us is naturally a potential student—an inner student corresponding to the inner master. And just as the master has always been within us, so the student, too, has always been there. That student's destiny is to accompany the archetypal master as the archetypal student—that is, the archetype of the man or woman prepared to follow unquestioningly on the way that leads to union with Being.

It is not always some great, cataclysmic event that wakes a person and turns him or her into a student. The slightest thing can suddenly provoke the inner change; for waking to studenthood has always been prepared for a long time beforehand by the anguish of true nature struggling to breathe. The greater the anguish, the greater the likelihood that some pinprick will trigger the change—some trivial incident that suddenly makes true nature ring out, unexpectedly reveals the hidden and unknown, and "initiates" the seeker, throwing open the door to the mystery and bringing something "totally different" palpably home. This first initiation experience of an outside element breaking into natural, worldly consciousness wakes us in this sense only if we understand what it demands of us—an effort wholly different in nature and purpose from anything we have ever been asked to do or not do before.

This first experience also opens up possibilities that make the whole of our previous existence seem blind, deaf, shallow, meaningless, and lonely. Suddenly a new possibility is offered, something that depends on inner change and not, like everything in our past life, on visibly doing well in a worldly sense. As new students, we are filled with a new happiness and a new sense of obligation because the law we must follow from now on is an inner, not an outer, one—indeed, we ourselves in our true nature are the law, and obeying it depends on ourselves and not on outside circumstances.

We wake to studenthood when we not only hear the summons from an old reality to a new one but are ready to obey it simply because we sense that the way to which it calls us is both the only way and the way we were personally meant to follow. We must travel it without knowing it, as if we had grasped the truth of the old Indian saying "Not knowing the way, I move forward on the way, with hands outstretched, with hands outstretched."

But when can a person call himself a student?

He can call himself a student only when he is consumed with longing, when anguish has brought him to the ultimate barrier and he feels that he must break through it or die.

He can call himself a student only when restlessness of heart holds him fast and will not let him go until he finds a way of stilling it.

He can call himself a student only when he has set foot on the way, knows that he cannot turn back, and is willing to be led forward and obey.

He can call himself a student only when he is capable of unquestioning faith, can follow without understanding, and is ready to face and endure any trial.

He can call himself a student only when he can be hard with himself and is prepared to leave everything for the sake of the One that is forcing its way within him toward the light.

It is only when the unconditional has seized him that he can accept every condition and endure all the hardships of the way on which the master leads him.

ALL OR NOTHING is written in large characters above the door through which the student passes on his way to the exercise room. He must leave everything behind, but can take one certainty with him: it is not caprice that awaits him, but the clear-sighted wisdom of the master, who focuses unwaveringly on what he really is and spares no effort to bring it to life; a kind of dying is expected of him, but its meaning is not death, but Life beyond life and death; not the destruction of existence, but Being that irradiates it.²

When the student is born, the inner master is born too. Although he cannot know the meaning of the term *master*, the new student still intuits it; for the master within has woken in the form of a new conscience. This conscience is mandatory primal knowledge of the innate way in our true nature that leads to total change and perfects us as mediums for Being. It has nothing in common with primitive conscience, which is simply a fear of punishment and operates only when punishment seems imminent. Similarly, absolute conscience has nothing in common with the voice of worldly obligation—the voice with which people, projects, or communities speak when we disobey their rules and which embodies the principle "What the whole is determines how the parts behave." The inner master's voice demands only that we be totally faithful to the inner core experienced in our own soul.

The omnipresence of the Absolute expresses itself as absolute conscience in the person who has woken to studenthood. The inner master's voice is uncompromising, and no one can call himself a student unless he is willing to obey it. This obedience also implies unconditional discipline.

There are two types of discipline—imposed and accepted. Imposed discipline means subjection to an outside authority which is experienced as an alien force and a limitation on freedom. Accepted discipline expresses fidelity to a personal decision concerning our true nature—the source of all true freedom.

In accepted discipline, we trade freedom of the ego (freedom to do or not do whatever the ego wants) for freedom from the ego (freedom to do what our true nature wants). Here, we ourselves are, as the inner master in our own true nature, the guiding authority. Even contact with the outer master serves only as a repeated, revitalizing spur to the inner master. If there is no inner master, the outer master has no power to transform—indeed, there are no masters. This is also why a genuine master repeatedly withdraws, leaving the student to himself. In doing this, he is testing and summoning the inner master—and making way for him.

A person who has woken to studenthood is moving toward new human status—the status of being on the way to the Way. Waking to studenthood is not a single step but a multistage process. It begins when the inner call is experienced, listened to, and first obeyed. This marks the entry to the Way. A distinction must therefore be drawn between two stages: waking to the possibility and waking to the actuality of studenthood.

And Eastern master was once asked to define the difference between students and masters, and answered: "When a person can really call himself a student, he's already where the master is—on the Way—only you can see it more clearly in the master's case." This means that people who have really become students are no longer in danger, in their constant battles with the worldly ego, of betraying the never-ending process of change that leads to manifestation of the Absolute—that is, of rebelling against the master. Those, on the other hand, who have merely opened their eyes to the possibility of studenthood are still a doubtful quantity. It is true that the Absolute has already touched them, that they are willing to follow and may even have promised to perform the first exercises—but they are still not totally committed to the Way. They are on the way to the Way, but

have not yet passed through the gate of total change, beyond which there is no turning back. Take the eternal prayers as a benchmark: we can say that students have passed through the gate when they no longer utter the prayer but when the prayer utters them. They remain human, of course, and are thus repeatedly tempted to stand still, but the real danger is past. To say that they are on the Way in this sense is really to say that the Way has got them—and will keep them.

People touched by Being are facing a totally new challenge, are radiantly, gloriously bathed in a new light. Quite simply, they know that a wholly new reality has emerged within, or more accurately, that they have emerged to a new reality, or more accurately still, that they each have genuinely emerged as a wholly different person from the person they had previously supposed themselves to be. But to become this person in and for the world as well, they need a master.

1   Cf. Lama Anagarika Govinda, *Der Weg der Weissen Wolken* (Munich: O. W. Barth Verlag, n.d.).

2   Karlfried Graf Dürckheim, *Zen and Us*, trans. Vincent Nash (New York: E.P. Dutton, 1987) 76-77.

From Dürckheim, Karlfried Graf. *The Call for the Master.* Trans. Vincent Nash (New York: E.P. Dutton, 1989).

Parabola
Volume: 15.3
Liberation

THE TEN OXHERDING PICTURES
William Segal

*The meaning and spirit of this Oriental allegory, composed
in the twelfth century as a training guide for Chinese Buddhist monks, has managed to survive many versions and
interpretations. Concerned with absolute as contrasted with
relative liberation, it is still used today as a teaching manual
in Zen monasteries in Japan. but the experience of relating to a
unifying element within oneself is not confined to Zen followers. Nor are the disciplinary approaches toward this experience,
so vividly indicated by the different stages of training the ox,
exclusively Zen.*

*People look for the Way in all directions—their search may
bring them to the ends of the earth. But the Way, it is indicated, is not far. It is as near as oneself, as close as one's breath.
The Way itself lies in wait for the seeker. The spell of Open
Sesame, of finding the liberating treasure that is right in front
of one, repeats itself in all traditions. The seeker, however, must
seek—and this is the core of his difficulty. For he cannot know
what he is looking for until he finds it.*

*Like all authentic manuals of spiritual instruction, the
oxherding theme is simple. But at the same time it is profound*

and subtle, pointing to the ultimate meaning of man's existence on earth.

What could be more simple than a man looking for his ox? But when we realize what the ox is, what could be more profound?

The Ten Oxherding Pictures reproduced here, and the introductory words attached to them, are by Kaku-an Shien, a Zen master of the Sung dynasty. (Some sources attribute the Kaku-an pictures to the fifteenth-century sumiye painter, Shubun.) There are earlier versions with five and eight pictures, ending with number eight, the empty circle. But Kaku-an realized that this was not the end of the story. It had to be shown, as now appears in number nine—Returning to the Source—that the ox from the beginning had never been missing. And further, that the ultimate stage of the search was neither the Void nor Nirvana, but the return of the enlightened seeker to the world of men.

Kaku-an reached that stage of development where detachment and compassion, like eternity and time, are not incompatible. His world is free from differentiation and discrimination. He does not keep his humanity

distinct from his divinity. The quest is not merely to discover the treasure of freedom for oneself, but to share it with others, "to enter the city with bliss-bestowing hands."

To find out who you are, and to know that the ox beyond constriction and limitation is never missing, is not easy. Probably Kaku-an, kind-hearted Kaku-an, made these wonderful drawings because he knows how difficult it is to describe this experience in words. So he wills us these oxherding pictures and asks only that we look at them with an open heart.

Then … maybe, AHH!

—William Segal

I. Searching for the Ox: the boy has only vague presentiments of its existence. The beast has never gone astray and what is the use of searching? The reason why the oxherd is not on intimate terms with him is because the oxherd has violated his own innermost nature. The beast is lost, for the oxherd has been led out of the way through his deluding senses. His home is receding further from him, confused by byways and crossways.

III. Seeing the Ox: he begins to have a glimpse of his own reality. The boy finds the way by the sound he hears; all his senses are in harmonious order; he sees thereby into the origin of things. In all his activities, it is manifest. It is like the salt in water and like glue in color. It is there although not distinguishable as an individual entity. When the eye is properly directed, he will find that it is no other than himself.

II. Finding the Tracks: in writings and teachings he begins to get clues. By the aid of the scriptures and by inquiring into the doctrines, he has come to understand something; he has found the traces. He now knows that vessels, however varied in form, are all of gold, and that the objective world is a reflection of the Self. Yet, he is unable to distinguish what is good from what is not, his mind is still confused as to truth and falsehood.

IV. Catching the Ox: long lost in the wilderness, the boy has at last found the ox and his hands are on him. But, owing to the overwhelming pressure of the outside world, the ox is hard to keep under control. Constantly he longs for the old sweet-scented field. His wild nature is still unruly, and altogether refuses to be broken.

V. Herding the Ox: when a thought moves, another follows, and then another— an endless train of thoughts is thus awakened. Through enlightenment all this turns into truth; but falsehood asserts itself when confusion prevails. Things oppress us not because of an objective world, but because of a self-deceiving mind.

VII. Lo, the Ox is no more: the boy's whip and rope idly lying about—not needed. The ox is symbolic. When you know that what you need is not the snare or net but the hare or fish, it is like gold separated from the dross, or the moon rising out of the clouds. The one ray of light, serene and penetrating, has always shone—even before days of creation.

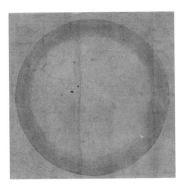

VI. Coming Home: on the ox's back he tunefully and leisurely plays his flute. The struggle is over; with gain and loss, the man is no more concerned. He hums a rustic woodman's tune; he sings a simple village boy's song. Straddling the ox's back, his eyes are fixed on things not of the earth. Even if he is called, he will not turn his head; however enticed he will not look back.

VIII. Gone, gone, altogether gone: the boy and ox are both gone. The boy's confusion has been set aside and serenity alone prevails; even the idea of holiness does not obtain. He does not linger about where the Buddha is, and where there is no Buddha he speedily passes by. When no dualism, no forms exist, even a thousand eyes fail to detect a loophole.

The introduction and commentaries (the latter based on D. T. Suzuki's translation of the original Japanese texts by Kaku-an) appeared, in slightly different versions, in *Search: Journey on the Inner Path*. Ed. Jean Sulzberger. New York: Harper & Row, 1979; and Segal, William. *The Ten Oxherding Pictures*. Brattleboro, VT: Green River Press, 1988.

IX. Back to the Source: he is neither for nor against the transformations that are going on. From the very beginning, pure and immaculate, the man has never been affected by defilement. He watches the growth of things, while himself abiding in the immovable serenity of non-assertion. He does not identify himself with the transformations that are going on about him.

X. The old man in the market: no glimpses of his inner life are to be caught—barefooted he goes to the marketplace. His cottage gate is closed, and even the wisest know him not, for he goes on his own way without following the steps of the ancient sages. Carrying a bowl he goes out, leaning against a staff he comes home.

Parabola
Volume: 3.4
Androgyny

TAMING THE WILD HORSE
Interview with Lobsang Lhalungpa

*"A tradition is a world," Lobsang Lhalungpa has written;
and on meeting him, one recognizes instantly the citizen of
such a world, so rooted and grounded that now it is as though
he were one with it, and can move with equal certainty in any
other. In his presence one meets his world, without the
awkward or resistant reaction that comes, perhaps, from the
fear of losing one's own footing. Lhalungpa's sureness and grace
have a liberating effect. He opens a window for you to look
through and stands beside you, friendly and tolerant, laughing
at times his wonderful laugh, and boundaries disappear.*

*Lhalungpa was born in Lhasa in 1926 and studied under
many eminent lamas of various orders. He tells us a little
about two of them: the extraordinary woman lama H. E.
Jetsun Lochen Rinpoche, and Gonsar Tse Rinpoche who was
his granduncle. From the age of fifteen to twenty-one he was a
member of the Ecclesiastical Service of the Tibetan government
and served at the Grand Secretariat of His Holiness the
Dalai Lama.*

*At twenty-one he was sent to India by the Dalai Lama
as cultural and educational representative of Tibet. He was
twenty-five, and the communists had already taken over*

China (but not yet Tibet) when the order went out from the Red Army to return home. Lhalungpa refused to go, and remained in India trying to prepare a place of refuge for his countrymen and the treasures of their tradition in the tragic conditions which he foresaw were coming. He founded the Indo-Tibetan Buddhist Cultural Institute, and directed it for several years.

Before and after the Chinese take-over of Tibet he continued to work for his people in India, until he began to feel it necessary to devote his special training and capacities more wholly to the translation of sacred texts, now greatly needed for exiled Tibetan Buddhism in its search for a new home. In 1971 he left India and went to Canada where he taught for a year at the University of British Columbia, continued his own work, studies, and translations, and since 1975 has been translating ancient texts and manuscripts for the Institute for Advanced Studies of World Religions at the Stony Brook campus of New York State University.

His works in English include two books on Tibetan music, a Textbook of Colloquial Tibetan *(co-authored by George Roerich), chapters in* Buddhism in Tibet *(edited by Kenneth Morgan) and in* The Way of Inward Discovery *(edited by Jacob Needleman and Dennis Lewis), and a new translation of* The Life of Milarepa, *in collaboration with Far West Translations, published by E. P. Dutton in 1977.*

East is East and West is West, but when we talked with Lhalungpa we knew they could not only meet but communicate; not mix, but exchange. The Buddhist demand for "compassion for all sentient beings" ceased for a moment to be just an idea (and an Oriental one at that) and we felt our common kinship in the human situation and the human search. So we believe that Lhalungpa is a "translator" of more than ancient texts. We would need rounder words than labels to cover the multi-dimensionality of the capacity he has to be a connector, a bridge between people and between worlds.

Parabola: *We are very much impressed by your introduction to* The Life of Milarepa *which you translated with Far West Press, and it seems that in the difference between Milarepa and Marpa we find an aspect of the relation* *of two forces, which is the subject of this issue of* Parabola. *Marpa the Translator is fully engaged in every aspect of life and Milarepa practices extreme austerities and complete renunciation. You seem to have a special feeling and admiration for Milarepa. And yet, wouldn't you call yourself more a follower in the footsteps of Marpa?*

Lobsang Lhalungpa: (Laughing) Yes, quite!

Parabola: *How do you look at that? You've chosen Marpa's way.*

LL: The kind of life I've finally come to live is closest to what we call a lay yogin, a devotee. I certainly have no such achievement and qualities as Marpa had. To follow the kind of life Milarepa led requires tremendous sacrifice and devotion and determination. As I explained in that introduction, Milarepa came at a time when Tibet was beginning to revive the Buddhism which had been introduced there and then destroyed. At that time there was a need for a teacher of Milarepa's tenacity, determination, and sacrifice. At the same time there were a number of other teachers who had a different approach, and each of them in their own way was able to contribute to the revival of Buddhism in Tibet.

Parabola: *Do you mean that Milarepa's way is more difficult?*

LL: There is an instance in his own life when Milarepa was already functioning as a teacher and quite a number of people were gathered around him who had a very deep feeling of veneration for him. And they said to him, "We really admire your capacity to sacrifice, to go through tremendous hardship and asceticism. We consider you to be the reincarnation of a great soul; this kind of sacrifice would be impossible for an ordinary individual." And Milarepa said, "As a religious practice perhaps it is good that you have this great admiration for me. But it is a great obstacle to your own achievement. By attributing to me an extraordinary, superhuman capacity, you deny your own possibilities. I was just an ordinary man. What I have done is within the possibility of each individual, with determination and sacrifice."

Parabola: *Didn't Milarepa also say at one time that he was incapable of following Marpa's way? Didn't he say he would be "like a hare following the footsteps of a lion" and that he could not maintain that spiritual force in the midst of life, as Marpa did? So it's a question which way is the most difficult.*

LL: It is a very interesting question, and the answer is implied by an essential and unique aspect of Buddhism in Tibet. In other countries such as Ceylon and Burma, no layman ever claims to reach the level of a monk who has devoted his life to meditation and study and spiritual development. The observances there are very disciplined and formalized. In Tibetan Buddhism too, there is a monastic community in the ortho-dox tradition where lamas have the necessary learning and experience for guiding the lay community. At the same time there are many lay people who have received the teachings from the lamas outside of monastic establishments and carry on the same kind of religious activities—some of them becoming teachers themselves. Both ways are recognized within the Tibetan tradition.

Parabola: *What is your own work now? Do you plan to translate more texts?*

LL: I have recently completed the translation of a major text called *Mahamudra* which was written in the fifteenth century by a very great lama and required tremendous effort to translate. There are not simple and clear-cut Western equivalents for the concepts and techniques of higher meditation, and so many subjects have to be treated with great care.

Parabola: *So it is a text which contains exercises and practices?*

LL: Yes, practices and theoretical training. The two go hand in hand, certainly. I did it at the request of the Institute for Advanced Studies of World Religions at Stony Brook, and

because of my own traditional obli-gations I had to ask the high lamas for permission. Before, it was very difficult to get permission.

Parabola: *Why do you think it has changed now?*

LL: I think now they see the need in the West. Some of the lamas have their own religious centers in Europe, America, Canada, and they are training people in this discipline. I think they are coming to a stage where they need serious materials for their students' study and use. Not all of them can study Tibetan and read the original. The lamas seem to recognize that these texts have a very important bearing on the life of these new students.

Parabola: *Do you think that the need for the teacher still remains?*

LL: Well, it all depends, certainly. If one is interested in a tradition like Tibetan Buddhism, no one ever thinks of going without teachers, without studies. And, almost all the texts are written in such a way that no individual student on his own can read and understand them fully. They were so designed that each student would have to discuss them with the teacher. This is especially true of the esoteric texts. There are so many important points that are deliberately made vague or sim-ply alluded to and not explained.

Sometimes symbolic terms are used which could mean many things. And I think there is a reason for that.

There are certainly a lot of people who have the intellectual capacity to go ahead on their own, but they lack the necessary experiential training. Whatever is written in the text has to grow within them, beyond the level of intellectual comprehension; they have to understand. So if somebody uses these techniques without knowing how this process is gradually carried on, it can cause a lot of problems, certainly. A lot of the meditations, even simple meditations, can cause problems for people—not knowing what to do at that stage or in what way emotional problems can be dealt with. And all these things suggest that some experiential guidance is necessary.

Parabola: *I see what you mean, that to a certain extent in the more important texts there's a sort of built-in safeguard; they are really hidden from anyone who has not prepared himself. At the same time, don't you think it can be harmful when people do think they understand and begin then to experiment? There are so many techniques being spread around, nowadays, techniques of real inner work, that are not really understood.*

LL: That's true. It's amazing how in these last years all kinds of techniques have come out of traditional contexts and are being made popular.

Years ago even Hindu hatha yoga was never practiced as a separate kind of physical exercise. It is still true with us. We can't use these hatha yoga practices simply for daily physical exercises. They have to be part of one's intensive meditational course.

There are examples of this in Milarepa's life: he runs into some difficulty at a particular stage and then he opens a little scroll Marpa left him and finds that at that point—which Marpa had foreseen—he must eat a certain type of food and do a certain type of exercise. One has to reach a certain stage of inner development and then appropriate physical techniques can support and further it. While the interest in Buddhism grows, the right approach and understanding still remain an enigma to many students. The formal aspects of the Dharma seem to take the place of understanding the spirit of it. Intellectual communication seems to supersede inner self-transformation. Thus strange things do happen. I can think of a specific case where some students who had recently received an initiation from a great lama quite innocently spoke of their intention of giving the same initiation to their friends back home. Any intelligent person can emulate a lama by giving an esoteric initiation, but without the requisite understanding and inner attainment it will be an exercise in futility. Certainly anybody can imitate a lama, and read the texts, and so on, but it means absolutely nothing! (Laughs)

Parabola: *What do you think will be the effect? What will really happen to people like this?*

LL: You know, it all depends on how serious they are. People who are very, very serious will never do these kinds of things. They will go to the proper people and gain experience. I think that people who wish for exciting experiences have a tendency to explore without going deeper into the disciplines. So they never gain any real experiences in the first place, simply because they have not given enough devotion. But if they go far enough, it could certainly create some problems.

I have known quite a few people who thought that by reading certain esoteric books they had sufficient understanding to do these practices on their own; and finally it created serious psychological problems. I remember translating for a couple of people who were discussing their problems in front of some lamas. (A deeply thoughtful pause) But with most of these very serious traditional practices, if the students are serious and trained properly, I think they really do learn very fast. We have quite a few Western Buddhist students who have not only acquired theoretical knowledge, but also meditational experiences and some of them even started a three-year retreat. For the first time, we have a group in France,

entirely Western, some men, some women, all of them doing a three-year retreat. So far there are no problems; everybody seems to be doing very well.

Parabola: *Can anyone learn, then?*

LL: Anyone can learn. That's why the lamas seem now to be very receptive if people show interest. And this was unthinkable even, in Tibet, years ago. Esoteric teachings were not given simply because someone came and asked for them. The lamas would wait and see if that person was ready or if he needed some more training to prepare himself to receive the teaching. We very often say: There is no use giving a child a wild horse if he isn't trained to ride. If he tries, it will be to his own disadvantage. So he has to learn the art and train the wild horse; then he will be able to ride.

Parabola: *Look what Milarepa had to go through!*

LL: (Laughs) Yes, that was tremendous.

Parabola: *You say some very strong things in your introduction to Milarepa about the qualities of a true lama and of the difficulties nowadays for people to find a true lama. The prevalence today of teachings without teachers is sometimes rather alarming.*

LL: Certain things in this age of technology are beyond the control of teachers, in spite of their wish to impart the traditions properly. But we are certainly very aware of this problem of good teachers and this is certainly very disturbing, having lost our own country and so many hundreds of teachers in Tibet. Quite a few have come out, however. But this generation of teachers is the last one—the younger ones have not come to their level yet.

And another problem is that our young monks and lamas have for the first time been exposed to completely different, new, modern ways of life. I think the younger people are going to be in many way quite different as teachers. They certainly seem to have a much wider understanding of modern life, which is in a way healthy, but at the same time it is necessary to prepare themselves to lead modern lives, and they must spend time doing many things such as learning different languages. I think this does have one disturbing effect: the quality of the training of the young teacher is never going to be as intensive or as good as it used to be. But modern teachers will know much more in terms of intellectual things.

Parabola: *But that's not the whole thing, is it?*

LL: That's not the whole thing. This is where the disturbing factor comes in. If ultimately the inner quality and the spiritual attainment of a teacher is important, then all that goes to make a teacher a good teacher, like spiritual training, is important. But then the young lamas are busy, and there are many distractions also, so it's not easy.

Parabola: *Taking Marpa, for instance, as a model, isn't it so that part of the function of the teacher is to make sure that the pupil has a hard enough time? Doesn't one get by too easily now? Nowadays we think of a teacher as somebody who can make it easy for the pupil, but I think it's quite the opposite. We don't have enough teachers who know how to make it hard!*

LL: (Laughs) I know. This is one of the modern phenomena and I think in some respects the teachers themselves are helpless. They see that their own time is so very limited; and they're very anxious to train a lot of young students. It really presents a problem for the teachers—how to bring about a sensible scheme of training which will give a really good ground for inner, spiritual strength. We have a few students who are unmindful of the distractions and just carry on the program of training—some are very serious-minded young people, but their number is very limited. And with more and more new centers coming up in various parts of the Western world, there is pressure on the teachers and the monasteries to produce quickly—

a demand for instant teachers!

As a result, young monks who have some knowledge are quickly given language training and then sent out here, there … That probably is unavoidable, and in some respects maybe they have a role to play. As long as the senior, learned, experienced lamas are available, I don't see anything wrong with the younger ones taking a certain role; and that is part of their training, to learn to go about facing new situations and meeting new people. It prepares them for higher teachings. In that respect, I see some useful role for these young monks. But they cannot substitute for the old teachers, not at this stage.

Parabola: *Would you tell us about your own teachers?*

LL: Fortunately I have had quite a number of teachers. I was admitted to a monastery but my father wouldn't allow me to stay there; he wanted me to stay with him and study privately under great lamas. This I did. It proved to be very effective and beneficial to me. Some of them are still alive in India.

I had a woman lama in Tibet, an extraordinary woman. Her name was Jetsun Lochen Rinpoche. She had very close connections with my family. Two of my cousins became nuns at her nunnery. It wasn't a nunnery in the strict sense of the word, but a kind of institution where old or young women—any-one—could go and spend time with her for different teachings, and then stay at the establishment and carry on their practices. There were many nuns and lay people as well.

She belonged to the order known in the West as the Red Hat sect, the *Nyingmapa* order, but actually she was eclectic. In giving teachings to students or disciples, she would always speak in comparative terms and encourage them to develop understanding of every teaching of the different schools and traditions. She herself was certainly respected by all the great monasteries in Tibet; she was one of the most widely respected women teachers that have lived in Tibet. She lived to one hundred and fifteen years of age and had a tremendous following throughout the country. She never traveled very widely, but people came to her at her mountain retreat. An extraordinary woman! Not so much in terms of deep learning; while she knew a good deal about Buddhism itself, it was her own inner development, inner experience and attainment that was so great. A lot of people who didn't actually study with her still received from her directly. Just being present there in front of her, they seemed to experience some deep sort of change.

Parabola: *Did she receive people up until her death at that age?*

LL: Up until her death. She never stopped—never stopped. Maybe only at night when she went to her bedchamber. At that time she went into meditation. She never actually slept. She trained herself in that way. She was always in a high meditational state of mind—very alert. I was able to spend a good deal of time listening to her and she really gave me many things.

Parabola: *She came out of Tibet into India?*

LL: No, she died a few years before the Chinese invaded Tibet.

Parabola: *Would you consider her your chief teacher?*

LL: I have had many great teachers, but this woman lama, Jetsun Lochen Rinpoche, gave me tremendous insight into the spiritual life. I was interested in devoting myself wholly to meditation, but she said: "Right now stay where you are and carry on your studies and practices. After you have done this for some time you will achieve the inner realization."

Parabola: *We still have a question as to whether the kind of tradition you come from can be available to anyone. It seems to me that it can't; that there are great differences between being Eastern and being Western.*

LL: I've been in close touch with the various Tibetan lamas who have centers in the West. We have a few who think there's a need to present the traditional teachings and techniques in a new, modern, simple, acceptable form. People like Chögyam Trungpa Rinpoche who first devoted himself to learning the Western approach and Western psychology. By and by he started presenting Buddhist teachings to Western students in a suitable form.

The more traditional lamas, on the other hand, are cautious and unwilling to start a mass movement to popularize Buddhism. They seem to think that those who have a deep urge for a living spiritual experience will find teachers who have the adequate knowledge and experience providing they are ready to go through the necessary training. These students might then form a nucleus of Dharma practitioners able to present the same teachings to their fellow-beings in an exemplary manner with true understanding and a sensible approach to modern life, its promises and perils.

The great lamas seem to have chosen a surer but slower way of bringing the Dharma to the people. They are anxious to prevent the Dharma from becoming the tool of exploitation in the highly commercialized and changing societies of the West.

Parabola: *Do you think a tradition can be made acceptable, as you say, without distorting or weakening it?*

LL: Oh yes, certainly. The Buddhist tradition can and must be adapted to the need and ingenuity of Western people and their culture. I have some Western friends who, strictly speaking, have not really gone through a very traditional training, but who, with their intellectual background and capacity, studied and discussed with lamas and did their own practice and have come to more or less the same kind of understanding, the same kind of spiritual experience. I'm speaking of people who already have a well-organized, disciplined life.

I don't think essentially there's so much difference between the Eastern and Western approaches to understanding the problems of life; it's only a matter of formal differences, differences of a certain approach, also the conceptual understanding or interpretation of things.

Parabola: *And the symbolism, I think. For instance, the symbolism of Tantric Buddhism is simply incomprehensible to most Westerners.*

LL: I think what happened in the West was that before esoteric Buddhism was introduced or understood properly, some of the Western pioneers, like Evans-Wentz, took up such highly esoteric books as the *Book of the Dead* and translated it, and a lot of people read it, for various reasons. Recently I happened to read a chapter with some of the explanations that he gives. Some of the wrathful deities are designated as "blood-drinking deities"; and the symbolism of blood was given in a footnote. I was shocked! It indicated to me that Dr. Evans-Wentz, with all his learning, his enthusiasm, his sincerity and hard work, still had not solved the problem of the inner symbolic meanings. These were understood only by lamas who were not available at that time in Sikkim, or in any of the Himalayan areas outside Tibet. In those days it was difficult to find a very learned lama in these areas.

Someone who is interested in inner, spiritual development may be horrified to read about "wrathful blood-drinking deities"; but when one is ready to understand the language of a symbolism, then certainly it is a great aid to understanding and realization. For example, the text speaks of blood, and the footnote says that blood symbolizes existence, life itself. But that is not really a symbolic meaning. That is a literal meaning. Blood is certainly an essential part of life, without which there is no life. The blood symbolizes the highest meditational experience: supreme bliss itself. This is endowed with the two attributes of enlightenment, boundless compassion and transcending awareness. That is what Tantric Buddhism explains, for we may not be fully aware of this tremendous spiritual potential within us. And a substance such as blood, which we ordinarily abhor even to talk about, is an indication of all these forces, these inner elements. If you ignore them, well, you have lost a precious gem, but if you understand the true significance and the deeper spiritual potential, then this will be a tremendous aid to your own inner development.

Parabola: I think we—perhaps especially Westerners—tend to confuse form and content. Here perhaps is one way in which modern science is beginning to come to some real inner truth in the "new" idea that energy and matter are not separable, that they are really aspects of the same thing. But I think we still tend in our culture to make an absolute division: this is flesh and blood which is matter, energy is something entirely different—something that we can't really come to grips with.

LL: This is a very important point. Buddhism believes and teaches the interrelationship of everything. Philosophers have made this tremendous division, either speaking of absolute eternal existence as reality, or, on the other hand, the materialistic approach which is a complete negation of everything beyond that which is visible or tangible: life is simply an aggregate of matters, material forces, and beyond that is nothing; once a man dies, he dies and nothing remains, and there is therefore no spiritual factor involved.

But Buddhism doesn't believe in either view. There is an intimate interrelationship between mind and matter, matter and energy—especially in esoteric Buddhism. When mind is spoken of, it always refers to higher energy. The deities that we see in so many paintings, the union of male/female which is so often depicted, all explain in the simplest form the union of compassion and wisdom; mind/matter, and the appearance of phenomena and its inherent emptiness. So there is nothing you can conceive of as a completely distinct duality. One cannot separate mind as higher energy from what one ordinarily understands as mind and mental forces. Similarly, speaking of the good and evil forces as an example of two opposite forces: while Buddhism did accept some of the ancient beliefs of the cosmic forces of good and evil, it teaches that you cannot divide the good and evil into two completely distinct and separate entities, whether you are speaking of the cosmic universe itself or your own human cosmos of the mind, the body, and everything that goes to form one individual. After all, good and evil are concepts that originate from the mind; in their common origin they have a basic interrelationship. If we understand things according to the causal relation, cause and effect, cause and condition, then we understand why there cannot be an evil which is absolute on the one hand, and good which is absolute on the other; if this were so, we would either be completely perfect or completely imperfect, absolutely evil with no possibility of improvement.

On the other hand, a third approach is that in everything there is a combination, the forces are combined. There are plants and animals, for instance, that can thrive on poison. If we understand this, then we understand human nature itself. You cannot say: this man is absolutely evil. Even a bad man has many good qualities; like everything else, he is mixed. I think what Buddhism is trying to say is that the intrinsic nature of man is incorruptible, is in a way pure in itself, the true nature of the human mind is perfect; but what has happened is that there are internal and external conditions that contribute to a change into different levels of consciousness, either understanding or lack of understanding, which bring about either realization or lack of realization. With the lack of realization, one becomes the victim of one's own inner delusion, and so every action that a man does brings about its own reaction, in an unending vicious circle. I think it depends on each human being, according to his own intellectual and spiritual capacity, to develop his inner potentiality. Not necessarily following one certain teaching—you know, there are so many different paths one can follow. But there are also those human beings who can on their own find new ways of understanding their own true nature, and thereby find out how to go about living in a way that is more meaningful to them and to others, more beneficial to them and to others.

Parabola: *The difficulty we've found in this issue about androgyny is that while the separation you speak of is clear, what we're trying to understand is the union of these two forces. The relationship of the one, the two, and the three. Instead we get a constant contradiction, a going away instead of a coming together. Wouldn't you say that it's necessary to understand this apparent division before there can be the right relationship?*

LL: Well—it's a very fundamental question, very fundamental, universal, having great, widespread implications, cosmic as well as individual. Certainly various traditions have concepts of the nature and the function of these two forces manifesting in many ways.

We can take the example of these two forces, good and evil, in terms of Buddhist ideas. How does Buddhism define good? Basically in terms of the individual; that is the most important thing, because religion, psychology, metaphysics, all these first of all must have the fundamental root within the individual himself, the basis of understanding from which he starts. So, in terms of the individual life, what is good? Good is something that does not bring any injury to him or others, something that brings great benefits to him and to other fellow beings. Good is something that has to be not only harmless but helpful, beneficial, not only to himself but to all others. The same things applies to evil. Evil is something that brings injury to you and to others. So we understand what good and bad actually mean.

Once that is established, how does an individual go about devoting himself to those things that he thinks are good and trying to get rid of what is evil? There are three avenues of action: these are physical, vocal and mental. If his actions, if his speech, if his thought are all good, good for himself and good for others, that is goodness. And the reaction or result that it brings certainly will be helpful, beneficial to him and perhaps to his fellow beings and to his environment as well. You have always to think and to speak in terms of something good and something right. But here another problem arises that has to be understood: why is one interested in this question of good and evil? Here comes the main problem: the root of all happiness, and all misery, lies in a person's consciousness of self. That is the root. Therefore, if he is anxious to develop, to do something good, is it "good" to think only in terms of his own good? That is where the different approaches come in. From the very beginning a human being must have a sensitive, humanistic approach, not only thinking in terms of his own problems but the problems of other human beings, and therefore be will-

ing to work for others and share the good and bad, misery and everything else. But if he is only an individual who is deeply interested in spiritual matters and is, say, very egotistic, in all his strict observation of rules and moral principles his motivation is very limited. He's still only concerned with his own good, and so has mixed motivation bringing mixed results.

Also, the "evil" aspect plays a very important role in every sphere of life. Instead of insisting that from the outset the evil aspect has to be eliminated, you could understand that you have to use the force that you have. The negative aspect has a tremendous force, you know, and therefore you must know how to use it. There are people who have the capacity to use this force in a very effective way, from the start. There are those who think: I must first pursue my own good and then think of others. The concern for oneself and one's actions is important, but the motivation to work for oneself must change in order to reach higher teachings.

If someone is to receive initiation and go through esoteric training, he must first understand that this aspect of evil that he has been using for his own good must now be reoriented and turned, not inwardly but outwardly, to others. Therefore, from that moment the tremendous concern for the self has to change completely—he has reached a point where the self-concern with which he began is an evil; so evil is relative.

His ego must undergo a big transformation if everything he does is to focus itself on others; and this is the fundamental ground on which to receive the initiation. All the symbolism which is painted, carved, or sculptured explains this essential aspect. It explains two things: understanding of the measure of human beings, of human minds; and the need for limitless compassion. But this too one can cultivate. You can be a *naturally* compassionate person but you have to go through the discipline and bring about this inner change. A process, a gradual change, is necessary.

With the first approach, anger is bad, hatred is bad, therefore they must be eliminated. But in terms of esoteric teaching about mind and mental forces, energies and all the psychological factors, each thing must be understood properly. By understanding the nature of hatred itself, you can open up new kinds of spiritual vision. Hatred is bad in a way, but don't reject it because there is great force that is produced with it, an energy that can be put to immediate use.

Parabola: *So the first necessity then is seeing.*

LL: Yes, exactly, *inside* seeing; it is that which esoteric teaching can bring about.

Parabola: *Discrimination, really.*

LL: Yes, therefore, straight away evil and hatred can be turned into something positive and good. It's a different approach that is necessary. Instead of centering around your own person, you are diffusing this tremendous energy in relation with the good of others. This is what esoteric Buddhism teaches. And therefore, all these people that you see in union in Buddhist art are all symbols of compassion and wisdom. They also represent the reality with its apparent form and its inherent, absolute nature. These dual aspects of phenomena are not separate realities, they are not two completely separate things. One is what we see when we look at things; but we don't see the true nature itself. It's beyond our ordinary senses. It requires a tremendous understanding, a certain level of mind; and that you can reach through meditation. That level is certainly possible for everybody to reach.

Parabola: *Meditation, then, is the tool for a sharpening of the inner vision?*

LL: Yes, exactly.

Parabola: *You have been speaking about training of mind. In the introduction to* Milarepa, *you spoke about the training of the emotions. That interested me very much.*

LL: Training of mind is a very essential factor in Buddhism, whether we are speaking of the exoteric or esoteric teaching. In exoteric Buddhism it is simple and straight-forward mind training: making students be aware of the consequences of their actions, good, bad, and neutral actions. But in esoteric Buddhism, the student is taught how to deliberately develop or bring about emotions. Emotion to us is either a disturbed or an elevated state of mind; so disturbed emotions are those like anger and delusion of mind.

Esoteric Buddhism teaches a man to straight away observe the very first moment when he is overcome with a certain kind of emotion. Then he must try to find out the nature of the emotion itself, and what it is doing to him. Also, in his meditation he could go further, beyond the analytical sort of investigation, to a level which is a combination of this contemplative analysis with something that is beyond ordinary cerebral, mental faculties. Here he sees the final calming down of the emotions, and then a deeper awareness manifests itself, where he is not consciously trying to do anything or to activate himself, but is just aware of what is now taking place in himself. I think in this kind of training, the vast energy that is produced by all of these strong emotions can become a great aid to elevating the spiritual experience and understanding, and also lead to final realization.

Parabola: *Is there a distinction between the kind of emotions you're speaking of, which are mostly violent, negative reactions, and real feeling which is a feeling-perception of the situation, or of another person? What would that kind of "feeling-perception" be? I am trying to get at the connection between what you call in Buddhism compassion, which I connect with this feeling-perception. If you are aware and really perceive yourself and the human condition, I'm sure this is the beginning of compassion. But what is the connection between that and our ordinary emotional states? Are compassion and emotion contradictory?*

LL: Well, it depends; disturbing emotions can bring about different reactions. If a person is overcome with some kind of problem, naturally it is necessary for him to sympathize with human beings who have similar problems and are afflicted with the same kind of misery. Compassion is certainly essentially emotion; and it is considered the primary virtue because its center is not directed toward oneself, but directed elsewhere, outwardly. It's not ego-oriented; it's ego-less. The moment a person is compassionate, then he doesn't care what happens to him.

But this gives me the chance to explain that because compassion is an emotion, though of a very special kind, a man can also be *overcome* with compassion. And then he goes all out to do something good for others, and in the process, if he's not fully awakened, or if he has no deeper spiritual capacity to sustain himself, or to sustain this tremendous emotion and its forces, he may do all kinds of things and go through various problems and difficulties, but his strength gradually declines and he is left without protection. So compassion and wisdom must always go together. This is what Buddhism says. You must first know the nature of compassion, the nature of yourself. You must have this deeper strength, so that when you really sacrifice something for people, it will not ultimately destroy you, but will bring you to your highest spiritual level, and also closer to final realization, to understanding and wisdom itself. Wisdom simply means the understanding of the true nature of man, or the true nature of things.

Parabola: *And that has to come first?*

LL: They have to come hand in hand together. That's why the male/female union always symbolizes these important things.

Parabola: *What do you think will happen with Tibetan Buddhism in India? And in Tibet itself?*

LL: Well, in Tibet it's a completely different story now. First, after the uprising, the Chinese deliberately suppressed religious practices and did everything to force the monks to leave the monasteries and join the labor forces or go to the villages to work. A lot of the monasteries were destroyed; only a few of the very famous ones are still maintained as museums. The Chinese make a point of taking the foreign visitors there to tour them, but it is quite obvious even to the visitors that in what had been a huge monastic town housing tens of thousands of monks, now there are only a dozen or so old monks looking after the buildings. During the cultural revolution, I think the final destruction came about; whatever was left was destroyed by the Red Guards.

Also in ordinary life, everything is organized in such a way that nobody can now say or do anything to suggest that he is doing some kind of religious exercise; if he does, he is in trouble. Life is organized very strictly in the totalitarian way. It's incredible how the Chinese could have such a hold over people. Organization is the weapon they use. They organize every ten families into some kind of group or commune, and then every movement and every word is listened to or watched. There are group meetings where they have "criticisms" and "self-criticisms," and where incredible things happen—sometimes the children accusing their parents—incredible! History has never known such cruel methods for tormenting human beings and depriving them of their freedom.

Our original society may have been backward, but I was born and grew up in that system and it was certainly not an oppressive regime. Maybe there were a lot of poor people, but I never saw any restrictions being placed on anybody, on his movements or on what he said. If he didn't like the government, he could openly say so; he could make up songs about it and sing them! There were no restrictions whatsoever. It was a very liberal society, in a way. People always tried to be pious and to help each other.

Parabola: *So will your tradition have a chance of surviving in a politicized atmosphere like India's?*

LL: I think it still has a sixty percent chance. Firstly, the settlements are rather isolated. Secondly, because Buddhism originally came from India, and although there are a lot of undercurrents and sometimes you sense a kind of anti-Buddhist feeling, there's no active antagonism toward Tibetans. I think Tibetans have brought a tremendous enrichment to the Indian culture by their experience and their artistic and other talents, as well as the manuscripts and things they brought with them. Sensible Indians really appreciate this; they say very openly that our people have brought a tremendous gift.

Parabola: *I was wondering how you see your role in the preservation of your tradition. We heard that you spent a lot of time and energy helping the refugees.*

LL: Yes, I came out of Tibet long before the refugees came. I had a rather unusual experience with my granduncle who was a very famous lama. Before I left Tibet, in 1945, I spent a good deal of time with him at his monastery. He was in Mongolia in the early 20's before the Bolshevik revolution in Russia. He had a number of followers both in Inner and Outer Mongolia, and he was able to talk to them in the Mongolian language. Then suddenly the Russian revolution affected Outer Mongolia because the Mongolian radicals had the support of the Bolshevik army.

In 1945, when nobody could foresee the fall of China to Communism yet, my granduncle and teacher Gonsar Tse Rinponche told me that our country would soon be invaded and occupied by Chinese Communists who would carry out an unprecedented destruction of life, culture and religion. He was in tears when he said this. Before long I went to India to look after the Tibetan cultural and educational projects on behalf of the Dalai Lama's government.

In 1950-51 the Chinese Red Army invaded Tibet and occupied it. I have always felt that I have an obligation to help preserve some of the essential aspects of our Tibetan spiritual tradition and that my extensive training and personal experience have put me in a unique position to do so. Under the leadership of the Dalai Lama we have been able to revive Buddhism and to reestablish the monasteries of all the four major orders of Tibetan Buddhism in India and Nepal. Already before leaving India I had the strong desire to work on a series of translations of selected Buddhist texts into English with a view to providing a basic literature for new Dharma students in the West. Great lamas of the various orders have asked me to include in my translation project texts which they have chosen and consider important. This endeavor has also received the blessing of His Holiness the Dalai Lama. Most of these texts are written as teaching manuals which can be understood only with tutorial explanations. Now I am facing certain problems such as lack of financial support and finding—or inventing—suitable terms to explain complex Tibetan ideas and subtle thoughts. But I am trying hard and still feel that these translations will be a very substantial contribution. In addition I intend to write and give lectures on different aspects of Buddhism and Tibetan culture.

Parabola: *I hope you will do some more writing for Western people, such as the introduction to* Milarepa, *because I think you have the capacity to make the bridge. The wonderful thing is the personal connection you have with the material which comes through to the reader; it's as if you know the people you write about. Most translators don't have that; they are separate from their texts.*

LL: Thank you! Perhaps that is because my father and my family were intersectarian, and from early childhood I tried to open up to many things at the same time. In the pro-

cess I managed to go to many different teachers and study a little bit here and there. In a way, this did help me a good deal; it broadened my understanding. That's why I feel that all of these different Tibetan traditions are like little pieces of a mosaic that you fit in to a more total pattern and each one has something important to offer, and if one is missing, then something important is missing.

So this is how I look at the different schools and the different approaches they represent. I try to follow whatever my limited understanding of a particular school is, and to expand my personal connections with the lamas of the different schools. They understand what I am up to and so I have no problem getting their cooperation. They have different ways of looking at the same thing, but when you really understand them all, you know, it's just a matter of different methods and emphasis. This is the result of the original approach of Buddha himself. He would not hand out one set of teachings and say, "You follow this, or just forget it." He said to each individual, "Your need is this, and your need is this." So he opened a different way for each one. And this has survived through the various schools of Buddhism.

Parabola: *The great teachers were all more liberal than their disciples!*

LL: (Laughs) Right! The people who are high up can see the totality of things, and they can tell you all kinds of things in a simple way. People in the valleys don't see much. So they are limited. It's very strange; but that's the way things are.

Parabola
Volume: 5.1
The Old Ones

THE TRANSMISSION OF BLESSINGS
Interview with Deshung Rinpoche

It was our good fortune to be present when the follow-ing dialogue between the Venerable Deshung Rinpoche and translator J. Douglas Rhotan took place at the Jetsun Sakya Center in New York. Helen Mendoza and Susan Mesinai helped to express questions and transcribed the replies, leaving us free to listen and receive impressions, which were many and strong. Deshung Rinpoche, after greeting us from where he sat under a scarlet canopy in his white-walled room, offered us tea and cakes and occasionally a penetrating glance or a kindly smile. Otherwise he gave his full attention, with the utmost tranquility, to one of two things. When a question was put to him, he gave a very long and thoughtful reply, which was apparently memorized by the extraordinarily well-trained Mr. Rhotan. While his answer was being translated, he returned to his prayer beads with a constant quiet movement of lips and fingers. There seemed to be no discrepancy between the two occupations, nor between the alternating laughter and serious-ness with which he spoke. The strongest of all the impressions we received was that of witnessing the possibility of a move-ment between outer and inner as natural and as little contra-dictory as breathing.

Born in Tibet in 1906, the Venerable Deshung Rinpoche entered a monastery at the age of six. He was recognized as the third reincarnation of the line of Deshung Tulkus, and studied under many teachers from all the Tibetan traditions; he became the chief disciple of the noted lama Sakyapa Ngawang Legpa, whom he succeeded as Abbot of the Sakya Tharlam Monastery. He came to New York in 1977 and founded the Jetsun Sakya Center for Buddhist Studies and Meditation, where he now teaches Western students.

J. Douglas Rhotan: *I recall that in your meeting at the Jetsun Sakya with Grandfather David of the Hopi, you spoke to him with great respect for having attained so many years, and expressed the hope that you too might be so blessed. Would you kindly tell us, why in Tibetan Buddhism is it considered so important to achieve a long life? Why are there so many practices and prayers to promote a long life? And especially—given the conditions of life as suffering, why is this attainment desirable?*

Deshung Rinpoche: One must distinguish between longevity in a purely samsaric context or in a dharmic and religious context. The beings who inhabit samsara in the unfortunate states such as the hell realms, certain god realms, the animal realm,

and even in the human realm may be forced to exist for long periods of time in intense suffering. In the case of some sutras, they are said to last for an aeon. Such incredible periods of time spent in intense suffering are of no benefit, even to the beings themselves, since their existence is severely limited by all kinds of unfavorable conditions.

But in the dharmic context, even the brief lifespan of a human being—say, fifty to one hundred years—is spent in worthwhile efforts that promote increased understanding, so that even that short period of time is the cause of some good, and is considered by the Buddhist to be of great value. If a person spends a day, month, year, or years in sincere, diligent effort that leads to present well-being for himself and others, and eventually for the highest good of all, then that human life, those moments of time, are worthwhile. They become the basis of immeasurable good in the world. Every effort of the Buddhist, whether a follower of the arhat or bodhisattva ideal, who—mindful of impermanence—applies himself towards the accumulation of wisdom, becomes a source of good in this world.

It is in this light that long life is valued. The more moments a practitioner of dharma is able to spend in this world, with prospects of enlightenment, the more it follows this will bring much good to the world.

Thus, long life for the religious person is of much value, in contrast to humans who merely accumulate unwholesome habits and perpetuate unwholesome actions in this life, causing great harm to themselves and others. For such beings, long life has little value.

JDR: *We know that the transmission of the teachings traditionally must go from the more experienced to the less, and frequently that goes from the elder to the younger. In the lineage structure for the transmission of teachings, what is it that age and experience have passed from ancient to younger, how does it flow, and how is it returned?*

DR: In the world, a parent transmits knowledge to a child through verbal instruction, by way of example and the like. A foreman trains and instructs his workers. Apart from a sense of convention about what has to be done, there is room for innovation in this kind of education. This is usually the case in worldly life: that while there is a continuity of education, instruction does not *depend* on continuity.

The Buddhist or Tantric tradition is quite different. In the Tantric context, the transmission is all important. It is absolutely essential. Therefore, all the exoteric teachings found in the sutras have their origin in Sakyamuni Buddha himself, transmitted through an unbroken historic lineage to the present, and the esoteric

Tantric teachings have their origin in Vajradhara, the Tantric counterpart of Sakyamuni.

The process of transmission is one of interdependence, and has two main requisites. First, the Master must be truly endowed with spiritual qualities which are transmittable. Then the disciple must have an attitude of receptivity—of respect and trust, and of harmony so that he or she remains in agreement with the aims of the teacher. If both requisites are present, a transmission of blessings must take place. There are two kinds of transmission, the *Oral Transmission* and the *Direct*. Through the *Oral Transmission*, a teacher verbally reveals through words and concepts what the student needs to know, as well as accomplishing his own spiritual aims. Through *Direct Transmission*, such a teacher can transmit something of his spiritual qualities. This is called the Transmission of Blessings.

There are three kinds of blessings—of wisdom, compassion, and of spiritual power. An endowed teacher may transmit something of his own attainment to the students, thereby enabling himself to gain extra advantages in the achievement of his own spiritual goals. These blessings are not tangible, and yet transmission takes place. One wonders how such transmission takes place. It is much like the transmission of a flame from one candle to another. The second begins to burn, but the first is not extinguished. The two are now identical, yet still separate and coexistent. Interdependent Origination is the mechanism through which Tantric transmissions are possible. It is like using a fire-crystal or magnifying glass to light a fire. If the sun is shining and one holds the glass at the right angle over the tinder, then it will work. But if any one of the three—glass, sun, wood—is obscured or absent, there can be no fire. The same is true of the transmission of blessings. Without the requisite qualities in teacher and disciple, no transmission can take place; but if the Master is truly endowed with transmittable spiritual qualities and the student is receptive and harmonious, the transmission is assured.

JDR: *What are the characteristics of the relationship between a Buddhist master and his student?*

DR: In the Tibetan Buddhist tradition, faith is considered to be the first prerequisite in embarking on the spiritual path. In the Tibetan terminology, however, the word "faith" rather signifies "confidence," that is, confident reliance of one person upon another person within the context of spiritual practice. As the *Dashadharmasūtra* states:

Just as no sprout sprigs forth from a seed which fire has scorched, so the phenomena of holiness do not arise within a mind which lacks faith.

Although faith is only one of a number of essential factors which enable one to progress on the spiritual path and attain its results, it is of great importance, especially in the early stages.

According to the Mahayanist Buddhist tradition, it would be extremely difficult, almost impossible, for a person to attain enlightenment on his own without recourse to the guidance of an experienced teacher. It is taught, "Without the Master, even the name of the Buddha would not be possible. All the Enlightened Ones of the past have become Buddhas through reliance upon a teacher." Sakyamuni Buddha and the Buddhas of the past have all been indebted to teachers in former lifetimes, whose guidance brought them eventually to the attainment of enlightenment. One can understand from this that the relationship between teacher and student is one of much importance in the Buddhist tradition.

The relationship between the two is initiated when one person seeks out another and requests his guidance in living the spiritual life. Recognizing his own role as a student, the disciple is encouraged to think of his teacher from then on as being none other than the Buddha Himself, no matter how human he might appear. This, of course, reminds us of the notion that Buddhahood is obtainable only through the guidance of the Master.

Veneration is shown to the Master in a number of ways: by respectful salutation, by seating oneself lower than the Master, and, in general, by observing a commitment to follow his precepts. The Teacher, in turn, commits himself to the relationship by assuming responsibility for the spiritual growth of his student. He thinks, "This is my student," and undertakes to nurture him with material assistance, needed instructions, and blessings.

Between the two, there must be an agreement upon the value of the relationship, of confidence in the process of the spiritual training, and, finally, of their joint commitment to uphold their spiritual tradition. A tradition consists of this very rapport—these meetings and agreement of two minds; it is simply a succession of such relationships between teacher and student.

The student, in turn, must also have three virtues or essential basic qualities. The first is *faith* in the teacher—a trusting reliance, a willingness to trust, a confidence. The second is *zeal* to learn, zeal in the acquisition of knowledge. Thirdly, he must be *intelligent* by nature.

JDR: *If the life of the spirit is endless, is there never an end to learning?*

DR: The process of the spiritual life is, as you say, endless in the sense that from the time that one first consciously decides to strive for a spiritual goal right up to the attainment of that goal, there is no ceasing of effort. Even beyond that, in the Buddhist view, the spiritual activities of an Enlightened One become infinite.

After a Bodhisattva has attained the "Path of No More Learning," a fifth stage on the Bodhisattva Path whereon he does not have to study or train himself anymore, he achieves total enlightenment, yet he continues to act spontaneously on behalf of those countless beings who remain unenlightened. He is able to do this through his realization of the Void of Selflessness and by the strength of his former resolves and prayers on behalf of all beings. His actions flow out effortlessly and spontaneously, so long as beings remain in the bondage of worldly existence.

There is another way of regarding this idea of reliance upon external supports. The concept of reliance upon an external source of strength for guidance or refuge is called the *ordinary* approach. In the Tantric, or *extraordinary* method, one is taught that one's only *guru* is the ultimate nature of one's own mind.

Parabola
Volume: 10.1
Wholeness

Now What?

Janwillem van de Wetering

Sakyamuni sat down under the bodhi tree. He sat there for a good while, then he got up. What got up? The Buddha. "Budd" means "to know." The entity that got up knew. Knew what? He knew Why. He knew the first cause and the last effect. He knew what suffering is all about. He knew the meaning of life, the purpose of the quest, he had solved the great doubt. Was he at the end? A disciple asked him that question later and the Buddha replied that the end is the beginning.

But now what?

We've all experienced achievement. One moment we had to walk and then we could buy a bicycle. One moment we weren't too well off and then, suddenly, we were provided with a bonus, an inheritance, a winning ticket of some sort. Or, deliberately, we fantasized a goal and then we realized that goal. The others congratulated us and envied us. We felt great, then what?

There's always the next step. There is one step that makes us Adam, and then, after a lot of trouble, with pleasure in between, there'll be the next step that makes us Adam II.

Adam II knows, which means that he no longer doubts. His mind is at peace, the mind that, Zen masters claim, never existed at all. "Show me your original mind."

"I can't find it," the disciple will finally have to admit.

"Now your mind is at rest," the Zen master replies and the disciple is enlightened. All of a sudden he is there.

Yes, but where is he? Is it there? Not there? Or is it somewhere that is neither here nor there? Does such a place exist? We assume it exists if we want to avoid senseless depression that will slow down the quest or turn it around so that it bites its own tail. We must believe that Sakyamuni, when he got up under the Bodhi tree, knew. We must, not because of an outside force that tells us either/or, but because of the innate light that we cannot douse, switch off, destroy. By what authority do we believe? By the same authority that the Buddha claimed, when he put his hand on the ground and evoked all life to strengthen his purpose so that the demon of doubt would falter and fall.

The living ground that holds us down, the pain that hurts us, the very doubt that makes us squirm, those are the forces that will deliver us to freedom. Doubt, eventually, destroys doubt. Freedom? Free of what? There will be, we believe, a total upsurge of light that burns the forces away that kept us down. The cock of pride, the snake of jealousy, the pig of greed, the powers that keep us within the wheel, that make us live the lives of Adam I, again and again, will be no more. So then, how do we feel?

A little dizzy, like that time we got the bicycle, or the check.

There'll be no more need to carry our identity for we can carry any name we like. "What's your name?"

"Adam Two." That's a good name, it'll fill in a form. As Mr. Two we can pay taxes, get a job and introduce ourselves to the neighbors. But there's nothing there, really, for Two is the magic figure that stands for any number, including Zero that absorbs all the others. What a relief it will be not to have to look out for number One anymore.

Shall we take off? The Buddha didn't. His body did, at the proper time, because of bad pork.

Where did he go? Ask the master within and he'll get up and bow to the spot where you are. "You Buddha."

And there, at that spot, the answer rests.

Or, rather, *moves*. I beg your pardon.

•

CHAPTER SIX

PULLING WEEDS

And what then are the defilements of the heart?
Greed and covetousness, malevolence, anger, malice, hypocrisy,
spite, envy, stinginess, deceit, treachery, obstinacy,
empty-headed excitement, arrogance, pride, conceit, indolence.

—The Buddha, *Majjhima Nikaya*

Parabola
Volume: 12.2
Addiction

THE MIDDLE WAY

Robert Aitken

Yen-yang asked Chao-chou, "What if I have nothing with me?"

Chao-chou said, "Throw it away!"

Yen-yang said, "If I have nothing with me, what can I throw away?"

Chao-chou said, "In that case, keep holding it."[1]

Yen-yang suffered from "spiritual materialism," an affliction found in all epochs, but especially evident in times of religious awakening such as the T'ang period of Chao-chou or in our own New Age, beginning about fifteen years ago. One evening at the Maui Zendo, Katsuki Sekida finally lost his patience. "Non-attachment!" he cried. "All I hear is non-attachment. If you weren't attached, you'd be dead!" Like Chao-chou, Mr. Sekida was urging us to be detached even from our non-attachment.

In those days on Maui there were extreme cases of attachment to non-attachment—naked celibates who ate only fruit and practiced breathing in a carefully regulated manner so they could eventually subsist on air. I heard that one or two did actually die, and I know that some who began again to eat sensibly felt deeply disappointed in their spiritual inadequacies. They could not acknowledge that their asceticism had never really been spiritual.

New Age people reacted against certain compulsions in society—the tracks of education, family, and career.

Many substituted their own compulsions—no education, no family, and no career. Only a few could find the middle way of no compulsion—that might or might not include an education and a family, and most certainly would include a career.

Everybody has a career. Everybody pursues a particular course. The question is, in its process, how do we handle circumstances as they arise?

A monk asked Chao-chou, "How should I use the twenty-four hours?"

Chao-chou said, "You are used by the twenty-four hours. This old monk uses the twenty-four hours. In what hour do you ask your question?"[2]

Chao-chou warns the monk and the rest of us that we are not paying attention, and so we allow the twenty-four hours and their contents to carry us along. As Wu-men says, we are like ghosts, clinging to bushes and grasses.[3]

We can see this behavior clearly in others. The psychotic compulsive at the fringes of restless humanity must cough twice before rising, take a set number of steps to the bathroom, and use toothbrush before washcloth—never the reverse. If something interrupts this exact sequence, the victim collapses in terror.

The psychotic compulsive is not merely the other fellow, of course. Yet while it is possible to acknowledge one's own addictions, to some degree, it is not easy to see into them clearly.

A drastic lesson may be necessary. One of my friends had a heart attack while at the beach. The lifeguard called an ambulance, and he was rushed to the hospital, diagnosed, treated, and bedded down. When everything was quiet, he reached for a cigarette that wasn't there, in a pocket that wasn't there. A moment of truth.

At quiet times we reach for a cigarette, the TV switch, or we open our mouths for some inanity. (David Hume turned to backgammon with his friends.) We fear the empty night that we glimpse in idle moments, and we program our lives to avoid it.

It has not always been so. In the West, some of our religious ancestors accepted the night as their context and named it the Valley of the Shadow of Death, the Dark Night of the Soul, the Fear of God. Ultimately the courageous ones could take a further step and welcome the night, by whatever name, as their true nature.

We needn't become mystics to take this step. You and I are products of the night just as we are, coming forth from the undifferentiated darkness, and calling out "Good morning." Then we pause for the other to respond, "Good morning!"

"Good morning" is a greeting in itself, and it is not merely a step to coffee, toast, and the ride to work. Coffee is not a step, but it is a right—a sip, and the rush of flavor from the roasted berries. The toast too has its virtues: buttery and crisp. Gridlock on the freeway becomes a chance to share oneself with members of the car pool. Yet even the most mindful of us forget, as Wu-men says:

Students of the Way do not know truth;

They only know their consciousness up to now;

This is the source of endless birth and death;

The fool calls it the original self.[4]

Even Zen students are bound to a drive that carries them from their earliest memories to their present, and on to the next thing and the next. They suppose this sequence is their true nature, bearing them from life to life, from home to job to vacation cabin to oxygen tent.

A monk asked Chung Kuo-shih, "What is the essential body of Vairocana Buddha?"

The Kuo-shih said, "Pass me that water jug." The monk did so.

The Kuo-shih said, "Put it back where it was."

The monk asked again. "What is the essential body of Vairocana Buddha?"

The Kuo-shih said, "That old Buddha passed away a long time ago."[5]

The monk did not notice the one point as it appeared, and then appeared again. If he had stopped at either of the Kuo-shih's requests, he would have found the pure and clear essential body in each one of his own thoughts:

Thought after thought arises in mind;

Thought after thought is not separate from mind.[6]

This is the ending of the short Kuan-yin Sūtra "of Eternal Life" that is part of the religious service of most Zen students. Thought follows thought in endless droplets of the great ocean. Each thought is the great ocean.

We know the sequence. We neglect the thought-moments. When we focus on the sequence, we lose touch with its source and allow ourselves to be carried along, grasping at bushes and grasses. When we see into the thought itself as it appears, we stand on our own feet and let go of the things that sustained us in our anxieties. We see right through ourselves, and the great ocean too.

One thought sees eternity;

Eternity is in the now;

When you see through this one thought;

You see through the one who sees.[7]

Thought and idea are not sharply distinguished in English, but in Asian languages the two are distinct. Nen in Japanese (Chinese, nien) refers to the vehicle of ideas. One nen is one frame of thought. "Nen after nen is not separate from mind." "One nen sees eternity."

The ideograph for *nen* has an interesting formation, and through its etymology we can trace the middle way to freedom from addictions and compulsions. The top part of the ideograph means "the present," and by itself means "now" in ordinary usage. The bottom part is charged with ambiguity, and by itself it can mean "heart," the human organ and the source of feeling—and also "mind," the organ of thought and Mind in the broadest metaphysical moment. Thus *nen* is the heart-mind of this moment. The heart-mind of the universe comes forth as this *nen*.

Pure Land Buddhists bring the Buddha forth in each consecutive *nen*. Their term *nenbutsu* means "to think [or] recall Buddha" and is the name of their mantra: "*Namu Amida Butsu*" ("Veneration to Amitābha Buddha"). In practice this mantra is a vehicle of religious gratitude, but etymologically the title Nenbutsu is Buddha as the heart-mind of this moment.

When my heart-mind is the Buddha, even Amitābha as savior vanishes. Shākyamuni as the Enlightened One is nowhere to be seen. Indeed, *Nenma* (*ma* meaning "devil") might also be the title of this practice—"to think or recall Mārā," the incarnation of greed, hatred, and ignorance. Buddha and Mārā are the same fellow, as Thich Nhat Hanh is always reminding us. If we stress only Buddha, we tend to become goody-goodies and Pollyannas. Our true nature, vast and fathomless, includes dark and destructive possibilities as well as light and constructive ones.[8]

No wonder you and I and other compulsives are afraid. A single thought can blow up the world. So we say "*Namu Amida Butsu*" to shut out our evil ways. We use breath counting and kōan study to cut off our desires. There we are at the brink of the stream, but we shy off. We misuse the skillful means of the Buddha: to focus upon a single point of inquiry—and we cover over the universe that that point includes.

Pursuing a single point of inquiry is freedom even from truth. "Students of the Way do not know truth." They do not know that truth is a structure that is already collapsing. They do not know that Buddha is merely a name. They do not know that truth is Mārā. Amichai knows:

The Place Where We Are Right

From the place where we are right
flowers will never grow
in the spring.

The place where we are right
is hard and trampled
like a yard.

But doubts and loves
dig up the world
like a mole, a plow.

And a whisper will be heard in the
*   place*
where the ruined
house once stood.[9]

Notes:

1 Hung-chih Cheng-chüeh, *Ts'ung-jung lu* case 57. English translation by Kōun Yamada and Robert Aitken in "The Shōyōroku," unpublished manuscript (Koko An Zendo, Honolulu).

2. Akizuki Ryūmin, ed., *Jōshū Roku, Zen no Goroku,* vol. 11 (Tokyo: Chikuma Shōbō, 1972) 52.

3 Wu-men Hui-k'ai, *Wu-men kuan* case 1. Cf. Kōun Yamada, *Gateless Gate* (Los Angeles: Center Publications, 1979) 13.

4 Cf. Hui-k'ai 66-67.

5 Hung-chich, *Ts'ung-jung lu* case 42.

6 *Enmei Jikku Kannon Gyō.* Cf. D.T. Suzuki, *Manual of Zen Buddhism* (New York: Grove Press, 1960) 16.

7 *Wu-men kuan* case 47. Cf. Yamada 237.

8 I am grateful to the Pure Land scholar Benjamin Lynn Olson for clarifying this point about *Nenbutsu* and *Nenma* for me. (In spoken Japanese, Nenbutsu is pronounced *Nembutsu* for euphony.) Personal letter of 8 November 1986.

9 Yehuda Amichai, "The Place Where We are Right," *Selected Poems of Yehuda Amichai,* ed. and newly trans. Chana Bloch and Stephen Mitchell. (New York: Harper & Row Publishers, Inc., 1986).

Parabola
Volume: 29.2
Web of Life

THE REAL AND THE MIRAGE

An Interview with Mu Soeng

Mu Soeng is the Director of the Barre Center for Buddhist Studies, which is devoted to the integration of scholarly understanding with meditative insight. Born in India, he trained in the Zen tradition, was a monk for eleven years, and is the author of Heart Sutra: Ancient Buddhist Wisdom in the Light of Quantum Theory *and* The Diamond Sutra: Transforming the Way We Perceive the World, *among others.*

Parabola *interviewed him for an issue on "The Web of Life" expecting to explore with him the interrelatedness of all sentient beings, the first noble truth that all life is suffering, and the need for compassion for all beings endowed with Buddha nature. We asked our Consulting Editor, Richard Smoley, to visit with Mu Soeng, and were surprised by the result of their encounter.*

Our expectations turned out to be based on false assumptions, but nonetheless brought a vital lesson home. While we are all part of the web of life, it is of the utmost importance that we recognize the subtlety of what it is that relates us, and do not project unexamined preconceptions on other traditions and cultures. Mu Soeng helps us toward the vigilance, rigor,

and inhibition necessary to make space
for what is totally other to appear.
—Parabola *Editors*

Richard Smoley: *One of the funda-mental teachings of Buddhism is that of Buddha nature, the quality of mind that all things, animate and inanimate, seem to share.*

Mu Soeng: I would like to put a little light here, because the notion of Buddha nature is not in the Pali tradition, which is the foundational tradition of the Buddha. Whenever we discuss Buddha nature, we are dealing with a concept that comes from much later, from the Tibetan tradition. While it's somewhat present in the language of the Chinese Zen, it is not quite as prominent as in the Tibetan tradition. Because of this, I would not accept that it's a fundamental teaching.

RS: *I see.*

MS: The term "Buddha nature" itself is suggestive. Language and how we use it is critical. When the term "Buddha nature" is used, there is often an unexamined notion of substantialism. Some schools of Tibetan Buddhism talk about a granular-like substance that's both part of the human body and at the same time independent of it. This goes back to the notion of the *atman* in the Hindu tradition, not the Buddha.

RS: *In that case, what if anything unites the world, the manifest reality, living beings, non-living beings? Is there a concept that underlies that, or is it emptiness?*

MS: Well, both the teachings of emptiness and the teaching of dependent arising—that nothing has an independent existence—are relevant here. Everything, whether it is animate or inanimate, is as subject to dependent arising as human beings are. The time frame may be different for each being and each person, but all beings, whether they are sentient or not, are going through the same process of arising, stabilizing, decay, and dissolution. So that unites all creation.

The Mahayana tradition used the term emptiness as a synonym for this dependent arising. The basic notion is that things don't have any core of their own. There is a term, *svabhava*, which is "own being"; because things don't have their own being, they are empty of being.

RS: *If you say that something is empty of being, what would satisfy the criterion of being?*

MS: There is a term, *bhava*, that I have translated as "being and becoming"—being, with a small "b," and becoming. The problem arises when you translate *bhava* as "Being," with a capital "B," and an element of substantiality is assigned to it. I see *bhava* as a process of constant change, becoming with a small "b." Once this is your frame of reference, the whole issue of being or nonbeing becomes irrelevant.

RS: *Would you say that an important part of spiritual practice would be to let go of this clinging, or what's sometimes called desire?*

MS: Let's go back to the terms you are using. From the Buddhist perspective, the use of the term "spiritual" becomes very problematic, because "spiritual" implies, at least in the Western intellectual tradition, that it has something to do with the spirit, which is independent of the mind and the body. We are saying in some unexamined way that there is a spirit, that spirit is good, and that's what spirituality is. There is no comparable word in the Buddhist tradition. This idea of spirit and spirituality then becomes a form of Orientalism, because it's a term imposed on the Buddhist meditative tradition. In effect we are saying that since the Judeo-Christian tradition talks about a spirituality based on the perfection of spirit, it must also be so in the Buddhist tradition.

The proper term in the Buddhist tradition is purification. The Buddha spoke of purification all the time—from greed, anger, and delusion. Purification has to do with karma and rebirth, but it does not have anything to do with spirituality, at least

not in the sense that spirituality is understood in the West. In my mind, that is a very important distinction to make.

RS: *Well, to go back to the term "purification," at least to a Western mind, it seems to contain the supposition that there's something there to be purified. And I gather this is not really true in Buddhism. What is the difference?*

MS: The purification is of the negative qualities of the human mind. It is a very human experience, regardless of who we are, to suffer because we have negative qualities in the mind—anger, frustration, envy. It's the purification of these negative qualities in the mind which becomes the basic building block in Buddhist thought.

RS: *In essence, mind is what is being purified?*

MS: Yes. The Buddha was the first thinker to focus on how the mind works, and what he spoke of was the science of mind. That's why contemporary psychology is finding resonance in Buddhist teachings: they address the same structures of mind, the same processes of mind, as Freudian and Jungian psychologists talk about.

RS: *There probably is some difference, because Western psychology tends* *to regard mind as a by-product of the brain.*

MS: I don't mean to say that there's an exact one-on-one equivalent, certainly, because in the Buddha's system, it's not an understanding of mind alone, but how the positive or negative mental qualities work toward the karmic process. By purifying the negative qualities of mind, one is also purifying all the karmic residues. The Buddha is a person in which all the negative qualities have been eliminated, and all the positive qualities are advanced. That's one understanding of Nirvana—all the negative qualities have come to cessation.

RS: *One element that seems to be a common theme in many traditions is that powers are conferred by the practice of austerities. Why do you think that is? Why is power conferred by denial and austerity?*

MS: Our brain has a tripartite system: we have inherited the reptilian brain and the limbic brain, and now we are prisoners of the neocortex. What happens in the deep meditation experience is that we drop down into the limbic system, and whenever we practice austerities and discipline, it takes us deeper and deeper into the limbic system, and eventually into the reptilian system. And the reptilian system is wide open, like an antenna that's receptive to everything

that's going on. Our energy is usually going into preserving and protecting ourselves, so when we go deeper into the limbic system we come into contact with all kinds of phenomena. The phenomena have always been there, but because we are so concerned with the layers of self-protection, we are not in touch with them.

RS: *How can one experience for oneself the truth that everything around us, which feels so real, is in fact empty of substance?*

MS: One of the schools of the Yogachara, in the Tibetan tradition, explains it through the metaphor of the mirage. If there is a traveler in the desert, he sees water and runs after it. But when he reaches his goal, he finds there is no water at all. The mirage is created by thirst, and that's what desire is. We are seeing imprinted on the world outside the qualities that would satisfy our basic longings. The qualities are actually not there; we project them, like a mirage.

This is insidious. We can see it in shopping addiction, for example. We go to a shopping mall, and we think, oh, oh, we could get this thing today and be happy. But when we actually get it, then very soon we find that this is not what we are looking for. So the illusory nature of the world is better understood as the projection of our longing, and trying to find in phenomena things that will satisfy us.

RS: *What, then, in this process is doing the projecting, and what is being projected?*

MS: Our longings. Longings named, and unnamed longings.

RS: *Longings of the mind?*

MS: The longings are essentially emotional. They are there because at our very core, we have a fear. This is the fear of mortality, and we try to cover up the fear in many different ways. Whether it's through religion or the shopping mall, everything that we do in an unexamined life is an attempt to cover up that basic fear of death.

One of the stories from the Zen tradition is about a great Taoist adept who performed austerities and denials until his body turned into a tree. He was still aware of his humanness, a living presence, yet his body had turned into a tree. He lived like this for a thousand years. Then one day a big wave came in from the ocean and started breaking onto the tree, and the adept tasted salt for the first time in a thousand years. The taste of salt was very enticing, and he tasted more and more and more and more, and as he reveled in the taste of the salt, his body turned back from a tree into a thousand-year-old human body, and within a few seconds it fell apart and turned into dust.

RS: *Marvelous story.*

MS: [laughs] So that's what Zen people say: What's the point of having a thousand-year-old body if you're so wound up that you give in to the first temptation? It's better to use the salt moderately in everyday life, in a way that keeps your body together, because that's the body's true purpose. And when it's time to die, it's time to die. There's no need to live a thousand years, and yet have this longing, this desire for eternal life.

RS: *The first of the fourfold noble truths is the existence of suffering.*

MS: No.

RS: *It's not?*

MS: No, no. Again, the person who talks about the existence of suffering is being very Orientalist. When it is translated properly, *dukkha* can mean "anguish," or "stress," or "sense of incompleteness," but when we translate it as "suffering," we are projecting a very Judeo-Christian idea onto it. The idea of the existence of suffering contradicts everything in Buddhism.

All conditioned phenomena have the characteristics of distress, anguish, unsatisfactoriness, incompleteness. That is a more accurate description of the first noble truth.

RS: *I see. Is that the way you would answer Western-oriented critics who sometimes say that Buddhism is world-denying and nihilistic?*

MS: Yes, certainly. There has been a tremendous misreading of the entire Buddhist tradition for a very long time. There has never been any indication of either world-denying or a higher state, because those words do not exist in Pali or Sanskrit. Whenever a word is used in the English language, see how it is expressed in Pali or Sanskrit, and for me you will have a much more solid frame of reference.

RS: *Apart from what we've already discussed, which misunderstandings of Buddhism in the West seem to you the most significant and most wrong?*

MS: The teachings of Buddhism try to deconstruct all our conditioning. That's a very necessary step. If you look at the Bodhisattva model in the Mahayana tradition, if the deconstruction is not taking place in a very powerful, deeply-felt way, then the Bodhisattva model just becomes another slogan.

In the West I think there has been a kind of—I don't mean to use a harsh word here—a kind of insidious commodification of the Bodhisattva model. The whole idea of being a Bodhisattva becomes just another expression of one's emotional or psychological values—wanting to do good, out of motives that one does not really understand. This can

become a very complex, sometimes very unwise engagement. Again, this lack of understanding as to what a Bodhisattva is, or what the Buddhist tradition understands the training of a Bodhisattva to be, is certainly a grave misunderstanding. It takes very, very long time—we talk about aeons upon aeons upon aeons—to become a Bodhisattva. In the training of the Bodhisattva, the deconstructing of all identities, all conditioning, is a necessary first step, and only then can one move into the space of helping all human beings.

RS: *Are you saying that someone has to attain a certain stage of realization or insight before one can truly do good in the world?*

MS: If one's trying to do good simply because one wants to do good, sometimes you're apt to do more harm than good. People have done terrible things in the name of helping others.

RS: *One thing that occurs to me is how Zen has entered into the popular consciousness. I was walking down a supermarket aisle a couple of days ago, and saw a packet of Zen Coffee.*

MS: [laughs] In my thirty years or so of involvement with the Zen Buddhist tradition, I find that the elements of consumerism and commodification are so powerful in the American culture that everything gets commodified, everything becomes a consumer item. Even well-meaning people end up being purveyors of consumer items. That's the power of the culture, and it's inescapable.

Everyone in America wants to be a teacher in the shortest possible time. I just find it quite amazing. In medieval China, for example, the ratio of teacher to students was so much higher than here in America. That is in itself a very subtle form of commodification. Look in the back of *Tricycle* magazine, and you find so many centers, so many teachers, all saying "Come, buy my product." On the face of it, it seems harmless, it seems healthy, perhaps, but this culture is very powerful, you know? This culture commodifies everything—the suffering of Christ, as Mel Gibson is doing—whatever.

One thing I see again and again is that Buddhism in America is a middle-class, bourgeois movement, and it is the nature of a bourgeois middle-class movement that everything be commodified. What the Buddha was trying to tell us is to throw all the furniture out the living room, but what we are trying to do is to just move the furniture around. People don't really want to change. We are not willing to throw all the furniture out. First of all, the culture will not allow it, and secondly because if we're throwing it out, there is the fear that everything will collapse. But if you throw the furniture out there is empty space—and a relationship with the space—that is

more open, more spacious. In every religion, the financial and the political support has always come from the middle classes, and Buddhism is not an exception; Buddhism in America is not an exception.

RS: *If a person is serious about taking all the furniture out of the room, and lives in the middle-class bourgeois environment in America, how would you suggest they do it?*

MS: I have known some who have gone to Korea or Japan, and lived in monasteries there for a number of years, and the changes that take place in them may be hard to quantify, but they're taking a risk. It's a complex phenomenon, of course, whatever happens, but at least within the framework of the American class culture, they are making a very public statement, and that is one step.

RS: *Most of the people you teach and encounter are in fact middle-class Americans. How do you view your work in this context?*

MS: Well, you know, I more or less say these teachings are about more than moving the furniture around the living room. I ask, "Do you want to do that?" Short of pushing people into going to monasteries, that's the only thing I can do. It's not simply about being a better person. It's not simply about thinking about making the world a better place. The place to start is by throwing the furniture out.

RS: *Given all this, what kind of future do you see for Buddhist teaching in America? That's pretty much the context it's come into, and it would be very difficult to change it.*

MS: Well, I can see it surviving in some small corners. At many places people come and they get some benefit, some stress reduction. But I am less and less optimistic about the promise that I saw in the late 60s and early 70s. Perhaps the Buddhist teachings might become a form of stress reduction.

RS: *Are you hopeful that there will be an authentic lineage of Buddhist teachers that are indigenous to America?*

MS: I am not so much concerned about lineage, because lineage becomes very institutionalized. But certainly in the last twenty-five years the language that we have created to talk about the Buddhist teaching is just amazing; that has been a really positive outcome of Buddhism coming to America. It's a very sophisticated language that traditions in India, China, and Japan never used. That language can be a valuable agent for some positive changes.

For example, we use the terms *decentering* and *recentering*. Using that language articulates how we are locked into our fixations about our-

selves and about the world. Knowing how we are creating these fixations show us that the first step is to completely decenter ourselves. Decentering is a psychological process, it's an emotional process; it's also a very difficult process. So it cannot be done outside of meditation, it's not something that you can think your way through. A very deep meditative experience is necessary, but if the cognitive framework of decentering is there, you can take it into the meditation retreat and it can be tremendously beneficial.

RS: *We've focused up to now on the weaknesses and problems of the American spiritual scene, which as you say are real enough. Do you see any positive signs to counterbalance these?*

MS: The interface between the scientific traditions and the Buddhist tradition I personally find very exciting. In some of my writings I've used David Bohm's model of the implicate order and the explicate order. That kind of language, those cognitive science and quantum physics models, can stand side by side with the Buddhist tradition and can speak wonderfully well to each other.

RS: *If a person were just beginning to explore the Buddhist tradition in the middle-class context, how would you suggest they go about it?*

MS: Most of the time what happens is that people hear that Richard Gere is doing something with Buddhism, or Steven Segal, and they want to as well. I would suggest they first read some good, reliable books and form basic ideas of what the teachings are trying to do. If the teachings resonate with them, they should go out and find a meditation center. Certainly knowing the cognitive framework in which the Buddhist tradition is trying to work is important, rather than just trying to have an experience of meditation or wanting to be a Buddhist without knowing what it is.

RS: *I think many seekers today are asking themselves, consciously or not, "How am I doing? How far along am I?" How do you deal with this concern?*

MS: I see it as a problem of the understanding of time. In the Judeo-Christian tradition, time is linear. It is going from point A to point B. Along that continuum, there is progress anchored by markers. People have an idea that we are going somewhere, and progress becomes a consumer item, a résumé item. In this country people are so very locked into how other people see them.

When you look at the Buddhist notion of time, it is circular. Within this circularity, we are reworking our karma over and over again. This is compost, and out of it the lotus flower emerges. You strive, and you shake off the dirt out of which it's

emerging. That's a manifestation of purified mind. But it's not progress in the linear sense that we understand progress to be. In the Western intellectual tradition, history means that we are evolving from some undesirable state to some desirable state. In the Buddhist, history is circular.

RS: *Because there are very few cultural frames of reference for Buddhism, some may be uncertain about whether they're on the right track. Some of it, as you say, is the result of this progress model, but might some of it be a concern over whether this is the right tradition?*

MS: Well, I suggest that a beginner should pick out one practice that suits them, do that one practice for ten years, and then step back into the spiritual supermarket and look at what's there. There is a qualitative difference between those two lookings. If you do one practice sincerely for ten years, you will never waste your time. No matter what it is—*vipassana* practice, Dzogchen practice, Zen practice, Mahamudra practice—if you do it for ten years, the experiential structure will reveal itself. And then once you come out of that practice it's not a problem at all to see what's beneficial and what's not.

•

CHAPTER SEVEN

Upon Awakening: Buddhist Ethics

*And thus as the Bodhisatta sat in his beautiful palaces day after day
surrounded by all the physical and intellectual pleasures
that could be devised by love or art, he felt an ever more insistent call
to the fulfillment of his spiritual destiny.*

—Ananda Coomaraswamy, *Buddha and the Gospel of Buddhism*

*Not by matted hair, by clan, or by birth,
is one a brahman.
Whoever has truth & rectitude:
he is a pure one,
he, a brahman.*

*What's the use of your matted hair, you dullard?
What's the use of your deerskin cloak?
The tangle's inside you.
You comb the outside.*

—*Dhammapada*

Parabola
Volume: 11.3
Sadness

HIGH RESOLVE

Interview with Tara Tulku, Rinpoche

The first noble truth enunciated by the Buddha over 2,500 years ago was the pervasiveness of suffering (dukkha). *With this in mind,* Parabola *arranged a conversation about suffering and the sadness it engenders with the Venerable Tara Tulku, Rinpoche, a remarkable Tibetan Buddhist monk already familiar to readers of* Parabola *(see Vol. IX, No. 3, "Pilgrimage"). Born in 1927 in eastern Tibet, Tara Tulku studied for nearly three decades in the monasteries of Sendru and Drepung, making him one of the last of his countrymen to receive a comprehensive monastic training on his native soil. During the great Tibetan diaspora of 1959, he fled to India where he became abbot and then abbot emeritus of Gyüto Tantric Monastery. Among his many duties, he currently teaches the Dharma to Westerners in Bodhgaya (where the Buddha achieved enlightenment) and occasionally in America.*

Our talk with Tara Tulku took place in the Office of Tibet in New York City. Robert A. F. Thurman, professor of religion at Amherst College, kindly agreed to translate for us, as he has many times in the past. Throughout the conversation, Rinpoche responded to our questions with the same great patience and enthusiasm he offered during our last conversation. His bright

crimson robes and orange prayer beads
served to remind us of just how far
he had traveled, geographically and
culturally, to bring his Vajrayana
tradition to the attention of the West.
                                    -Philip Zaleski

Parabola: *We understand sadness to be*
an attitude toward suffering, an atti-
tude that can go in two directions: in
a positive way toward compassion, or
in a negative way toward self-pity and
other destructive emotions. Does this
accord with Rinpoche's understanding?

Tara Tulku: I think this is how it is.
According to the Buddha's teaching,
when one feels strong sorrow, the
superior method for dealing with it
is to examine its causes. One always
finds two major classes of cause: one,
the inner, evolutionary forces coming
from one's previous actions in this
and former lives, and two, external
circumstances, things that happen
outside oneself. By the meeting of
these two streams of causality, suffering will invariably be produced.

If someone makes the mistake—
as I think it often is made—of thinking that the major cause of suffering
is outer circumstances, then it is very
difficult to develop a method to free
oneself of sorrow. But if one takes
on the responsibility of realizing
the major cause will always be one's
internal stream of causality, coming
from one's past evolutionary actions
and relating to the state of one's own

mind, then it will not be too difficult
to remove sorrow from one's mind.
Our trouble is that when someone
causes us distress, we usually don't
feel that we have brought this sorrow upon ourselves. Rather, we
simply focus on the external forces
involved. We say "that person or that
thing really makes me unhappy." This
makes our sorrow grow more powerful. On the other hand, if we say "it is
my responsibility that this happened
to me, it is my own evolutionary
action, if I can't see what I did then
I did it at some other time that I'm
unaware of," then whatever else may
happen, our sorrow will automatically become smaller and loosen its
hold over us.

To be concise, the intensity of
sorrow will vary in direct proportion
to the intensity of our feeling that "I
am important."

Parabola: *How then should one be in*
front of the suffering of another person?

TT: To begin with, one should not
differentiate between oneself and
others who are suffering. One should
take upon oneself the burden of their
suffering, thinking "maybe I don't feel
this suffering right now, but I have
felt it so many times in the past and
I will so many times in the future, so
really this suffering is my suffering."
This would be the beginning.

Furthermore, in our normal habit
there are at least three ways in which
we react to the suffering of others. If

the one who suffers is beloved by us, then even without trying we identify with their suffering. With those whom we dislike intensely, we not only do not identify with their suffering, we even enjoy it. Then there is the great majority to whom we have no special connection either positive or negative; we are more or less disconnected from the suffering of these people. This shows that our normal way of reacting depends very much on how we are thinking about the suffering of others. These three—the enemy, the beloved, the neutral—are suffering more or less the same. *We make the difference in our reactions.*

The Buddha said that the source of our reaction to these three relates to the three major poisons of the mind—desire, anger, and delusion. In the case of someone we love, desire creates a strong sense of identification with their suffering. In the case of someone we dislike, anger creates a strong sense of disassociation with their suffering, or even enjoyment of it. And with the one we don't care about, our delusion makes us fail to appreciate that they are suffering. Therefore we are controlled not by any objectivity of our own perception, but by the force of these three mental poisons. If one realizes this and can guard oneself against being carried away by one or another of these three negative emotions, then perceiving the suffering of others, even identifying with it and in a sense taking it upon oneself—that is,

feeling responsibility for it and trying to do something about it—will not cause one harm or discouragement, but will give one a more powerful incentive to act benevolently toward the sufferer.

The Buddha began his whole teaching from the fact of suffering. That is why this is called the holy fact of suffering.

Parabola: *It sounds as if Rinpoche were saying that suffering, properly understood, is a prelude to compassion, even a necessary road to compassion.*

TT: Oh, yes. The root of the attainment of liberation and freedom is the acknowledgement and full understanding of the fact of suffering. Similarly, the best way to experience viscerally the erroneousness of one's attitudes and the distortion of one's perception is to observe oneself while in the process of confronting suffering. By knowing how one's attitudes are distorted, and under what kind of delusions one is driven in one's wrong interactions with the world, the goodness of one's mind can be cultivated, and compassion, love, and wisdom can all be generated. But we never think that it has to do with our own attitudes, responses, and perceptions. We don't understand our own responsibility for what has happened. If we were really to understand how the mind works, and how to bring out its goodness and correct its distortions, then no matter what happened outside, nothing could make us sorrowful.

There's a beautiful example of this, a very ancient illustration. If you're in a country where there are many thorns, and you set out to destroy the thorns, thinking that the problem of the thorns is the thorns, you will never be finished. But if you put on a good strong pair of boots and chaps, then you can go where you like and the thorns will not harm you. As Shantideva said in *A Guide to the Bodhisattva's Way of Life*, it is really quite a bit easier to put on a pair of shoes than to cover the earth in shoe leather. If you get people to understand this, then you will have accomplished a great deal.

Parabola: *But the thorns don't go away.*

TT: The universe is full of thorns. It's not a matter of how many thorns there are, but that one's own mind is right at hand, and one can work with that. Of course, the thorns are only an example. The entire environment, every aspect of our body, all of our experiences and enjoyments and possessions, all are capable of causing us suffering. And they commonly do. Look at America, where in the question for the removal of suffering tremendous material progress has taken place—yet we have not yet heard it announced that suffering here has come to an end. In fact, we see suffering get greater and greater, in more and more subtle forms. Among peo-

ple who traditionally are considered to be more free of suffering—namely, those who are young, strong, healthy, and smart—we see in America the greatest kind of suffering, anxiety, misery, self-destructive behavior. The main problem is that their approach is to try to remove the suffering in the world and not to put on a good pair of boots and chaps.

Parabola: *But isn't there something further here? Beyond protecting oneself by wearing boots, can't one make use of the thorns or understand them in a constructive sort of way?*

TT: These are not two different things. The making of the shoes is not just an example of simply avoiding the thorns; it has to do with one's own subjectivity. It shows how, by understanding what the thorns are, and what the source of the pain is, one is enabled to fashion the shoes. Once one has fashioned the shoes of tolerance, enlightenment, and patience, then one can even go in those shoes to rescue others and to help them make their own shoes. But if instead one just rushes out into the thorns to save other people, one would end up being shot full of thorns, paralyzed, ruined oneself and unable to benefit anybody else.

Parabola: *Then the question is really how to make the shoes.*

TT: That's right. The beginning, of course, is the thorns. It is stepping on the thorns that gives us the wish to make a really strong pair of shoes. Without that pain, we would not have any desire to develop a method to make shoes. Therefore the Lord Buddha, when he turned the Wheel of Dharma for the first time, in Sarnath, near Benares, said "this is the holy fact of suffering."

Parabola: *In the beginning, Rinpoche said that when I see the suffering of another I should not identify with it—I free myself so I can help free others—and then he said that we should identify. If someone is suffering and I identify with their suffering, doesn't it cause more suffering?*

TT: The first process is not a question of not identifying with suffering, but rather of understanding its danger. The Bodhisattva would be multiplying suffering if he tried to run among the thorns without first having good shoes. Although from the beginning the Bodhisattva identifies with the suffering of others and wants to remove this suffering, nevertheless he realizes the necessity of developing an understanding of the nature of suffering, of its emptiness, before being able to benefit others.

Once the Bodhisattva has understood emptiness, he develops compassion. Compassion is a very strange thing. Looking upon the suffering of others, compassion wants to take that suffering upon itself, but it keeps failing. Instead of gathering more suffering, it gets happier. Compassion removes the suffering of others, and somehow that makes the Bodhisattva happier. Somehow, suffering disappears when it comes into the field of the understanding of emptiness. Rather than doubling the suffering, the Bodhisattva's action destroys the suffering.

Parabola: *The Dalai Lama said something about that in the interview we published in the* Wholeness *issue.*

TT: When many people are starving, it won't help to want to save them if you are too weak to move. You must get a bite to eat before gaining strength to get up and feed others.

Parabola: *Must I always look after feeding myself first, or can it be done at the same time as helping others?*

TT: They are done simultaneously in the sense of motivation. If you are just grabbing food because you are hungry, of course you are not satisfying the need of others as well as your own. But if in the process of eating you are simultaneously aware that only by doing so will you be able to gain the strength to feed others, you will actually have more power in getting that food, and greater motivation for helping others.

Parabola: *And the source of the motivation is correct understanding.*

TT: Yes, of course, it is the right knowledge of the nature of the reality of the situation, of the real facts of life, of relativity and emptiness. It is from this true knowledge of the situation that the motivation arises.

Parabola: *Compassion isn't a feeling. What is it? What is the real relation of compassion to suffering?*

TT: Compassion is a desire, a desire that others be free of suffering. Compassion not combined with wisdom is ineffectual in relieving suffering. In order to become effectual, compassion must be made indivisible with wisdom, which realizes the ultimate nonexistence of the other, of the desire, of the self, of the suffering, which sees the pure relativity of all these things and the emptiness of their intrinsic reality. This is defined as the great compassion which, perceiving living beings, wishes them to be free of suffering.

Parabola: *The acceptance of the suffering of oneself and others seems to be the key. In this acceptance, a force seems to grow.*

TT: It's a very strange thing about acceptance. Yes, the Bodhisattva accepts the suffering of himself and others, and the inexorable nature of relativity. But if that was all, the Bodhisattva would become like one completely overwhelmed by thorns. There is a moment in the Bodhisattva's career, just before generating the new spirit of enlightenment, when he has something called high resolve. This is a feeling of total acceptance of suffering and of his responsibility for eliminating it. It's a kind of madness, because how can anyone possibly do that? It's an endless job, and it's only you that are doing it. At that point, there must be a recognition that this is indivisible from wisdom. Then it is a curious fact that to the degree that wisdom does not accept any suffering of self or others—to the degree that wisdom sees that on the absolute level suffering is empty of intrinsic reality—to that degree the Bodhisattva becomes more and more capable of accepting the suffering of a wider and wider circle of human beings. So simultaneously there is a total acceptance of suffering, and a total refusal of suffering by seeing its emptiness. This is nonacceptance at the absolute level generating acceptance on the relative level.

Parabola: *Could Rinpoche share with us an example from his life of how he confronted suffering?*

TT: On March 12, 1959, I was in Drepung Monastery, teaching some new monks and studying with my own teachers. I was enjoying life there. On the tenth of March, as you know, there was a massacre in Lhasa. We all felt great sorrow and anxiety over this. We didn't know that His Holiness had escaped from the Palace; we were afraid that he was being harmed. In the morning I got up and went to the abbot, with whom I was very close. When he said that His Holiness had left the other night and had not been harmed, I became a bit more cheery. But still there was terrible suffering in Lhasa; many people were killed. The next day my disciples came early in the morning and urged me to leave right away, warning me that the Chinese planned to shell the monastery and that I might be killed. So I went with them. I was in the process of studying *The Essence of Eloquence* and wanted to continue with this, so I took a copy with me. But I took no clothes, no suitcase or backpack, no lunch. Some of the students brought a few blankets, a bag of barley flour, and a few other things.

As we were waiting up in the hills, it became dark. So, drawn by the fact that His Holiness had gone all the way to India, we decided to follow him. It was a very arduous and difficult journey, but we really weren't all that miserable. At no time did I think "the Chinese are awful, what they've done is dreadful." All I thought was "now we're wandering here, now we're going there." We thought all this was happening because of something we had done, and so we all prayed. We were praying all the time. This way we were expiating some negative, illusionary thing

that was with us. And by the time we had reached India, we were actually in a better state of mind than when we had started out! For a long time, we were filled with all kinds of virtuous thoughts, we had our very best mental attention, we were taking our teachings more deeply than we ever had. We thought more deeply about the holy fact of suffering, we looked at our texts more carefully, we meditated more intently than we might have otherwise. We were not able to feel great hatred or worry about the Chinese, although we knew on some level how awful they had been.

It is from that experience that I now presume to say that I am an expert in suffering!

Parabola: *It is as though you were already prepared for this catastrophe. You knew that allowing yourself to go in the direction of anger would be harmful to yourself and others. The Dharma was a great protection.*

TT: Yes, that's right. The Dharma is the greatest protection for the mind. I had thoroughly studied the various mind practices of the Dharma.

Parabola: *What advice would you give to those of us who aren't studying actively in the Buddhist tradition?*

TT: It's not a matter of Buddhist or not Buddhist, when one confronts, for instance, the fact that the idea of a rigid difference between self and other is a distortion of reality. My advice is to think as much as possible about the fact of the existence of suffering, without worrying about labels. If one can be just a little less concerned about oneself, and become a little more concerned about others—this is my main advice.

In this regard, a very good theme to reflect upon is the way in which others are of benefit to oneself. Whatever happiness one has depends upon the kindness of others. Clothes, shoes, food—all this comes from the labor of others; it is by their kindness that one has these things. If you fill your mind with such thoughts, then your mind will definitely improve. Of course, we have to know how to think. If we have something we like—a tape recorder, for example—we have to begin to analyze the origins of that tape recorder: why it was made, how, by whom, and so on. We begin to realize how that tape recorder is an aggregate of the beneficial intentions and actions of many other beings.

When we get up in the morning and drink a cup of tea, how does this depend on the kindness of others? But rather than thinking about the person who picked the tea leaves, the person who packed them, the person who supplied the water, and the gas that cooked it, our own inferior way of going about it is to think "I made this cup of tea." This is the way we really think. To think back, when we are in a restaurant, on the causality of the tea—this is the supreme advice I

have to give. To give another example, if a person has great wealth, they tend to think "It is my great fortune and karma, I don't depend on anyone else." But that wealth really depends on the kindness of others in a very complicated way. To develop a continuous thinking about that sort of thing is the best advice I know.

Parabola: *Could you explain more about what you mean by "the holy fact of suffering"?*

TT: It is not a fact for us ordinary people. We think a lot of things are fun or nice; we don't think they are suffering. But to a holy person, what we consider to be fun is really suffering. That is why this is called the "holy" fact of suffering. It is said that a holy person is like an eye, and we are like the palm of a hand. The tiniest speck of dust or hair is very unpleasant when in the eye—and the sensitivity and awareness of a holy person is like that. They are aware of the real suffering nature of something that to other people is fun. Others experience a piece of dust as if it were on the palm of the hand; they think nothing of it.

Parabola: *When it is said that all is suffering, it means that our pleasures and enjoyments are also suffering.*

TT: Exactly, all that we think of as happiness is called "the suffering of change." Only a holy person really knows that. It is factual for a holy person; it is not factual for other persons.

According to one analysis, the holy fact of suffering consists of three kinds of suffering. There is the suffering of change, the suffering of suffering, and cosmic suffering or the suffering of creation. The suffering of suffering is what we ordinarily recognize as suffering. Most of what makes us angry and irritable in our lives is really our confronting the suffering of suffering and failing to recognize it as such. The suffering of change is what we call ordinary pleasure, pleasure contaminated by egotism. If we don't recognize pleasure as the suffering of change, we generate desire for it. The third kind is cosmic suffering. By not recognizing it, we get steeped in delusion and ignorance. But if one knows well the nature of these three kinds of suffering, then one's anger, desire, and delusion will become less.

Meditation on the holy fact of suffering means to think upon one's experience: When I have become angry, what made me angry? When I became desirous, what made me desirous? When I became confused and deluded, what made me confused and deluded?

Parabola: *Would Rinpoche say something about cosmic suffering?*

TT: Cosmic suffering is existence itself. The aggregates themselves—of ideas, of consciousness, of sensations, of emotions, of forms—the very structure of the whole system is cosmic suffering. For example, my body now does not have contaminated happiness, nor does it have the suffering of suffering. My arm is not feeling pleasurable due to the suffering of change, nor miserable through the suffering of suffering. However, it has the nature of suffering; it has all the causes of suffering contained in it. A bit of heat applied to it will make it hurt. Or take a piece of clothing. Clothing is neither suffering nor pleasure. But if someone rips it, or it becomes frayed, or you spill tea or coffee on it, then it becomes a cause of suffering. Everything has this causal propensity to generate suffering. It is in the very fabric of reality. Wherever one dwells, there is suffering. We dwell in the universe, where there is cosmic suffering.

Parabola: *But if suffering is in the nature of everything, how can we get rid of it?*

TT: We must live in a different place, another world. Our friends, our house, our body, our food, our possessions, all are cosmic suffering. We need a whole new situation. In general, in Mahayana Buddhism, the creation of the Pure Land or Buddha Land by the Bodhisattva means the making of a new world. What is so notable about Vajrayana or Tibetan Buddhism is the ultimate elabora-

tion or technology of the creation of
a new world.

Parabola
Volume: 26.4
The Heart

THE EXCELLENCE OF *BODHICHITTA*

Pema Chödrön

When I was about six years old I received the essential *bodhichitta* teaching from an old woman sitting in the sun. I was walking by her house one day feeling lonely, unloved, and mad, kicking anything I could find. Laughing, she said to me, "Little girl, don't you go letting life harden your heart."

Right there, I received this pithy instruction: we can let the circumstances of our lives harden us so that we become increasingly resentful and afraid, or we can let them soften us and make us kinder and more open to what scares us. We always have this choice.

If we were to ask the Buddha, "What is bodhichitta?" he might tell us that this word is easier to understand than to translate. He might encourage us to seek out ways to find its meaning in our own lives. He might tantalize us by adding that it is only bodhichitta that heals, that bodhichitta is capable of transforming the hardest of hearts and the most prejudiced and fearful of minds.

Chitta means "mind" and also "heart" or "attitude." *Bodhi* means "awake," "enlightened," or "completely open." Sometimes the completely open heart and mind of bodhichitta is called the soft spot, a place as vulnerable and tender as an open wound. It is equated, in part, with our ability to love. Even the cruelest people have this soft spot. Even the most vicious animals love their offspring. As Trungpa Rinpoche put it, "Everybody loves something, even if it's only tortillas."

Bodhichitta is also equated, in part, with compassion—our ability to feel the pain that we share with others. Without realizing it we continually shield ourselves from this pain because it scares us. We put up protective walls made of opinions, prejudices, and strategies, barriers that are built on a deep fear of being hurt. These walls are further fortified by emotions of all kinds: anger, craving, indifference, jealousy and envy, arrogance and pride. But fortunately for us, the soft spot—our innate ability to love and to care about things—is like a crack in these walls we erect. It's a natural opening in the barriers we create when we're afraid. With practice we can learn to find this opening. We can learn to seize that vulnerable moment—love, gratitude, loneliness, embarrassment, inadequacy—to awaken bodhichitta.

An analogy for bodhichitta is the rawness of a broken heart. Sometimes this broken heart gives birth to anxiety and panic, sometimes to anger, resentment, and blame. But under the hardness of that armor there is the tenderness of genuine sadness. This is our link with all those who have ever loved. This genuine heart of sadness can teach us great compassion. It can humble us when we're arrogant and soften us when we are unkind. It awakens us when we prefer to sleep and pierces through our indifference. This continual ache of the heart is a blessing that when accepted fully can be shared with all.

The Buddha said that we are never separated from enlightenment. Even at the times we feel most stuck, we are never alienated from the awakened state. This is a revolutionary assertion. Even ordinary people like us with hang-ups and confusion have this mind of enlightenment called bodhichitta. The openness and warmth of bodhichitta is in fact our true nature and condition. Even when our neurosis feels far more basic than our wisdom, even when we're feeling most confused and hopeless, bodhichitta—like the open sky—is always here, undiminished by the clouds that temporarily cover it.

Given that we are so familiar with the clouds, of course, we may find the Buddha's teaching hard to believe. Yet the truth is that in the midst of our suffering, in the hardest of times, we can contact this noble heart of bodhichitta. It is always available, in pain as well as in joy.

A young woman wrote to me about finding herself in a small town in the Middle East surrounded by people jeering, yelling, and threatening to throw stones at her and her friends because they were Americans. Of course, she was terrified, and what happened to her is interesting. Suddenly she identified with every person throughout history who had ever been scorned and hated. She understood what it was like to be despised for any reason: ethnic group, racial background, sexual preference, gender. Something cracked wide open and she stood in the shoes of millions of oppressed people and saw with a new perspective. She even understood her shared humanity with those who hated her. This sense of deep connection, of belonging to the same family, is bodhichitta.

Bodhichitta exists on two levels. First there is unconditional bodhichitta, an immediate experience that is refreshingly free of concept, opinion, and our usual all-caught-upness. It's something hugely good that we are not able to pin down even slightly, like knowing at gut level that there's absolutely nothing to lose. Second there is relative bodhichitta, our ability to keep our hearts and minds open to suffering without shutting down.

Those who train wholeheartedly in awakening unconditional and relative bodhichitta are called *bodhisattvas* or warriors—not warriors who kill and harm but warriors of non-aggression who hear the cries of the world. These are men and women who are willing to train in the middle of the fire. Training in the middle of the fire can mean that warrior-bodhisattvas enter challenging situations in order to alleviate suffering. It also refers to their willingness to cut through personal reactivity and self-deception, to their dedication to uncovering the basic undistorted energy of bodhichitta. We have many examples of master warriors—people like Mother Teresa and Martin Luther King—who recognized that

the greatest harm comes from our own aggressive minds. They devoted their lives to helping others understand this truth. There are also many ordinary people who spend their lives training in opening their hearts and minds in order to help others do the same. Like them, we could learn to relate to ourselves and our world as warriors. We could train in awakening our courage and love.

There are both formal and informal methods for helping us to cultivate this bravery and kindness. There are practices for nurturing our capacity to rejoice, to let go, to love, and to shed a tear. There are those that teach us to stay open to uncertainty. There are others that help us to stay present at the times that we habitually shut down.

Wherever we are, we can train as a warrior. The practices of meditation, loving-kindness, compassion, joy, and equanimity are our tools. With the help of these practices, we can uncover the soft spot of bodhichitta. We will find that tenderness in sorrow and in gratitude. We will find it behind the hardness of rage and in the shakiness of fear. It is available in loneliness as well as in kindness.

Many of us prefer practices that will not cause discomfort, yet at the same time we want to be healed. But bodhichitta training doesn't work that way. A warrior accepts that we can never know what will happen to us next. We can try to control the uncontrollable by looking for security and predictability, always hoping to be comfortable and safe. But the truth is that we can never avoid uncertainty. This not knowing is part of the adventure, and it's also what makes us afraid.

Bodhichitta training offers no promise of happy endings. Rather, this "I" who wants to find security—who wants something to hold on to—can finally learn to grow up. The central question of a warrior's training is not how we avoid uncertainty and fear but how we relate to discomfort. How do we practice with difficulty, with our emotions, with the unpredictable encounters of an ordinary day?

All too frequently we relate like timid birds who don't dare to leave the nest. Here we sit in a nest that's getting pretty smelly and hasn't served its function for a very long time. No one is arriving to feed us. No one is protecting us and keeping us warm. And yet we keep hoping mother bird will arrive.

We could do ourselves the ultimate favor and finally get out of that nest. That this takes courage is obvious. That we could use some helpful hints is also clear. We may doubt that we're up to being a warrior-in-training. But we can ask ourselves this question: "Do I prefer to grow up and relate to life directly, or do I choose to live and die in fear?"

All beings have the capacity to feel tenderness—to experience heartbreak, pain, and uncertainty. Therefore the enlightened heart of bodhichitta

is available to us all. The insight meditation teacher Jack Kornfield tells of witnessing this in Cambodia during the time of the Khmer Rouge. Fifty thousand people had become communists at gunpoint, threatened with death if they continued their Buddhist practices. In spite of the danger, a temple was established in the refugee camp, and twenty thousand people attended the opening ceremony. There were no lectures or prayers but simply continuous chanting of one of the central teachings of the Buddha:

Hatred never ceases by hatred
But by love alone is healed.
This is an ancient and eternal law.

Thousands of people chanted and wept, knowing that the truth in these words was even greater than their suffering.

Bodhichitta has this kind of power. It will inspire and support us in good times and bad. It is like discovering a wisdom and courage we do not even know we have. Just as alchemy changes any metal into gold, bodhichitta can, if we let it, transform any activity, word, or thought into a vehicle for awakening our compassion.

From Chödrön, Pema. *The Places That Scare You: A Guide to Fearlessness in Difficult Times.* Boston: Shambhala Publications, Inc., 2001, 3-7.

Parabola
Volume: 5.3
Obstacles

CHANGING THE IMPOSSIBLE
Interview with His Holiness the Dalai Lama

*Through my own little experience I can feel benefit of love
and compassion and realization of human value, human dignity. I feel that as a result of this practice I am quite happy
person. Despite many difficult circumstances, I always feel: Oh!
I am happy! So that is my luck! If because of these difficulties I
always feel I am sad, it is not much use!*

—H. H. *the Dalai Lama*

*In 1935, a two-year-old Tibetan peasant boy named Tenzin
Gyatso was discovered as the Fourteenth Dalai Lama, the reincarnation of his predecessor on the Lion Throne, and supreme
temporal and spiritual ruler of Tibet. He began his training
at the age of four; he was fifteen when the Chinese invaded
Tibet, and he was forced to assume the full responsibility for
his beleaguered people. For the next eight years, continuing his
studies and training, he demonstrated the amazing depth of
his political and spiritual understanding, in a patient struggle
to negotiate with the Chinese and to bring Tibet's case before
the world.*

*Everyone knows of his dramatic and sacrificial flight from
Lhasa in an unsuccessful attempt to avert the bloodbath with
which the invaders were threatening his unarmed defenders.
And as everyone knows, he has since lived in India as an exile*

with the remnant of his people, includ-ing a large number of children, many of them orphans, who must be cared for. The struggle against odds continues; yet dur-ing his recent visit to the United States, what we saw was an overwhelming kind of triumph. He did not speak of obstacles or of struggle, except indirectly: "Enemy your greatest friend; without him, how learn patience?"

Who is the Dalai Lama? A god-king? An anachronism?

A tall thin man with dancing eyes, who seems to take a kind of eager delight in all that is human and all that is divine (with no division between the two), he bears the weight of his people and his own extraordinary destiny lightly and with joy. The eagerness and the joy were contagious and people responded to him, in such numbers that we were too late to obtain an interview with him. So when our friend the artist Ruth Wilson went to India, we pulled all the strings we could for her to see and talk with him for us. She writes of her experience as follows:

It is a misconception that the Dalai Lama is easily accessible! I devoted the entire time from March 12 to the end of my stay in India to getting this interview. *This is no complaint*—I knew from the start that it would be well worth every effort, and it was. The Tibetan office said that he was "out of station" at the moment and though he would return within the week, it was very, very difficult to see him in Dharamsala as he was fully booked before going out again. However he was to come to Delhi and there was a very good chance for an interview there. It was finally arranged for the 29th at 6 P.M. at his hotel, at an hour's drive from where I was staying.

My hostess and her fourteen-year-old son drove me over at the appointed time. There was a Tai conference going on and the hotel was flooded with Burmese wearing red roses. Luckily I had been given a room number on the fifth floor; we went there and found it locked. We were a little early, as the exact time I had been given was 6:10 P.M., so we sat down and waited in full view of the elevator, for about half an hour. Finally a group of Tibetans came; one of them stepped towards me and said he was extremely sorry to have kept me waiting, but His Holiness had been addressing a youth conference and had been delayed. Another half hour—and then—finally—a flurry of identical dark red robes, but not a fraction of a doubt as to which one of the crowd of monks he was! He walked quickly to his room followed by his escorts. Another few minutes while a monk who had also been wait-ing in the foyer took precedence, and then I was informed that "my party" was invited to come in with me. I first declined for them, but then the Dalai Lama himself appeared at the door and personally invited them in. Soon we were seated around the coffee table and His Holiness was plugging the microphone into my tape recorder. I brought out the microphone stand and while I was reaching into my handbag for my glasses which I needed for fitting it to the mike, he had taken both things and put them in working order, and set them up at an appropriate distance on the table. An audiovisual engineer couldn't have done a quicker or better job. This beginning of our interview took me by surprise; I had expected an august presence, a "holy person," and here was this easy, smiling, warmly kind man, completely free of any trace of strangeness or constraint. Yes, so free! That was the great impression. In a second, we were both involved in setting up equipment, both interested in getting to the question that you had asked a few weeks ago and several thousand miles away.

"The magazine *Parabola*," I told him, "comes out four times a year and every issue deals with a special theme, a specific question. Once the topic was 'Children' and another time it was 'Death.' The issue this talk is going into is on 'Obstacles.'"

His Holiness: Obstacles? Obstacles? Hm ... obstacles of what?

R. Wilson: *All kinds of obstacles. Your Holiness has had more experience in dealing with obstacles than almost anyone I can think of! There are, of course, the obstacles in life as the Tibetan nation has experienced them, and also the inner obstacles—obstacles to the evolution of the human spirit. A person strives, and circumstances get in the way. The question is, how can one utilize this situation, make use of these difficulties rather than saying that obstacles are only negative: What is their role in the life of the spirit?*

HH: That is difficult to explain. We may say this way: if you utilize obstacles properly, then it strengthens your courage, and it also gives you more intelligence, more wisdom. Because there is obstacle, you make attempt; so have to think, have to try something. Have to try certain way; so this gives strength and also wisdom and intelligence. If you use them in wrong way, then discourage, failure, depression. [Laughs]

RW: *Yes, very often this is the case; one feels low, incapable of taking the next step. What should be the spiritual attitude? How to overcome this feeling of depression? How can we look at the obstacle as something positive rather than negative?*

HH: That depends on the angle. One way, regard the obstacle as something negative; therefore, we try to overcome. Another way, it gives you, as

I mentioned earlier, a good result, in certain ways; therefore we may call them positive. I don't know; but generally, obstacle is obstacle! We do not want them; so that means we want to overcome. So that means negative. It depends on interpretation. And then, what is the interpretation of negative and positive itself? These things are relative. Negative depends on positive, positive depends on negative.

RW: *Is it just a question of the mind dealing with it?*

HH: Not only mind. Things are not controlled by mind fully. Things are things—but heavily depend on mind. But mind itself is not superior to everything. I mean, mind cannot change things—for example, this solid table cannot change into something liquid by mind force. (In some exceptional case may be possible, but generally not.) So that means mind depends on matter. So you see, matter depends on mind, mind depends on matter. In a sense, mind is superior: due to consciousness, due to mind, we utilize this matter in this direction or in that direction. Unless you get inner peace through mental improvement, mental upliftment, you cannot achieve real, lasting peace externally. So in that sense, the mind is superior.

RW: *In your book, you say that as a boy, when you entered school you had this resistance to learning certain things.*

When you started on dialectics, there was this resistance, and when you finally started to study metaphysics you even felt distressed. But you say that every time, after the first few days, you managed to get into your studies and not only to feel quite good about them but actually enjoy them. So you overcame something. What made you do that: was it obedience that helped you to overcome the obstruction?

HH: Obedience to whom?

RW: *Obedience to the teacher?*

HH: I think it was to my own brain. And making more attempt, more effort. I can understand, I can absorb that thing with my mind, so it becomes easier. So once you learn some difficult subject you feel very happy. That happiness is like a prize for the hard work.

RW: *In a word, it's a challenge that you accept.*

HH: Right!

RW: *I have just now been to Dharamsala to see how the Tibetans live, and I was very much impressed by the whole atmosphere there. It was remarkable to see how the people take their lot; they seem to be very happy, as far as I could see as an outsider.*

HH: Yes, they are jovial—jovial types. Generally they are quite happy. That's a gift. It is an advantage—despite many difficulties, they feel quite happy! [Laughs]

RW: *Do they feel they want to go back to Tibet?*

HH: Definitely; no doubt, no question. You see, every time they receive any fresh news from Tibet the reaction is very strong. That means the love for their country.

RW: *Do you think there is a possibility of going back?*

HH: I am hopeful. One day we can return. Things are changing.

RW: *I wish the whole world would understand what you and your people have understood. You have faced this great crisis—all people have their own problems, their own crises, but how many of them look at their problems in this way: that they are challenges they have to accept?*

HH: [Laughs] Is this the first time you mix with Tibetans?

RW: *Well, I have heard about Tibet as a child from my father who loved Tibet. He used to show me pictures of Lhasa and told me fascinating things about your country. So there was a picture in my mind, and also of course curiosity. Now, of course, Tibetans are all over the world; I have met some in Austria, and England, and America; and I have met Trungpa Rinpoche and been to his place*

in Vermont. Still, that does not make me know very much.

HH: But this time you gained more knowledge?

RW: *Yes. I have met several people studying at the Buddhist Center in lower Dharamsala—that's an excellent place. I also watched some of the celebrations at the temple: the chanting, the gongs and the Tibetan horns, and then the masks and the dancing—I was very impressed. Just to stand there and be part of that gathering was a tremendous experience.*

His Holiness chuckled, obviously pleased. Some more conversation followed that included everyone, and I then asked his permission to leave, as we had heard that His Holiness had to leave at 7:30. We were each presented with a white scarf and conducted to the door, His Holiness supporting my arm with both hands while pointing out a hardly visible step. His smiling face and his blessings accompanied us all the way home.

Human being can do anything. Determination, some sort of courage, self-confidence, that is the real force for victory, for success. If you have will-power and courage—reasonable courage, not blind courage; courage without pride—at a certain stage, because of that courage, because of effort, continued effort, sometimes the impossible can change into possible ...

—H. H. the Dalai Lama

This is a true story ...

A certain professor had the rare opportunity of getting an interview with the Dalai Lama at Dharamsala. A friend counseled him to write down his questions, so he would not forget them when the time came. The professor said nothing but thought he was quite clear about his questions and for someone so used to public speaking surely there was no need to write them down. As he approached the Dalai Lama's residence he noticed a monk working in the garden. "Excuse me," he said, "where should I go for an interview with the Dalai Lama?" "Just proceed and wait in the first room," the monk said, "he will be with you shortly." The professor did as he had been told and after a few minutes the Dalai Lama entered; to the professor's great surprise, he saw that it was the monk he had been talking to in the garden. He was so confounded by this unexpected revelation that he could not think of anything he had wanted to say. The Dalai Lama smiled and said, "If you were to ask me so and so, I would answer thus, and if your question were such and such, I would say this," and he answered all the questions that had been in the professor's mind.

The practical test comes when occasions of sorrow or suffering arise. The person whose mind is conditioned by the study and practice of religion faces these circumstances with patience and forbearance. The person who does not follow the path of religion may break under the impact of what he regards as calamities, and may end in either self-frustration, or else in pursuits which inflict unhappiness on others. Humanitarianism and true love for all beings can only stem from an awareness of the content of religion. In whatever name religion may be known, its understanding and practice are the essence of a peaceful mind and therefore of a peaceful world. If there is no peace in one's mind, there can be no peace in one's approach to others, and thus no peaceful relations between individuals or between nations.

—H. H. the Dalai Lama

Eastern or Western, even believer or non-believer, there is no difference, we are all the same. I am a human being, you are a human being, we all are the same. If we look this way on this planet, there are no boundaries, there is just one globe. So all these demarcations, these differences, actually we make them, I think. We make this color, that color, these separations. If we look from wider viewpoint, we can remain calm; with that we feel much inner peace. Even when in daily life all may not be successful, we can remain without losing inner peace and stability. That way you can minimize many inner problems; despite these problems and obstacles you remain peaceful and calm, and your neighbors also share that ...

—H. H. the Dalai Lama

Parabola
Volume: 12.3
Forgiveness

THE HOLY ANCHORITE
OF BHUTAN

Alexandra David-Neel

I got some idea of this teacher from the accounts of Dawasandup, who venerated him deeply. He must have resembled many lamas whom I have met later on, harboring in his mind a mixture of learning and superstitions, but, above all, a good and charitable man.

He was distinguished from his colleagues, however, by having had as master a veritable saint whose death is worth relating.

This holy lama was an anchorite who practiced mystic contemplation in a secluded spot in Bhutan. As it is often the case, one of his disciples shared his hermitage and served him.

One day a pious benefactor came to see the ascetic and left him a sum of money to purchase winter provisions. His disciple, urged on by covetousness, stabbed him and ran off with the silver. The aged lama was still alive, and came to his senses soon after the murderer had gone. His wounds caused him excruciating suffering, and to escape this torture he sank into meditation.

Concentration of thought is carried so far by Tibetan mystics that it becomes anaesthetic and they do not feel anything; or at a lower degree of power they can thus greatly lessen their pains.

When another disciple of the lama went to visit him a few days later he found him rolled up in a blanket and motionless. The smell from the festering wounds and the blood-stained blanket caught his attention. He questioned his master. The hermit then told him what had happened, but when the man wished to get a doctor from the nearest monastery he was forbidden to do so.

"If the lamas and villagers happen to hear about my condition they will search for the culprit," said the ascetic. "He cannot have got far. They would find him and, probably, condemn him to death. I cannot permit this. I wish to give him more time to escape. One day he will, perhaps, return to the right path and, in any case, I shall not have been the cause of his death. So do not tell anyone what you have seen here. Now go, leave me alone. While I meditate, I do not suffer, but when I become conscious of my body my pain is unbearable."

An Oriental disciple does not discuss an order of this kind. The man prostrated himself at his guru's feet and left. A few days later the hermit, all alone in his hut, passed away.

Although Dawasandup greatly admired the conduct of the holy lama, such moral summits were not for him. He humbly confessed it.

From Alexandra David-Neel, *Magic and Mystery in Tibet* (New York: Dover Publications, 1971) 15-16.

Parabola
Volume: 28.1
Compassion

It Doesn't Begin with Honesty

Robert Aitken, Zen Master Raven Tales

Saving the Many Beings

Mallard appeared in the circle after a trip and asked, "The first of our vows is to save the many beings. You told us that the Sixth Ancestor said this means 'You save them in your own mind.' Is that all there is to fulfilling this vow?"

Raven said, "Completely fulfilled."

Mallard said, "But what then?"

Raven said, "Not just your own skull."

Not Helping

After a talk by Raven about the precepts, Woodpecker said, "The cowbird lays her egg in the wren's nest, and the two wrens have to hustle to feed the cowbird's baby as well as their own. I don't see why the wrens stand for it, especially since the cowbird's baby is a lot bigger than theirs and has a huge appetite. Maybe the wrens are really bodhisattvas, selflessly devoted to helping others."

Raven said, "They aren't helping the cowbirds."

Compassion

Mole spoke up after a long silence one evening and asked, "What's compassion?"

Raven said, "That's an inside story."

Mole asked, "Inside what?"

Raven said, "Stars on your fur."

Watch Out!

Cougar's presence created a certain tension in the circle, but he didn't seem aware of it. One evening he asked, "If all things pass quickly away, why should we be concerned about the suffering of others?"

Mole abruptly excused himself with a bow and hurried off, muttering. Raven said, "Mara can quote sutras."[1]

Cougar said, "I'm serious."

Raven said, "All things pass quickly away."

Honesty

Black Bear came to a meeting late and said, "I'm feeling frazzled after dealing with my cubs. What if I don't feel compassionate?"

Raven said, "Fake it."

"That doesn't seem honest," said Black Bear.

"It doesn't begin with honesty," said Raven.

Mara

After an exchange about compassion, Badger said, "Well, I got my comeuppance on that one. I have another question—not really a question, more a confession. It's the one that's been on my mind for some time. I've sat with you all this time and not realized very much at all. I wake up in the night feeling guilty that I haven't made more of an effort. You devote yourself to us, and I feel that I've failed you."

Raven said, "Mara is prodding you."

Badger said, "It hurts."

Raven said, "It's the only way he knows."

Notes:

1   Mara: The Destroyer, the Evil One

•

CHAPTER EIGHT

TIBETAN BLESSINGS

This self-originated clear light is eternal and unborn.
How strange and marvelous!

Since it is unborn, it cannot die. How strange and marvelous!

Although it is absolute reality, there is no one to perceive it.
How strange and marvelous!

Although it wanders in samsara, it is undefiled by evil.
How strange and marvelous!

Although it sees the Buddha, it is unattached to good.
How strange and marvelous!

Although it is possessed by all beings, it is not recognized by them.
How strange and marvelous!

Although the clear light of reality shines inside their own mind, most people
look for it outside. How strange and marvelous!"

—Padmasambhava

The Lama of the Crystal Monastery appears to be a very happy man, and
yet I wonder how he feels about his isolation in the silences of Tsakang, which he
has not left in eight years now and, because of his legs, may never leave again. Since
Jang-bu seems uncomfortable with the Lama or with himself or perhaps
with us, I tell him not to inquire on this point if it seems to him impertinent, but
after a moment Jang-bu does so. And this holy man of great directness and
simplicity, big white teeth shining, laughs out loud in an infectious way at
Jang-bu's question. Indicating his twisted legs without a trace of self-pity
or bitterness, as if they belong to all of us, he casts his arms wide to the sky and
the snow mountains, the high sun and dancing sheep, and cries, "Of course I am
happy here! It's wonderful! Especially when I have no choice!"

—Peter Matthiessen, *The Snow Leopard*

Parabola
Volume: 10.2
Exile

Tibet: Mystic Nation in Exile

Robert A. F. Thurman

This center of heaven,
This core of the earth,
This heart of the world,
Fenced round by snow,
The headland of all rivers,
Where the mountains are high and the land is pure.
O country so good,
Where men are born sages and heroes![1]

In 1959, His Holiness the Dalai Lama had to flee the
invading Red Army of the People's Republic of China, to go
into exile in India. He was followed eventually by over one
hundred thousand Tibetans, with many more tens of thousands perishing in the attempt. Since then, those Tibetans
who could not get away have suffered genocidal occupation
by the Chinese Communists. And those in the diaspora
in India, Europe, and America have had to be responsible
for the preservation of the entire culture. They are having
a real experience of exile. Yet they have adapted amazingly
well to the homelessness of modernity, stepping effortlessly
across what seems to be a chasm of five centuries into the
world of industrial technology. They have preserved the life
and culture of their nation without their land, which floats
in the diamond sky over the Himalayas whence came their
ancestral king.

The exile has not daunted, has even strengthened the Tibetan people as a whole. But so many individuals have died, are dying, have suffered, and are suffering horribly. Reflecting on national tragedies, we must always remember the individual dimension. In many cases, the little death of exile became real death. Often there were insurmountable physical hardships on the flight over the high Himalayas and during the reacclimatization to the heat, low altitude, and germ-environment of India.

John F. Avedon, in his recent masterpiece, *In Exile from the Land of Snows*, poignantly recounts the trials and hardships of one little Tibetan family.[2] On a cool October night in 1959, Chopel Dhondub began a hastily planned flight from his village to the south, across the Himalayas. Unaware that the Dalai Lama had already gone the previous March, Chopel Dhondub and his wife were fleeing to save their ten-year-old son, Tempa, who was to be taken from them forcibly by the Chinese military authorities, and sent down to China for schooling. Mr. And Mrs. Dhondub had to carry their two infant daughters on their backs through the cold, deep snow. One of the little girls died of exposure in her mother's arms during the third day of the trek, just after they had succeeded in getting over the last pass at eighteen thousand feet. They had to bury her little body right there in the snow. With further great hardships,

they had to beg their way through Bhutan to reach India. After some months in an over-crowded refugee camp in a hot, humid climate they had never experienced, their second daughter died. The family was eventually transferred to a road-working camp in the hills, but Mrs. Dhondub had become withdrawn and listless from the shock of the loss of her daughters. The better climate of the road-camp did not revive her spirits, and after two more weeks, she also died, simply of a broken heart. Chopel Dhondub himself became very ill, and the eleven-year-old Tempa had to be taken into the Tibetan government nursery that was being set up in Dharamsala. In spite of tragedy that might have crushed such a young boy, Tempa somehow survived. He grew to serve the Dalai Lama and the government very ably as secretary and translator.

The Tibetan story is hundreds of thousands of such individual cases of human tragedy and suffering. The policy of the Chinese occupation forces was described as "genocidal" by the International Commission of Jurists in Geneva. Following Mao's ideological determination and his expansive geopolitical strategy, the mission of the Chinese generals in charge was to eradicate Tibetan culture and assimilate Tibetans into the Chinese race. They wanted to create *ex post facto* the appearance of legitimacy for their claim to a land that had never been part of China during its several thousand years of recorded history. Tibet has suffered a total loss of the physical setting of its civilization, monasteries, temples, palaces, elegant houses; a loss of at least one fifth of its population to war, mass executions, both militarily organized and class-struggle incited, attrition in gulag-style prison camps, mass deportation to China; and a loss of their national land and individual properties due to the carving of the eastern parts of Tibet into a new state, Qinghai, and into new districts of old states such as Sechuan, and due to the mass colonization of their ancestral lands by Chinese workers and soldiers.

In an exact sense, Tibet only exists in the refugee community in India, Nepal, Bhutan, and Sikkim, where His Holiness the Dalai Lama, his government-in-exile, and his by now roughly one hundred twenty thousand refugee subjects have preserved much of the old culture, while vigorously developing new forms of Tibetan living in the modern situation.[3] The capitol is in Dharamsala, a small town in the Himalayan foothills in the Indian state of Himachal Pradesh. The Dalai Lama has led the way in a monumental administrative job of reconstructing a government, with elected representative bodies, ministries of Home Affairs, Foreign Affairs, Religious and Cultural Affairs, and Education, and numerous smaller agencies. Hospitals,

practicing Tibetan medicine and western medicine both, have been constructed, large nursery schools for the many orphans and virtual orphans, monasteries, cultural associations for dance and drama, fine arts, carpentry, silver and goldsmithing, archives and museums—the energy and thoroughness with which the culture is selectively preserved and developed are remarkable. Education has been a major priority, and His Holiness received great understanding and assistance from Pandit Nehru in this, allowing him to create a special Tibetan school system for the Tibetan children. The Dalai Lama realized twenty-five years ago that the survival of his people depended on the education of the youth—they could lose their language and Tibetan culture in the Indian school system, or they could follow a curriculum that provided them with knowledge of their language and history and native culture as well as giving them the essentials of a modern education, including English and Hindi. The excellent implementation of the latter policy led to a whole generation of Tibetans with a well-balanced education, now able to enter and excel in institutions of higher learning anywhere in the world, restricted only by limited funding.

The Tibetans have also successfully developed industrial projects in various parts of India, as well as a thriving craft industry in rugs, metalwork, sweater manufacture, and other popular arts. They have done well in farming on the large tracts of underdeveloped lands generously given by the Indian government in various parts of the country. In fact, the degree of success they have achieved in only two decades has been stunning, resulting in many cases in their achieving a standard of living substantially better than that of the surrounding population. This has sometimes been a source of friction arising from envy on a local level, as happened in Bhutan, for example. Finally, the major industry of Tibetans will always be knowledge, especially their "Inner Science" knowledge. The Tibetan lama teachers have already had quite an impact on spiritual seekers in India, causing a renaissance of Buddhism in its original holy land. They have created substantial movements in Europe, Australia, and North America.

The Tibetan holocaust is a culminatory event in a sequence of calamities that bring us nearer to the bitter end of a certain flow of history. It is a warning for us all, a warning that confirms our clear sense of ultimate planetary danger. But most important is the opportunity for rebirth, the chance to understand the various levels of forces at work here, to see the reality of Tibet. We must find out how to benefit by its special knowledge, help it become reborn, by the power of truth against whatever odds, and let it help us become reborn again. As we stand on our own brink, we need whatever might be useful to turn it all around, to avert oblivion and realize a practical utopia.

Tibet, culturally including the previously scattered Mongolian peoples, represents a special civilization, which is not "traditional" in our usual sense of "pre-modern," but also is not "modern" in the western sense of modern. It is not a "medieval" or "feudal" civilization, as often even its most sympathetic students have assumed. It had its own "renaissance" and "reformation," developed its own form of "modernity," and its own form of "industrial revolution." But, where the western industrial modernity is "exterior," i.e. materialistic, secularistic, and aimed at ultimate transformation of the world as a physical, external environment, the Tibetan industrial modernity is spiritual, religious, and aimed at ultimate transformation of the world as an intersubjective, internal realm of mind.

Tibet/Mongolia was the only society on the planet in which Buddhism had become completely central, the only fully monasticized society in history. But have a care—this does not mean that it was a "pure land" or "Buddha-land," a land where all Buddhist ideals, both individual and social, were fulfilled. No land could ever satisfy the messianic aspirations of the Mahayana Bodhisattvas without the entire planet going along with it, according to the Buddhist view of the interconnectedness of all beings. Tibet showed her implicit awareness of her own imperfection in this sense in two ways; by seeking in the end to shut out the rest of the violent world, and by adopting the dream of Shambhala as central to her view of history. But Tibet was still a relatively, temporarily purified land to her people, a land chosen as sacred to the angelic messiah/Bodhisattva Avalokiteshvara, a land where the millennium had already arrived and the God of Compassion was manifestly and institutionally incarnate in the five-century-long line of the Dalai Lamas.

To understand what this means, we need to run through the thousand-year process by which Tibet/Mongolia became such an even temporary Buddhist paradise. At the time of the song at the beginning of this essay, Tibetans were a powerful race of conquerors, feared by the T'ang emperors, Muslim caliphs, Bengali and Nepali kings, and Inner Asian princes. In the seventh century, Songzen Gampo brought in Buddhism against the strenuous objections of his fierce feudal vassals, and it took his dynasty almost two hundred years to build the first monastery. The Dharma of non-violence, renunciation, love, and wisdom did not sit well right away with blood-thirsty tribal warriors. And a nation's support of a monastery, a nonutilitarian sacred space for the individual's spiritual development, is the threshold of its entry into the sphere of Buddhism as a way to enlightenment.

In the tenth through the fourteenth century, Tibet was slowly monasticized, as the nation's warrior energies turned more and more inward to the conquest of the inner enemies of ignorance, lust, and hate. The power of the feudal nobles still remained great, however, and the fortunes of the monastic Orders teetered in a precarious balance with the various dynasties, with foreign powers often involved, especially the as yet untamed Mongols. This was the period of the "feudal, medieval Tibetan society" so many think still existed until recently, due to the combination of Tibet's lack of "exterior modernity," the propaganda of the Chinese, ignorance, and the lack of even a concept of a form of personality and society that existed nowhere else, a form we can suitably call "interior modernity."

Then in the fifteenth through seventeenth centuries, something remarkable happened, something that did not happen anywhere else on the planet. The monastic, spiritually-centered institutions became the secular power, gradually assumed responsibility for the government, took over the management of resources, and developed a skillful bureaucracy. During these same centuries in northern Europe, the merchant classes backed secular kings to suppress the feudal nobles, the Protestant ideology destroyed the role of the monasteries by making "interior industry" irrelevant to a pre-determined salvation by faith alone and hence irrational, and the unification of the sacred/secular duality was accomplished by the collapse of the sacred into the secular. Max Weber has analyzed this process of "exterior" modernization quite well.[4] In Tibet, the monastic Orders employed Messianic and Apocalyptic Buddhist ideas to produce a Sacred King to control the feudal nobles, depriving them of much of their land and all feudal claims over the serfs. The monasteries became the seats of the national industry, the inner perfection of minds and souls through education and contemplation. And the Apocalyptic Buddhist ideology encouraged a sense of millennial immediacy of ultimate spiritual fruition that led to the sacred/secular nonduality being focused on the sacred (the exact reverse of the western secularistic "nonduality"). Although rough and tough individuals still roamed free, especially in the east of Tibet, the national policy was non-violence. There was no army and little police. There was total access to learning and wide social mobility through the universal monastic education system. The central government protected the lower classes from the greatly weakened nobility, whose landholdings had become dependent on their service of the government, and there was a new avenue of ennoblement through having the merit or good fortune to receive a reincarnate saint in the family by birth. Above all, the whole nation lived for the enlightenment of each individual, within a multilife time-frame, with a messianic and apocalyptic sense of the immanence of the divine benefactors of the world.

The magnificent edifice renowned as the Potala was completed during the seventeenth century, combining monastery, ancestral royal fortress-palace, apocalyptic mystery temple, and bureaucratic administrative hall of government. It symbolizes dramatically the synthesis I have so quickly sketched. At the nexus of this synthesis was, of course, the person of the Dalai Lama, Buddhist monk, Messiah/Bodhisattva Avalokiteshvara incarnate, Mystic Master of the Vajrayana, apocalyptic sacraments, and chief executive of the state. The reformation was conducted by the first four Dalai Lamas, and the Potala was begun by the Great Fifth (1617-1682), and finished by the Seventh (1708-1757). It symbolized the national center, the abode of the nationless, universal Bodhisattva of Great Compassion, incarnate to protect his people whose chosenness was their selflessness, whose identity was identitylessness, whose industry was enlightenment, and whose evolutionary destiny was imminently to be fulfilled in the unfolding of the mystic Wheel of time.

This is Tibet's "modernity," her "conquest" of the realms of the individual mind through a refined technology of self-perfecting education and contemplation, and her "industrial revolution" of producing powerful and beautiful, benevolent, magical energies to create new spaces of the human imagination, within which invisible horizon the imaginations of all peoples could flourish. This is not an intellectual game, a play on the words "conquest" and "industry," a way of dressing up in fine new clothes a quaint traditionality we should value for humanitarian reasons. No, I mean this in great seriousness. Opening a path of insight toward this social possibility can bring us to the concept of something as important, useful, even essential to us as an alternative modernity; a way of becoming modern that is equal and yet opposite to the one Europe chose; a way of modernity that may complement our own.

It is convenient that His Holiness the Dalai Lama has become more well-known, as his personality and the mythic sources of identity underlying it provide us with a good example of "interior modernity." Quite a bit has been written about him since Heinrich Harrer first knew him as a boy eager to dissect radios and assemble car engines,[5] and people are always surprised about how "contemporary" and "everyday" and "modern" he is. Tibetans in general have taken easily to technology and machinery, becoming skillful quite

rapidly, learning very well. Tibetan refugee colonies in India have tended quickly to become islands of Swiss-like order and precision in a sea of third-world shabbiness. His Holiness in his home in exile in Dharamsala relaxes doing scientific horticulture, repairing watches with a set of fine Swiss precision tools, soldering connections in home radio sets, as well as reading widely in the enormous Tibetan philosophical and mystical literature. He goes into his office and conducts businesslike and amiable conversations with people from all over the world. Or he holds a staff meeting with his Cabinet, or with officials from one of the Ministries or government institutions. Or he presides over an elaborate liturgy in his hierophantic regalia. Or he attends a philosophical debate or he lectures to graduate students. And occasionally he spends weeks or even months on retreats, practicing very disciplined contemplations. He travels widely, has quietly met most world leaders around the planet, and is well informed in many fields. He holds incisive views on a variety of subjects, yet he always maintains an open curiosity. What are the sources of identity of such a person?

His Holiness is a Buddhist monk, a Mendicant in the Community of Shakyamuni the historic Buddha. Shakyamuni Buddha was a famous exile, exile in the really cosmic sense of a "stranger in a strange land." In his mythic royal lives previous to his historic Buddhahood, he was often exiled, usually for being too good to be true. As Vessantara, the Prince of Generosity, he is exiled for giving away the national treasury and the key to the national defense. As Mahabodhi, the sage of ethics, he is exiled for giving counsel that was all too excellent. As Siddhartha in his final life, when his father seeks to imprison him in his royal role, he must escape into exile himself to gain his individual freedom, his enlightenment.

The Buddha undertook such an exile voluntarily, in keeping with his spiritual vision of ignorant life as an exile from enlightenment. After he had overcome such ignorance and the samsaric life cycle it controls, he formed a new Community, the precious Sangha. This was his historic invention of the monastic institution, which codified and made more widely available the "homeless" life. He expressed his fundamental insight into the nature of reality in the "lion's roar" of "selflessness." He saw through the illusion of fixed identity on every level, personal and biological as well as national and cultural. Thus, the Buddha provided the earliest preparation of people for modernity on record. He taught "homelessness" as a fundamental quality of the Buddhist experience from its beginnings. It is as if the Buddha were teaching a kind of selfless personality structure in anticipation of modernity.

It is because of the centrality of this teaching that the Tibetan nation achieved what we can only call a "national identity of identitylessness." And herein we see a foundational source of the "spiritual modernity" we are after. On this level of identity, His Holiness is an international, universal human figure, at home in homelessness, tolerant of wandering, forgiving of his enemies. It is from this monastic depth of his being that he is often heard to express sincere thanks to Mao Tse-tung as one who taught him the realities of impermanence and suffering. And he only possesses to a highly cultivated degree a trait shared by most Tibetans, coming from the same source.

His Holiness is considered the reincarnation of the messianic Bodhisattva Avalokiteshvara, the archangel of great compassion. There is a myth about Avalokiteshvara that is key to understanding his central role as patron deity of Tibet. He vowed to tame the wild beings of the Land of Snows many eons ago, when he lived in the Sukhavati in the presence of Buddha Amitabha. To stress his determination, he insisted that, should he ever become discouraged with that difficult task, his body should be torn into a thousand pieces and his head shattered into ten. He descended to the Red Mountain overlooking Lhasa and meditated for many centuries. Finally, he did become discouraged, for he found the

Tibetans to be incorrigibly difficult. At that moment his vow came true, and he was torn up into shreds. He cried out in agony and despair to his father, Amitabha, who appeared and stated, "All things are created from conditions. You should always take care about what you wish for: sooner or later you will get it!" Then he blessed the dismembered Bodhisattva, and the thousand pieces became the thousand arms of the thousand wheel-turning kings, each having in its palm one of the thousand eyes of the thousand Buddhas of our present Good Eon. The ten pieces of his head became ten heads, each symbolizing the vision of one of the ten stages of Bodhisattvahood. On the top of the stack of heads rested a miniature emanation of Buddha Amitabha himself. The Bodhisattva thus became gloriously resurrected as the embodiment of both royal power and spiritual wisdom. His topmost head was the head of Death, Yama, Lord of the underworld, symbolizing that he now could understand and deal effectively with evil without compromising his constitutional goodness of messianic great compassion.

The national myth understands that he emanates in innumerable forms to help the Tibetans: as the great King Songzen Gampo, who imported Buddhism in the seventh century; as the Great Adept, mystic anthropologist, Padma Sambhava, who tamed the shamanistic deities of the Tibetan tribes; as the lay disciple of Atisha, Drom, who established the seed of a viable form of monasticism in the eleventh century; and afterwards as kings and queens, lamas and nuns and ministers and lay men and women. He "manifests whatsoever is needed to tame whomsoever," in the words of the famous salutation. Finally, in the seventeenth century, after one thousand years of taming the wild Tibetans, he unifies church and state in a millennial fusion, emanating himself as the Great Fifth Dalai Lama and building the magnificent Potala on the ruins of Songzen's favorite palace.

At Lhasa beneath its imposing beauty, the Tibetan people have enjoyed a happiness unique on the planet during the last three centuries. Tibet was a nation enjoying its own millennium, with its own resurrected savior alive among its people, guiding them in day to day matters as well as blessing them in matters of spirit. On this level the present Dalai Lama is of course agonized by the holocaust that has overtaken his people, and he is committed never to abandon his effort to see them through to freedom and happiness again. He is also committed to the happy solution of planetary tensions and conflicts, and tries in an unassuming way to mediate any conflicts that come close to him. All Tibetans, whether accomplished or not, place great value on love and compassion, and seek to emulate the deeds of Avalokiteshvara. This gives them boundless industry and perseverance in struggling to make the world a better place, in trying to better themselves and help their fellow beings. It gives them a kind of modern universalism of world improvement, a messianic commitment to a better future.

Finally, His Holiness is a Great Adept, both ritually and on the strength of his contemplative virtuosity, a Vajra Master of Apocalyptic Buddhism, especially renowned for his expertise in the *Kalachakra Tantra*, the "Spiritual Technology of the Wheel of Time." In this role he can be identified in certain rituals and contemplative contexts with the Buddha in his most cosmic manifestation, as the *Time Machine* itself, a godlike presence that is fully aware of all time and all destinies, and is fully competent in benevolent strategies to assure the positive evolution of all forms of life toward freedom and happiness. The Tibetan sense of history is tied to the teachings of the *Kalacharkra*. They believe in the existence of a mythic country at the North Pole named "Shambhala," where there are thousands of enlightened Bodhisattvas with a highly developed spirituality and an effective technology. This country remains invisible to all the nations until a time in the near future when things seem all but lost to the forces of darkness, ignorance, and despotism. Then Shambhala becomes visible, there is a final battle between darkness and light, light prevails, and a golden age ensues all over the earth.

It is rather like the apocalyptic teachings of most religions. On this level of His Holiness' identity, he practices a contemplation that uses the artistic creative imagination to conceive a Mandalic universe of pure beauty, harmony, kindness, and wisdom, never losing faith in the essential spiritual fact that good is more powerful than evil. Again, although the Dalai Lama is the standard-setter for the nation, all Tibetans possess this identification with the positive evolutionary process symbolized by the *Kalachakra Time Machine*. It provides them with a resilient optimism in the midst of the worst difficulties and sufferings. It is a great asset in modern times.

These three strands of mythic identity combine in the complex Tibetan personality to constitute its "interior modernity." There is the basic, monastic "homeless mind" of the free individual, grounded well enough in the ultimate groundlessness to be tolerant and resigned and detached from many of the props of ordinary life. There is the messianic commitment to universal compassion that underlies a general friendliness, a sense of the "familiarity" of all beings that enables the Tibetan to get along so well in pluralistic situations. And finally there is the historical utopianism, or "Shambhalism," that enables him or her to keep up hope in the face of overwhelming odds, that preserves a sustaining faith and sense of grace even in the darkest moments of holocaust, torment, and death. In these three traits we have a concrete illustration of a "modernity" of personality that does not depend on external technology, modern industrial urban living arrangements and so on: the character constellation of "interior modernity."

Well, so what? What difference does it make if we call the form of society of Tibet "an interior modernity" rather than "medieval," or "feudal," or even "traditional"? Perhaps modernity itself is not so wonderful; there are those among us who have no great pride of progress, and esteem the values of good old traditionality. What is the point of this exercise?

There are several levels of answers to this. On the minimal level, "feudal" and "medieval" have been used by the Chinese Communists to justify their genocidal policy, trying to pretend that their theft and absorption of Tibet is a form of "progress," righting "feudal class injustice" and "medieval barbarities." It has been used by westerners seeking an excuse for their turning a blind eye on these atrocities, pragmatically resigning themselves to the inevitability of the disappearance of traditionality. Both these excuses disappear when we recognize the integrity of Tibetan civilization and the importance of allowing its development to continue on its own innovative line of progress.

On the next level, it is true that there are many drawbacks to our

form of modernity: the homeless mind is a painful alienation and a sorry way to live, and we are on the brink of destroying the earth itself in the process of breaking away from fettering traditionality. We have a great deal to learn from so-called "traditional" peoples, and every single one of them, each in its own way, presents an alternative form of modernity, in that it still exists somehow today. Granting these points, is it practical to try to take the world back into any existing form of traditional social reality? Is it desirable? Every form of romantic atavism I know of, including all forms of religious fundamentalism, tacitly admits the impossibility of turning back the momentum of "modern progress" by basing the plausibility of its worldview on an evident anticipation of the destruction of modernity in some form of planetary apocalypse. Not one of them considers that its social vision could be implemented by systematic design without the catalyst of doomsday. Secondly, although we moderns sometimes feel lonely, alienated, rootless, and restless, we also feel free, full of potential, and optimistic about the infinite horizon of positive evolution that lies before us. We want a refined postmodernity, not a regression to any premodern romantic fantasy.

On the other hand, the "interior modernity" of Tibet presents another way of having the freedom and pleasures of modernity without the dangerous alienation and destructive excesses of "exterior modernity." If our technologies of self exploration, self-conquest, and self-transformation were just as systematic and effective as our exterior technologies, then it would be extremely likely that self-restrained, enlightened, sensitive, and compassionate individuals could utilize such great power over the environment for human benefit instead of detriment. Such individuals would clearly adopt nonviolence in conflict resolution, and war, with its exorbitant expense, could be abandoned. War industries could become peace industries, the ghettoes could become elegant ethnic paradises, the Sahara could become a garden, the oceans farms, outer space resorts, schools and universities centers of enlightenment training, and monasteries could replace mental hospitals and prisons. Use your own imagination on how the one trillion plus yearly planetary war dollars could be spent to long-term human benefit.

The key is the Inner Sciences kept alive for us in Tibetan monastic universities and rooted in her unique cultureless culture. In brief, from Tibet's alternative, interior modernity, we can learn the Inner Science and Technology we need to balance knowledge with cultivated positive emotion, to complement our power over nature with power over self, to become interior conquistadors and discover our inner El Dorados, fountains of youth, and the vast Pacific vistas of the mind. This means we have much to learn, especially in the line of ethics, psychology, and philosophy included in Inner Science. And we can learn much from books, but more from people.

As people learn best by example, we have to observe the Tibetans themselves, to see how they combine our outer modernity with their own inner modernity. We are not the only active agents. It is not just a matter of how we use their knowledge. At least as important is how they will pick and choose among our knowledges and techniques. We may learn most of all about evolving a balanced modernity from how the Tibetans learn from us. There are two experiments going on: nations with exterior modernity trying to balance it with newly learned interior modernity, and the nation with interior modernity trying to balance it with newly learned exterior modernity. If, as the Indian and Tibetan sages have said all along, the Inner Science is the more important, difficult, and valuable, then they should have the easier time and develop an integrated modernity before us. Thus, it is they who would lead us by example into Shambhala, and not the other way around. And we cannot know how they will do that until they are free to evolve in their own space, their own freedom, their own time. So it is part of the complex project of continuously saving the world not to cease the struggle to return the Tibetan people to their own environment, to enable them to rebuild their institutions. And then how we will enjoy their happiness, watching them evolve in open international communication!

It is not only a moral imperative to stop the human rights abuse in Tibet and to base our policy there on the principle of freedom and self-determination. It is in our own interest and in the interests of the Chinese to see Tibetans free. We should not just enjoy the spiritual gift of the Tibetans, ignoring their relative, political plight. We should see that they regain their freedom, as a planetary priority, more important than any nation's face-saving or short-term interests, even a huge nation such as China. A free Tibet can do even more for the world than the Tibetans free in exile are now already doing.

A viable world order, what the Chinese called T'ian Ming, the "Will of Heaven," stands not on power or strategy, but on truth. The truth is that Tibet is free, its shattered pieces gloriously resurrected into a thousand loving arms and knowing eyes, even floating in exile. Let the Bodhisattva have his feet back on the ground. Give back the Land of Snows.

Notes:

1 Ancient Tibetan Song, from H. Richardson, *Cultural History of Tibet* (London: Weidenfeld & Nicolson, 1968) 24-25.

2 John F. Avedon, *In Exile from the Land of Snows* (New York: Alfred A. Knopf, Inc., 1984) 73ff.

3 From *Tibetans in Exile, 1959-1980* (Dharamsala: Information Office of H.H. the Dalai Lama).

4 Max Weber, *The Protestant Ethic and the Spirit of Capitalism*, 1905.

5 Heinrich Harrer, *Seven Years in Tibet* (New York: E. P. Dutton & Co., Inc., 1953).

Parabola
Volume: 10.1
Wholeness

THE FULLNESS OF EMPTINESS

Interview with His Holiness the Dalai Lama

*His Holiness Tenzin Gyatso, the 14th Dalai Lama of Tibet,
has a number of principal identities. He is a Buddhist monk
in the Order founded by Shakyamuni Buddha around 525
B.C.E. and revitalized by Lama Tsong Khapa around 1400;
hence, a spokesman for the ancient educational tradition of the
Buddhists. He is a reincarnation of the Buddha Avalokatesh-
vara, the Mahayana Buddhist Archangel of Compassion, and
especially the Savior of Tibetans, the King of Tibet (tragically
in exile for the last twenty-five years); hence the defender of
rights and freedoms of the Tibetans. And he is a Vajra Master
of the esoteric Mandalas of the Unexcelled Yoga Tantras,
especially of the Kalachakra Wheel of Time; hence deeply and
perhaps prophetically concerned with the positive evolution of
all intelligent life in our sacred environment on this planet.*

*The following interview was conducted at the Deanery at
Westminster Abbey, where His Holiness was staying as the
guest of the Very Reverend Dean Edward and Mrs. Lilian
Carpenter. Under an original portrait of Queen Elizabeth I,
in a building built during the lifetime of Tsong Khapa, at the
ritual center of the English nation, I asked His Holiness to
share with* Parabola's *readers his vision of Wholeness.*

—Robert A. F. Thurman

Dr. Thurman is a professor of Religion at Amherst College, a founder of the American Institute of Buddhist Studies, and an old friend and student of His Holiness's since 1964. The interview was conducted in a mixture of Tibetan and English His Holiness and Professor Thurman tend to speak when they discuss the Dharma in terms of its relevance today.

Robert A. F. Thurman: *Your Holiness,* Parabola *magazine would like to ask you about "Wholeness"—the Whole Man, the Whole Person. They say: "We are defining the Whole Person as one who has in his being, to a very high degree, freedom, unity, consciousness, and will. What is your view?"*

His Holiness: What I call the human qualities are love, compassion, tolerance, will. To be warm-hearted—that is true human being. You see, not to have warm feeling in the heart, that is almost not to have fully the nature of a human.

RT: *Would you say, finally, that Buddha is Whole Man?*

HH: Yes—on a high level. Yes, certainly. But when I speak of the good qualities of a human being, that means our ordinary human being, on the human level. Buddha is already beyond the human level.

RT: *If Buddha is beyond ordinary human nature, then some people might think of Him as cold-hearted—someone sort of superhuman, that doesn't care.*

HH: No, no, no, no. What we call Buddha is warm-heartedness developed infinitely, love perfected. And also infinite enlightened consciousness—oh, yes.

RT: *Their next question is: "It has been said that the Whole Person is one who lives simultaneously in two worlds. Do you agree with this, and if so, what does it mean to you?"*

HH: This has different meanings. One: the person himself or herself reaches the highest level, but meantime, remains in world affairs—for the sake of other beings, out of altruism. In that way, "living in two worlds" can be said. Then again, maybe another meaning: a person who really practices well, and as a result, for himself or herself there is no sort of emotion, but equanimity. One is impartial; but in accordance with circumstances, taking certain action. In his inner world, there are no differences, but in his outer world he or she keeps aware of differences, and accordingly takes action. So you see, two worlds, I think, can be understood on different levels.

RT: *"Is there a fully realized, totally developed whole within every human being? Or does the process of struggling* *to free oneself of ignorance contribute to the perfection of the individual? In other words, is there only a seed of a liberated being within, which must grow through effort?"*

HH: I think this is correct. In other words, what we call the Buddha-nature—that is the Buddha seed. That means of course there are different aspects of Buddha nature. One aspect is *shunya*[1]: "the reality of the mind which needs not to abandon any taints." That is what we call Buddha nature, according to the *Ornament of Realizations*. Also, *Sugatagarbha*: according to the *Supreme Tantra*, that also is Buddha nature, and the ultimate nature of consciousness is also called Buddha nature: *Tathāgatagarbha*. So you see, from that viewpoint, the seed of liberated being comes right from the beginning; that seed is there. But that is not sufficient. Just by being there, there's no benefit, right? So you see, one needs effort, to develop, to purify oneself, on the basis of that nature.

RT: *Is it that the fact of that seed being there makes it possible to do it? Without it …*

HH: Without it that can't happen. There is no sense in purifying a stone, even though it has the nature of emptiness also. But because the other aspects of the Buddha nature are not there, we can't say that the stone ultimately becomes Buddha.

RT: *"Are human beings, as they are, in any way unfinished?"*

HH: In the spiritual sense?

RT: *Yes, and in the evolutionary sense also, perhaps. Have they reached the fulfillment of their evolution, perfected their brain and heart and understanding, or are they unfinished in that sense?*

HH: In that sense, I don't know. The human brain may develop or it may decrease. I am not at all sure.

RT: *But isn't a Buddha a being with a more developed brain?*

HH: But that's not natural evolution.

RT: *Isn't it? It is not test tube development!*

HH: (Gales of laughter.) I think, you see, without effort, that kind of evolution we are speaking about cannot take place. For example, first an animal goes on four legs, then on two legs, then it is easier to run around, yes? Now that is without effort, isn't it?

RT: *I don't think it is without effort.*

HH: Not in the sense that, for example, those four-legged creatures needed some effort to go on two legs—that kind of effort, yes. But I speak of evolution in the Buddhist sense: for example, in the primordial eon, beings do not depend on grosser food. Then they go down, and finally reach a ten-year life span. That period is the worst the human race can reach. Then again another rise, and finally they reach the time of Maitreya's teaching. That we may call "evolution." And that without special effort.

RT: *I see what you mean.*

HH: Simply as you see the seasons changing, these are cycles. We are still, you see, on the line of decline …

RT: *Unfortunately.*

HH: (Laughing.) You can't say unfortunately. That's just the way it is.

RT: *But, an individual who is reborn after an effort in his individual life— for example, one who creates the spirit of enlightenment, who conceives that higher mind—then he advances in evolution, even though he is in a world like this.*

HH: You see, the human level of mental development, of course, is not a finished one—even in the ordinary sense, within our inner state there are still many things to explore. This has nothing to do with religious ideology; this is spiritual. I think some part of the brain's capability may be fully utilized only through deep meditation. But meantime, there are certain things still to be explored in the ordi-

nary way. So from that viewpoint, the human being is unfinished.

RT: *(Laughing.) Does Buddha have more brain, do you think, in His ushnisha?[2]*

HH: It is not a question of that. The grosser consciousness depends heavily on particles of matter; so it is the grosser level that has very much to do with the brain. The subtler consciousness is more independent. So the innermost subtle consciousness does not depend so much on the brain. If it did, it couldn't exist without the brain; and you see, in the Buddha state, the grosser mind completely disappears. Luminance, radiance, imminence—the three states of the subtle mind—all of these disappear in the clear light, the clear light of supreme innermost subtle consciousness.

RT: *Exactly, exactly! Now: "What is the realization which the Whole Person enjoys?" Would you say, like Shantideva, that the more a person is aware of others, the more they approach wholeness?*

HH: Right!

RT: *So in a sense, to a human being, compassion is almost natural.*

HH: Right, right. As I already said, there are many different levels of the Whole Person. For example, one sees a dog beaten by someone; a Whole

Man, on a certain level, then feels a certain kind of pain. Although he is not beaten physically himself, yet mentally he feels he himself gets some kind of blow. If one sees a bug killed before one, one feels a shiver of identification.

RT: *Yes. So though people say that human beings are aggressive, like apes, like tigers, would you say rather that the essence of human nature was not aggression but compassion—differentiating him from the animal?*

HH: I think so. I think so. If the basic human nature was aggressive, we would have gotten animal claws and huge teeth—but ours are very short, very pretty, very weak! So that means we are not well equipped to be aggressive beings. Even the size of our mouths is very limited. So I think the basic nature of the human being should be gentle.

RT: *Now* Parabola *asks: "What does it mean to be free and open?"*

HH: I understand the meaning of "open" as just like open door: it can open very easily, without difficulty. Then "free," that is also the same. And as a result of being free and open, the more you receive new ideas, that makes you want to give out more your own energy. That way, I think, each helps the other. The more new ideas come, the more you see the way open for your own expression or thought to go out. That I think is very useful, very necessary, especially these days.

RT: *Don't you think "openness" is a matter of views, primarily—of not what we call "holding one's own view as superior"? For example, a prejudiced person, who thinks he already knows everything, is not exactly open, is he? So in a sense, doesn't "open" mean "free of wrong views"?*

HH: That's right. The more pride, the greater arrogance, then the less open one is. Yes, we do call that holding one's own belief as highest, not accepting other beliefs. Now, there is a different meaning there. The self realizes that our knowledge and our mental development are not fully developed, and feels that there are a lot of new things to be understood; in that sense one is open and free-minded. But there are certain things one investigated oneself, for a long time, and found a conclusion, with reason. On those subjects, you should be very firm. That does not mean you are not open-minded. But since you fully investigated, and you found the firm answer, you accept that as ultimately true. Openness does not mean you are wishy-washy, or that if someone comes and says, "Oh, this is not that," then you change; and another person says the opposite and again you change. It is not like that! Conceit about a view means a certain wrong view of reality, a dogmatic attitude. That is view-conceit. But holding truth as true, without prejudice—there is no pride there.

RT: *But isn't that also not only because the ultimate truth is the right view, but also because the Buddhist view, of absolute negation, selflessness, truthlessness, emptiness, cannot be a dogmatic conviction? One can't hold selflessness as a self, can one? Therefore, there is something about the view itself, since it is absolute negation, that in itself creates openness, wouldn't you say?*

HH: That's a difficult subject. For example, the cognition that ascertains realitylessness just recognizes the mere negation of intrinsic reality. Beyond that, there is no ascertainment of the existence of a realitylessness other than that, nor is there any thought that "it is something other than that." There are no such things. There is the mere recognition of the negation of hypothetical intrinsic reality. Now, in the wake of such an understanding, there is no clinging to any other thing.

RT: *In short, there is not much "Oh, I am; I know." That kind of view-conceit can't easily arise with respect to selflessness.*

HH: Such does not arise.

RT: *Without an "I" it's hard to be self-conceited. I'm sure somebody can manage it, but it's not easy!*

HH: (Laughing.) It will come!

RT: *"How do you see openness in the sense of the non-obstruction of life-force?"*
  Coming back to fanaticism and dogmatism about views, there is the field of race-relationships: "I am white," "I am black," "I am Chinese," "I am American." For such persons, even some little hints of emptiness temper their fanatic ideology, don't you think? It might dawn on them that their deepest identity was something beyond their race or nationality.

HH: Now, here, you see, two things are involved, so we should be very clear. There are two levels of the strong feeling that I am of this race or that race: one, the conventional level—just the mere recognition that "I am an Easterner" or "I am an American," which is true. There is nothing wrong with that. It is reality. In order to make harmony between races, the basis is difference; there are different types, and it is thus harmony comes. The realization of emptiness in no way harms this feeling. Even I think it supports it. Now this is the level of conventional recognition. Then there is another thing. With this realization, then the other strong feeling, the truth-habit, arises. When that joins this mere recognition, it starts trouble. It is that feeling that becomes racism; the prejudices of the truth-habit are very much involved. Now, the view of the realization of emptiness is quite contrary to that feeling of truth-habit; it is the antidote for that. For example, I see something good: I appreciate it, it's a good thing. Here there's nothing wrong. Then I go beyond that: "Oh, it is very beautiful!" and I become very much attached to it; then there is something wrong. So you see, the exaggerated identity feeling on the second level, not on the first level. The first level, if we misapply emptiness on the conventional level of surface reality, then confusion will arise, nothing can be distinguished, then it will go into nihilism.

RT: *Yes; that's very precise. That's great …*
  Now, another question: "I understand your teaching to say that the Buddha nature is inherent in every person. There is also an expression, especially in Zen Buddhism, 'effortless effort,' which is often misunderstood to mean an inner passivity. What kind of active inner effort is necessary for the liberation of the Whole Person within?"

HH: This "effortless effort" is what is called the effortless striving. Right. Now in the meditation of mental quiescence, in the nine states of mind, there is a state where striving must be abandoned; an effortless concentration is necessary at a certain stage. It is effortless; that means, your mind becomes very tranquil—with good qualities, with its character complete. At that moment, if you make effort, that disturbs the tranquility. So in order to maintain that pure tranquility, the sort of effortless effort must be used. Of course, it is a kind of effort. You have to make at least a mental effort: "Now, I don't want to make effort!" That means effort, in order to have less disturbance of meditation.

RT: *So there's a kind of wisdom …*

HH: No, not a kind of wisdom, a kind of concentration.

RT: *What about the non-perception of three sectors?*

HH: No, no, no. It has nothing to do with that. Before this moment, when your mind tends to depression, then you need some effort to raise up your mind, intensify it. When your mind becomes active and ready to go to different objects in distraction, at that time your mind should be quieted. So that effort must be made. When your mind becomes even, with no more fluctuations, you need to stabilize it; that is the effortless effort. That is the simple effort to heighten any tendency to depression, lower any tendency to excitement. It is effortless in the sense of subtly balanced. It has nothing to do with emptiness. Of course you need an active inner effort.

RT: *"Can you explain what is meant by compassion and why it seems so little accessible?"*

HH: Now, our compassion is not just sheer emotion by itself. One must think over some reasons; it comes with reasons: thinking that all beings want happiness, do not want suffering; thinking over such reasons, wishing to free them from suffering.

RT: *Besides, from the Buddhist point of view, is it really "so little accessible"? Isn't it quite accessible for a human being?*

HH: Yes, it's not far away from human beings. Their using compassion depends on whether or not they know how to think it over, how to cultivate it in their minds, or whether they make effort. The key is how to use the mind, how to open the mind through reasons, and then make the effort.

RT: Parabola's *next question: "Are lower energies to be purified in the sense of removed, or are they to be transformed? In what sense can the lower forces be a help?"*

In other words, must the lower energies only be suppressed, or can they be carried into the path and be an actual help, if rightly treated?

HH: Yes, they can, in some cases. I think the different stages must be considered. The initial, preliminary stage is when the person is not yet much developed in the wisdom field; during that time, the lower energies should be controlled. Then when there is more wisdom power, and also

some other technique, then they can be transformed—so that the lower force becomes, instead of an obstacle, a help.

RT: *But if you try to do that too soon …*

HH: Without other factors, then by itself it will not work; it is dangerous. For instance, there are certain very powerful poisons, say morphine, which in certain cases can be used for medicine. Aryadeva, in one of his works, put up a great argument: "The various substances enjoyed in the Tantric practice according to the vows, these things can be used in that practice … for example, poison can be used effectively as medicine. If it helps, it is no longer poison, but medicine. As it helps, it is to be used."

RT: *Now, "What would be a fruitful attitude for me to hold towards those things in myself which I would like to change? Should I hate these aspects of myself? Study them? Try to eliminate them? Learn to accept them?"*

HH: That depends on your own inner strength. There are different techniques. If it is someone who knows, and who has the capability, that is one thing; if not, the only thing is to eliminate. And after all, the ultimate aim is to eliminate these. But the method sometimes makes use of these negative forces; for example, insects born from wood eat the very wood—it's like that. Those persons who are using these lower energies or wrong thoughts—that does not mean they accept these thoughts, only that a different method is being used. It's something like wrathfully killing one's enemy in the open, or using stealth and deception to kill him; in both cases, the essential point is to kill the enemy. In one case, with a very wrathful face, in the other, a very polite one, and then exploiting his own weakness.

RT: *Yes, like judo.*

HH: Exactly.

RT: *Now they ask, "Is there a relationship with one's own suffering which is not usually understood?"*

III: In Christian teaching, suffering has some powerful meaning, doesn't it? For example, Jesus took the suffering himself. Now that, you see, was not in the ordinary sense, but something very meaningful. Now in Buddhist tradition, we have every right to avoid, to overcome suffering; but when the suffering actually happens, then, instead of being discouraged or mentally distressed, you simply utilize that occasion in such a way that it will benefit you. For the moment, you will minimize your mental disturbance, and for the long run, you develop a certain kind of motivation that will help you to gain more virtue.

RT: *Your Holiness always says that suffering increases your inner strength.*

HH: That is right.

RT: *But some people might think: well then, I should seek more suffering in order to become stronger.*

HH: (Laughing.) This I don't mean.

RT: *But voluntary suffering—in a way, isn't that what it is? Don't Bodhisattvas sometimes seek suffering on purpose?*

HH: Oh yes, they do. "I want to take on myself all the sufferings of living beings." They directly enter into suffering that way. But in that case, you see, actually the suffering does not come!

RT: *Ahh! Is that so? When they seek the suffering, they don't get any?*

HH: No, never. The wishing for suffering makes the suffering disappear.

RT: *That's beautiful.*
Another question: "Is significant growth of being possible outside of serious religious practice?"

HH: In terms of human happiness, I feel it is not necessary to accept one particular religion. Without accepting a religion, but simply developing a realization of the importance of compassion and love, and with that more concern and respect for others, a kind of spiritual development is very possible for those persons who are outside of religion.

RT: *And you feel that development can be significant?*

HH: So long as you are a human being, a member of the human family, you need the others' warm feeling, and therefore it is most important that you try to get more warm feeling, be warm-hearted. I always put emphasis on that. That is actually the base of all spiritual teaching. Without that, there is no other thing, no so-called spiritual practice. Isn't it so? With this, the spiritual development will come. And now you see, if someone lives with these qualities, even an extreme atheist, the Buddhist viewpoint is that when life ends, if a person has lived within this life very honestly and as a good person, then because of that behavior, he will get a good result in the next life. On the contrary, one who has talked about the future life and Nirvana very much without that practice, although that person belonged to the category of the spiritual groups, in reality he will face more problems. This I believe.

RT: *Then: "In light of the plurality of religious traditions living side by side in the world today, many people find it impossible to move wholeheartedly into any one tradition; such is the dilemma of modern western man. Yet to draw a little from this tradition and a little from that seems too often to lead to a featureless pudding. What advice can you give to those in this predicament?"*

HH: What is "pudding"?

RT: Thugpa—*everything boiled down to a mush.*

HH: (Laughing.) Oh, oh, oh, oh …

At the initial stage, I think there is nothing wrong in taking something from this tradition and other things from that tradition—not necessarily becoming a follower of a particular tradition but simply remaining as a good human being. I think that is possible; not only possible, I think it is good. Then if you want further development, a deeper level—it is like education. On the school level, you learn this subject a little, that subject a little. Then you become interested in one field; then you have to choose one particular subject, and train, and become an expert in that line. In the spiritual line also, when you want to deepen your understanding and your experience, then you should follow one tradition. And develop.

RT: *Yes. I was struck yesterday by your use of the metaphor "spiritual supermarket" to mean something good; I thought it was very beautiful. Usually people use that expression to mean something bad, but you meant that a supermarket offers many choices, many options.*

HH: Ah-hah! Do they usually think of it as something bad? Why?

RT: *Precisely because of the idea that with a little bit of everything it will become* thugpa, *a hodgepodge, as in the question. But you turned it around, and I agree with your interpretation, definitely: "supermarket" means you have more possibility, more different kinds of people can get what they need. You're not stuck with the one thing they have in the little village store. That's wonderful, and it applies here.*

Now, "What advice would you give to an ordinary Western man or woman who is concerned about discovering his or her true inner nature?"

HH: I think, to try to get at least some time, with quiet and relaxation, to think more inwardly and to investigate the inner world. That may help. Then sometimes, when one is very much involved in hatred or attachment, if there is time or possibility during that very moment, just to try to look inward: "What is attachment? What is the nature of anger?" That also is good.

RT: *"What is the proper relationship of knowledge to feeling in one's search for the Whole Person within, and what role does the body play in this search?" In other words, is intellectual understanding helpful at all, or is it just an obstacle?*

HH: Ah, but you see, generally speaking, the intellect is not at all an obstacle for searching inner truth. But certain experiences are reached at certain times without using the intellectual side, simply through a kind of direct feeling; that also is possible, from the Buddhist viewpoint. But usually, reasonings are essential. Nevertheless, when you practice the path of Unexcelled Yoga Tantra, when you cultivate the bliss-void-indivisible samadhi, you don't practice analytic meditation, you proceed by concentrative, non-discursive meditation alone. It's the same with the Great Perfection and Great Soul teachings. Now that does not mean that intellect is fundamentally useless. These are different times and different circumstances.

RT: *Especially during the time of learning and reflection prior to meditation. You can't just proceed on faith.*

HH: That's it.

RT: *So would you say that intellectual knowledge initially is crucial?*

HH: Yes. And then in connection with the role of the body, you see, when intellectual work is carried on, the brain and its physical particles is very much involved. So you see usually these intellectual thoughts are a grosser level of mind, which is very much connected with the cell particles. In a state wherein the grosser mind becomes inactive, then the subtler mind becomes more active, and at that moment the relation of the subtler mind and the body cells is left behind, so at that time the intellectual work also is left behind.

RT: *However, isn't it true that to enter the subtle mind state, the blueprint of the structures—of channels, winds, drops, the four lights, luminance, radiance, imminence, clear light—the image of these structures must be in the imagination. This must be said to be a kind of intellectual activity, mustn't it? The mind must hold these images as targets.*

HH: Quite so. Now there are two ways: one method is the meditation of not-thinking—these are the methods of the Great Perfection and Great Seal. Through the non-conception practice, one should reach clear light. There are other methods, through *tummo* heat yoga, through *Vajra* incantation, through breathing practice and so on. But in every case, in the initial stage, the other factor must be there. Even for the practice of the Great Perfection, it requires renunciation, it requires the spirit of enlightenment. Again now, the intellectual function is indispensable.

RT: *There is an intellectual decision to excise intellect, isn't there? For example, "I am not going to think, I am going to cancel intellect and dwell in clear, blank voidness." To decide this one must use* an image of blank voidness, a negative image—isn't that so?

HH: That is certainly so. I don't know the exact meaning of the word "intellect" in English, but if it is our Tibetan *togba*, conceptual thought, then the decision, "I am going to meditate in a thoughtless state," is itself a thought.

RT: *Could one use the simile of shooting a gun? Your sight, aiming at the target, is the concept. To hit the target you must sight accurately, have the right concept. The actual shooting is not a concept; the bullet just goes where it is aimed. So that is the non-conceptual concentration. But of course, the aiming is crucial. Is that a fair example?*

HH: Yes, that's fine. It's quite useful... Of course, there are still some problems. When we talk of the thoughtless state, we are talking really of a deeper level.

RT: *Yes, of course*
The next question is: "What Buddhist concepts are most misunderstood by Westerners, and what troubles you most about the consequences of this misunderstanding?"

HH: I think *shunya* is one of them, and also some Tantric practices; and something like "the blood-drinking deities."

RT: *(Laughing.) Cannibal activity!*

HH: For example, Vajrabhairava, the tutelary deity, is very easy to misunderstand; it really looks like some kind of devil. And one can only slowly understand its function as a symbol of the union of the wisdom of great bliss and voidness after an awful lot of explanations. Otherwise, it is very misunderstandable. And sex!

RT: *Yes, certainly; there was a lot of confusion about Tantra based on poorly translated Hindu sources.*

HH: What is troubling is the simple fact of the misunderstanding preventing people from getting the right idea. Some people who don't really know anything and pretend to know a lot about it cause the most trouble. And if it is thought that Tibetan Buddhism is some kind of strange business, this is very harmful to Tibetans, as it makes people not respect their culture and so not defend their human rights, not cry out against their national tragedy.

RT: *Now it is asked: "Are true religious teachings fragile? Is the greatest threat to their potency and vigor from inside or from outside? And if from inside, what are the threats?"*

HH: I don't think religious teaching is easy to wipe out, but very difficult. Once it is deep-rooted, I don't think it is easy to destroy. The actual threat comes from the inside. That means, you see, those so-called "religious persons" who do not practice well, do not follow a proper way. That is the most dangerous, the greatest threat. In our own Tibetan case, there is the outside threat. Of course, it can easily destroy the temples and monasteries, but it is very difficult to destroy the inner feeling. But suppose one Tibetan monk or lama behaves badly, then that can do very much harm. That can really destroy the inner faith, the inner feeling. So the actual threat comes from within. And also, using religion as the instrument for division; that also is a threat. And then I think in some cases, you yourself can have too much attachment to the ideology and lose the basic aim of religion, of helping humankind.

RT: *We come to the last question: "What is the task of the Whole Man, and what fundamental questions are you concerned with in relation to your sojourn on earth?"*

HH: The task of the Whole Man is to help others; that's my firm teaching, that's my message. That is my own belief. For me, the fundamental question is better relations, better relations among human beings—and whatever I can contribute to that.

Notes:

1 The doctrine of emptiness.

2 The cranial dome. Buddha's was unusually large.

Parabola
Volume: 23.2
Ecstasy

DELIGHT IN THIS WORLD
Tantric Buddhism as a Path of Bliss

Miranda Shaw

One who desires Buddhahood
Should practice what is to be practiced.
To renounce the sense objects
Is to torture oneself by asceticism—don't do it!
When you see form, look!
Similarly, listen to sounds,
Inhale scents,
Taste delicious flavors,
And feel textures.
Use the objects of the five senses and
You will quickly attain supreme Buddhahood.[1]

Tantric Buddhism, or *Vajrayana*, the Diamond Way, was founded on the principle that ecstasy is the essence of the world. Divine ecstasy is ever-present at the core of every sense experience, mind-state, and emotion, yet the human heart has lost its capacity to fully surrender to the bliss that is its birthright. For this, a journey of transformation must be undertaken. The pioneers of the Tantric movement offered numerous practices as paths leading back to the blissful source and ground of being. Their methods drew upon the sources of bliss that are ready at hand in ordinary human experience: the joy of embodiment, the communion of sexual union, loss of self in rhythmic dance, artistic creativity, and the abundant richness of taste, touch, smell, sound, and sight. They wove these natural sources of ecstasy into their spiritual disciplines, following the principle that "bliss is meditatively derived from bliss."[2] They believed that sensual pleasures, cultivated and refined through metaphysical insight, are the mind's portal to the transcendent bliss of supreme enlightenment.

Tantric Buddhism arose in the seventh and eighth centuries in India and the Himalayas, and survives as a living tradition today in the Buddhism of Nepal and Tibet. The spiritual disciplines and sacred arts of this movement all seek to cultivate the ability to recognize the intrinsic ecstasy of being at every moment. There are as many ways to accomplish this as there are people. Tantric gurus down through the ages have tailored the path to the needs and predispositions of the disciples, assigning to a given student whatever practices they deem most appropriate. Some practitioners adopt an itinerant lifestyle, meditating in caves and forests and congregating for rituals at the holy places that serve as Tantric meeting grounds. Others choose to interweave their meditative practice into their daily life and occupational pursuits. For example, a musician might concentrate on the sound of music to attain nondual awareness, a winemaker might envision herself as distilling bliss from the grapes of experience, a shoemaker could imagine that he was sewing the leather of passion with the thread of freedom to produce shoes of enlightenment, and

a king on his throne could meditate upon the radiant purity of all phenomena while gazing at his gleaming golden jewelry.

Although Tantric practice can be pursued in any setting and is open to every social class, it is particularly appropriate for passionate people. Passion is one of the most powerful forces in the psyche; its energies can be harnessed in the service of inner transformation. There is a Tantric saying that "there is no greater sin than dispassion." Passion—raw emotion, intensity of feeling—is simply an outward expression of an inner hunger for divine ecstasy. Although passion is a major source of worldly entanglement when it is fueled by the delusory belief that some person or thing holds the key to the happiness we seek, it also conceals within it the seeds of the fruit of bliss.

The Tantrics have always recognized the necessary connection between bodily discipline and ecstasy. The inherent blissfulness of embodiment is for them the point of departure for a range of practices that enhance the capacity of the body to serve as a vessel for increasingly potent and transformative states of ecstasy. Here the Tantrics have drawn upon ancient Indian yogic techniques. Flexibility of limb, suppleness of spine, and mastery of the breath provide the physical basis for heightened states of awareness. Tantrics also pursue inner forms of yoga that operate on more subtle levels of somatic experience. These inner yogas serve to concentrate energy near the base of the spine, where it ignites an inner fire that consumes the dross of dualistic mind-states and negative emotions. This inner flame produces intense feelings of bliss as it moves up the central energy-pathway of the body and reaches the crown of the head, where the tip of its tonguelike flame illuminates a thousand-petaled lotus of light. The lotus in turn rains a stream of nectar that permeates the body with even higher forms of bliss.

The blissful ambiance of Vajrayana practice is epitomized by the Tantric feast. Remote locations, cremation grounds, and deserted temple court-yards are favored for these esoteric gatherings. The ideal time for the Tantric feast is twilight, for the softly darkening sunset sky is conducive to the expansion and refinement of inner vision. Participants don special insignia, like bone ornaments and crowns, and use musical instruments of archaic design—skull drums, thighbone trumpets, and conch horns—to accompany their sacred dance and song. Celebrants sit in a nonhierarchical circle and partake of sacramental meat and wine served in skull cups. A new genre of Tantric literature was born in this setting, as the revelers, intoxicated by spiritual rapture, regaled one another with spontaneous "songs of realization."

Fortunately, a body of their inspired verses has been preserved. These festal songs offer an exhilarating taste of the blissful clarity that is the fruit of Tantric practice:

KYE HO! Wonderful!
Whatever appears is enlightened awareness,
Ornamented by the objects of the five senses.
You cannot enter or leave your natural state—
Run on the plain of great bliss.

It should not be surprising that bliss itself is a recurrent topic of their mystical poetry:

KYE HO! Wonderful!
This spontaneous wellspring of great ecstatic wisdom—
Without realization, one cannot describe it;
After realization, why speak?
Taste it and you're struck dumb, speechless![13]

The ultimate state of consciousness may be inexpressible, but I am grateful that all who attain it do not remain speechless. Otherwise, we would not have this precious poetic legacy of ecstatic inner freedom.

For the Tantrics, the joy of artistic creativity could be heightened by transposing it into the sacred realm of visionary wonder. Every aspect of the creation process could be approached with a sense of ritual focus, beginning with the preparation of the materials. For such a numinous painting, ordinary canvas does not suffice: it must be fabric woven from thread spun by female practitioners. The artist should carve his or her stylus from human bone and fashion a brush out of hair procured from a corpse. A bowl made from a human skull makes the ideal palette. Five colors are used: white, blue, red, yellow, and green, the rainbow hues of the five Buddha-wisdoms.

The act of painting, too, is undertaken as a yogic discipline. The practitioner should paint at night during the dark of the moon, in an isolated natural setting, having shed all clothing, donned bone ornaments, and partaken of some wine to attain "a ferocious state of mind."[4] The source of inspiration should be the artist's concourse with deities, for only one who has beheld a deity can convey the splendor of the divine presence. The Tantric consort should be seated nearby. Some of the early Tantric paintings, presumably produced in such a manner, are stylistically crude but vibrant with energy and with the unmistakable print of an ecstatic mind at play.

An intrepid Tantric might even seek to cultivate bliss by confronting reality in its most repulsive, shocking, or terrifying aspects, in order directly and swiftly to break down conventional patterns of dualistic thought. Such was the case with Luipa, a former prince who had made great progress in yogic practice but still harbored a lingering trace of royal pride when he went to beg for some food at a tavern owned, unbeknownst to him, by a female adept. With her clairvoyant vision, she perceived a small but obdurate knot of royal pride in his heart. She saw that Luipa was clinging to the dualism of purity and impurity, so instead of giving him something from the menu, she served him a bowl of moldy leftovers. Luipa threw the bowl into the street in disgust and shouted, "How dare you serve garbage to a yogi?" She shot back, "How can a connoisseur attain enlightenment?" Stunned by the accuracy of her insight, which revealed his final obstacle to enlightenment, Luipa repaired to a nearby riverbank and began to live on food that was fit only for dogs and other scavengers, namely, the entrails discarded by fishermen. Through this practice, Luipa attained a state of uninterrupted bliss and realized that ultimately there is no difference between fish entrails and ambrosial nectar, since all experience is blissful in essence.[5]

The ancient Tantrics reinterpreted the biography of Shakyamuni Buddha to render it more compatible with their distinctive doctrines. Illustrative of this is their treatment of Shakyamuni's departure from his wife and the opulent life of the palace in order to pursue solitary ascetic disciplines in the forest. From the Tantric point of view, a desire repressed is not a desire mastered; therefore, abandonment of conjugal intimacy was not necessary to his spiritual progress. According to the

Tantric version of this event in the Candamaharoshana-tantra, it was in actuality the bliss that Shakyamuni experienced in union with his wife, Gopa, rather than his subsequent ascetic practices, that enabled him to attain enlightenment:

Along with Gopa, he experienced bliss.
By uniting the diamond scepter and lotus,
He attained the fruit of bliss.
Buddhahood is obtained from bliss, and
Apart from women there will not be bliss.[6]

The same text explains that the Buddha's period of renunciation was merely a display, a liberative drama that he offered for the benefit of those who might be caught up in the delusory pursuit of superficial pleasures and material gain. Such people must first be inspired to yearn for higher truths and led onto the path of spiritual aspiration before they can scale the lofty heights of bliss and wisdom.

It is natural that the Tantrics' disciplined pursuit of ecstasy should find abundant fuel for spiritual growth in the pleasure of erotic intimacy. Sexual union provides a context for advanced inner yogas and meditations upon emptiness. A female adept named Sahajayogini-cinta, author of a classical treatise on the yoga of union, taught that the man and woman should envision one another as a male and female Buddha and, with one-pointed concentration

upon bodily pleasure, should traverse the stages of erotic play as deepening levels of meditative awareness. Their passion will eventually lead beyond itself into the sphere of uncondi-tional bliss. Because it is the nature of the mind to seek bliss, the mind can finally come to rest in its "primordial essence of holy bliss."[7] This state of transcendent bliss is so supremely sat-isfying that the senses will no longer wish to wander in the desolate cities created by hunger and desire, when they can be opulently entertained in palaces spun of bliss and luminosity. At this point, as Sahajayoginicinta promised, every experience will have the "same flavor":

When one has entered the palaces of the
sense organs, experiencing abundant
delights, this very world attains the
singular taste of spiritual ecstasy.

This realization reveals the world to be a paradise, a perfect Buddha-land, when every sensation, thought, and emotion becomes saturated with "holy bliss."[8]

Tantric iconographers developed a new visual vocabulary to express their unique vision of enlighten-ment. The peaceful, beatific figures of the Mahayana pantheon gave way to dynamic Tantric Buddhas who embody the capacity for ecstatic wholeness of all persons, both male and female. In these works, the female Buddhas are generally red in color, the hue of passion. They are naked, except for their billowing hair and delicate bone ornaments, and dance in exuberant poses that reveal their bodies in all their female glory, without shame or fear. Their eyes blaze with ecstasy and intensity as they gaze into the depths of reality. Each female Buddha brandishes a skull bowl, overflowing with the nectar of bliss that she distills from every experience, and a curved knife that she uses to sever all bondage and illusion at the root. Male Tantric Buddhas, often blue in color, are portrayed in wrathful guise, with upward-streaming hair and a grimacing face contorted by the ferocity of direct awareness and flow of primal passion. They are ornamented by snakes, adorned with a tiger skin, and encircled by a ring of fiery energy. Sometimes the male and female Buddhas are depicted as couples in sacred union, displaying the Tantric belief that men and women can traverse the spiritual path as intimate companions and even inhabit its summit together in cosmic embrace.

Vajrayana proclaims as its goal the attainment of Buddhahood in the present lifetime and present body. A Buddha is one who has completed the path to bliss and total wisdom. An enlightened being no longer has a selfish thirst for existence, but neither is he or she impelled to escape the world, having discovered it to be a perfect realm of bliss. Indeed, a Buddha does not abandon those who still suffer, because acting for the benefit of others is the most sublime delight of an awakened soul. Therefore, the highest state of ecstasy naturally gives rise to a stream of compassionate activities. Every Buddha engages in the creative process of generating new ways to express enlightenment and to instruct, inspire, and liberate others. Only one who has perfected the art of ecstasy can extend the hope of joy to a suffering world. A Buddha's eternal smile is a beacon of invitation to the true destiny of all beings: the ecstasy of Buddhahood, the ultimate bliss that can never be destroyed.

Notes:

1 *Candamaharoshana-tantra*, trans. Miranda Shaw.

2 *Cittavishuddhiprakarana.*

3 Miranda Shaw, *Passionate Enlightenment: Women in Tantric Buddhism* (Princeton: Princeton University Press, 1994) 93-94.

4 *The Hevajra Tantra: A Critical Study,* trans. and ed. David Snellgrove (London: Oxford University Press, 1959) 114-15.

5 Keith Dowman, *Masters of Enchantment* (Rochester, VT: Inner Traditions, 1988) 33-34.

6 *Candamaharoshana-tantra.*

7 Shaw 188.

8 Shaw 188-89.

Parabola
Volume: 19.4
Hidden Treasure

THE REAL IS IN YOU

Yeshe Tsogyel

Yeshe Tsogyel (757?–817?) was initiated into Buddhism by an Indian teacher, Padma Sam-bhava; together they then helped bring Buddhist teaching to Tibet. Her poem (taken from a terma, *or secret teaching hidden for future discovery) is part of a discourse given to her students near the end of her life. It speaks not only of the oneness of teacher and student, but also of the fact that awakening to that unity inevitably awakens the disciple also to the Oneness of all beings, all worlds.*

Listen,
O brothers and sisters,
you who have mastered the teaching—
If you recognize me,
Queen of the Lake of Awareness,
who encompasses
both emptiness and form,
know that I live in the minds
of all beings who live.
Know that I live
in the body of mind

and the field of the senses,
that the twelve kinds of matter
are only my bones and my skin.
We are not two,
yet you look for me outside;
when you find me within yourself,
your own naked mind,
that Single Awareness
will fill all worlds.
Then the joy of the One
will hold you like a lake—
its fish with gold-seeing eyes
will grow many and fat.
Hold to that knowledge and pleasure,
and the Creative will be your wings.
You will leap through the green meadows
of earthly appearance,
enter the sky-fields, and vanish.

                    —Yeshe Tsogyel

•

CHAPTER NINE

BUDDHA-FIELDS

The color of the mountains is the Buddha's pure body.
The sound of running water is the Buddha's great speech.

Zen Master Dogen

Parabola
Volume: 23.1
Millennium

BUILDING THE BUDDHA-FIELD

J. L. Walker

In this blessed Buddha-land of irrevocable enlightenment,

In the lofty abode of openness, the intrinsic nature of things,
having neutralized surface, depth, width, the limits of
any dimension, on the highest plane where there is neither
inner nor outer: the windows of vision are flooded with light.

—*Pema Kathang*
(Terton Orgyan Lingpa, 1326)

It is four in the morning. In a large white tent atop a mountain in California, five all-but-comatose men and women are completing a six-foot sand mandala for a ceremony that is to begin with our closing of the circle of wisdom fire that is the outermost circumference of the celestial palace. Sleep-deprived, we can barely see, but still we work. Suddenly, a quiet laugh breaks our concentration. Hands, dripping delicate trails of sand from metal funnels, pause. Our teacher, Lama Tharchin Rinpoche, stands by the mandala table as if he had appeared by magic. He tells us how much he loves us, how much he appreciates our work, how we are inseparable in this mandala forever. We smile, oddly refreshing tears in our eyes. Soon we finish and hobble off to find a bite of breakfast and relief for weary legs long past bending. Others come and fill the corners bordering the mandala with deep blue sand. The Buddha-field now rests in its space, waiting.

It is July 1992; the place is Pema Osel Ling, the Land of Lotus Light, retreat center and home of the Vajrayana

Foundation. Those of us gathered here are celebrating the miraculous birth of Padmasambhava, known in Tibet as Guru Rinpoche. The great adept who brought Vajrayana Buddhism to Tibet, he is the center of all of the mandalas that come together for this extensive traditional celebration. These mandalas exist on many levels: our physical gathering together from many places, the construction of the supports of our practice—from the statue of Guru Rinpoche to the sand mandala, from masks and costumes to shrine room tent and kitchens— and the luminous sphere of the inner mandala raised by the practitioners in meditation. By the end of the third week of this summer retreat, the sand mandala is completed, to be consecrated and brought to life on the first morning of the final week. This is to be a *drupchen* or intensive seven days of continuous round-the-clock meditation practice and mantra recitation. On the last day of the retreat, we will perform the sacred dance cycle of the Eight Manifestations of Guru Rinpoche, bringing the manifestation of the mandala deities visibly into our midst.

The practice of a traditional art, whether it is ritual, the crafting of beautiful and useful things, or the art of creating community, is essentially about education. The work itself educes or draws out of the one who works a wholeness, transforming the environment and everything accomplished in it. The making of this man-dala was the end of the world I knew, and, though I didn't recognize it at the time, the beginning of a radically new one. By creating not just a sand mandala but the entire physical and ritual context of its traditional setting, we created a world, and as that world grew up around us, we grew into it.

To understand what it means to "grow into" the mandala—to build the mandala world into oneself, whether by the mental arts of meditation and visualization or by creating with paint or colored sand—one must know what a Buddha-field is actually made of. It can be thought of as a door into an inner universe, a memory system in the form of a palace and its surrounding country. In the West, ancient rhetoricians memorized vast amounts of information by visualizing a mansion with all the objects in its many rooms imprinted with details of their discourse. For us as meditators, however, the aim is higher: the crafting of a fully enlightened being.

The "myth" of a mandala—any mandala—is a story of how one becomes many, and how the many return to one. It teaches integration which begins and ends at the center. As the bodhisattva purifies and perfects qualities, these begin to radiate into the field of his or her activity: a pure world in the making. As this force builds, it creates an environment in which other aspiring beings can develop the same qualities, realizing the Buddha-nature inherent in everyone. As the perfection of patience grows, for example, a multiplicity of opportunity for positive thought and virtuous application follows. Each perfected quality creates a harmony and order where imagination can act clearly. The Buddha-field is a liberative art in that its very structure invites movement, a rhythm essential to life and growth, like the breath. The practitioner becomes a field of accumulating merit for others—the Lama's realization is the field in which students develop and mature. The universe could be imagined as a gigantic set of these lucent, interpenetrating spheres, each with an Awakened One at its center.

Our creation of the pure Buddha-world depends on our movement through our experience in a mindful way. This in turn depends on our intention. The Tibetans have a saying: "If the mind is pure, everyone is a Buddha. If the mind is impure, everyone is ordinary." The process of purifying the mind requires becoming vulnerable to greater possibility, so that vulnerability becomes a conduit of the blessing we need in order to melt barriers that obstruct our path. The Buddha-field is made, therefore, of such elements as the six perfections—generosity, discipline, patience, devotion, meditation, and wisdom—and the four immeasurable qualities of love, compassion, sympathetic joy, and equanimity. In building a sand mandala, there is no place for ego, pride, or self-assertion. There is no way to separate oneself from the world when one brings a world into being beneath one's own hands. Making the mandala changed and continues to change our relationship with the world. Throughout the process, we worked on ourselves and on each other in myriad and often unexpected ways.

A friend and I were sitting by the mandala late in the evening. The base drawing had been completed, silvery webs on a pale grey foundation of faultlessly smooth paint. Everything was prepared; orderly pots of colored sand and funnels lay ready. Rinpoche came and joined us for a while, and we knew from what he did not say that it was past time to start sanding. In that silent mountain night, the hollow, rhythmic sound of vibrating metal funnels that would be background to our lives for weeks to come began. Unable to reach the center of the mandala from the ground, we two women sat on it as the monks do, forehead to forehead. We worked without speaking, at one with each other and with the work, until at last in the still hours of the morning the first four lotus petals had emerged, outlines of deep garnet red, their flourishes ornamented with gold. Guru Rinpoche's seat awaited him.

The ways of sand became my teacher. Years ago, learning the process of lost-wax casting, I discovered the languages of wax and fire, plaster and molten metals. As a painter, I know the language of pigment and canvas, ink and brushes and paper. Here I learned yet another new language: sand, vibration, time, and patience. Sometimes a single detail is one solitary grain, falling with the weight of the mountain behind it: the eye in a tiny face, a jewel writ small. Stonemasons say that every stone is a law unto itself, and I discovered that sand grains have this quality in miniature. Particles lie against each other in precise ways, edges cohere, layers converge according to the vibrations of the metal funnel. To play the rasp of the funnel becomes a kind of musical skill, as much intuition as instrument. Perhaps all artists learn to know in this way.

As with any craft, the material molded our mental set, and even our bodies. One day, after working many hours without a break, I sat at lunch and watched my plate of beans and rice dissolve into tiny grains. The table went as well, and as I lifted my eyes to the dining hall, countless moving specks were all I saw, as if the spaces between our molecules had all been expanded.

The process of bringing the perfect world of the mandala into our world is analagous to the translation of humanity from one condition or state of being to another. As the millennium approaches, what seems to be trying to manifest is a new order of being, a new kind of existence altogether. We are seeing the beginnings of a reintegration of our culture, and perhaps of the world itself. The challenge of making our present chaotic changes into a better reality for everyone is reflected in the creation of the mandala, and in its accompanying rituals and sacred dances.

While these Buddha-worlds are ultimately the play of luminosity and emptiness of intrinsic awareness, from our present state they must arise from our development of the qualities of enlightened mind. Our mandalas—the one of sand and the one of our living selves—were built by our individual and collective devotion, our determination, and our hands. Consecrated and brought to life by the Lamas, they consecrated and brought us to new life as well.

Parabola
Volume: 24.1
Nature

THIS QUIET PLACE THAT
BUDDHAS LOVE

J. L. Walker

Enchanting caves and fields in peaceful forests

*Adorned with flowers moving in dance and streams
sounding Lhung,*

*In them, may we without wavering contemplate our
tired minds,*

*And remain there to fulfill the purposes of precious
human life.*

In that place, not having encountered any wild beings,

*Having pacified emotional defilements, and having
achieved the seven noble qualities,*

At the time of leaving the living body,

May we attain the king of the mind, the primordial state.

—*Longchen Rabjam (1308–1363)*[1]

"O this quiet place that Buddhas love,"[2] begins a song
by Milarepa, one of Tibet's greatest poet-adepts. He sings
the praises of his Red Rock Valley hermitage in all its natural splendor, full of life and sound. Trees dance, and animals
large and small play and sing there. Bees hum melodi-
ously in fragrant flowers. As clouds float by the mountain
top, he describes the place of the yogin in the scene: "I,
Milarepa, practice meditation; I, the yogin, practice the

heart of enlightenment." Thus the world of nature is made meaningful.

We often think of nature, "this quiet place," in terms of a refuge from the world of action, driven by desire and necessity. But the true refuge lies not in the ever-changing natural world with its objective beauty, or even in a subjective state of peace and solitude within that, but in apprehending the very *nature* of nature beyond and within its objective content. The healing potential of nature depends on finding this non-ordinary, transformative, "vertical" aspect of nature. Otherwise all we have is another "horizontal" translation of it, another way of looking at it, rather than a powerful force of real change in our lives as we must live them in the world.

In Buddhist cosmology the world of appearances arises out of its nondual and indestructible Base, described as unborn, the perfectly unobstructed and unchangeable state that is self-liberated and perfect from the beginning. This state of perfect, discriminating awareness is called the natural mind, which cannot be contrived. From this limitless origination, the conditioned existence of universes and beings arises. *Samsara*, or conditioned existence, is created by beings mistaking the external and temporal appearances of things for their ultimate nature. This ultimate nature of the mind is forever beyond the intellect, and yet they are inseparably intertwined in a dance of interdependence.

The arising of manifestation begins with *sunyata*, or emptiness. From out of this ground arises the completely pure Wind of the Mind. This wind is endowed with the potential to generate our universe. Above this vast Wind of the Mind arises the actual mandala of the wind element of the universe. The mandala of the wind billows and storms and pervades everywhere. Other winds arise above this, which each perform various functions in the creation of the material universe. The Roughening Wind scatters in all directions. The Gathering Wind causes clouds to gather, and the Stabilizing Wind causes the basic foundation of the universe to settle. The Fire Wind ripens it. Above these winds arise the mandalas of the other elements: first Fire, then Water, then Earth. Thus the outer vessel of the universe is formed, and from these same elements living beings are manifested.

Everything that is generated from the Base or ground of existence has three aspects: essence, nature, and energy. The *essence* of anything refers to its emptiness of a permanent, independent self-existence. The *nature* aspect is the propensity in this emptiness to continually manifest, and the *energy* is how it manifests. The traditional analogy to illustrate this triple aspect of things is that of a mirror. Its fundamental clarity and purity, and the fact that it is not changed by any of the reflections that appear in it, represents its essence. Its nature is the inherent capacity of the mirror to reflect whatever is put in front of it, and the energy aspect is illustrated by the reflections themselves.

My first Buddhist teacher, Ch'an Master Nan Huai-chin, used to laugh at me when I told him I was going to the small mountain temple I often visited to do a little retreat. "Ha!" he would say. "You can't escape the red dust out there." He was right, of course. One cannot escape anywhere. We take our world with us because it is the reflections we hold before the mirror of our mind: our limited awareness, our attachment, our illusions, all the dust of our habitual ways of perceiving ourselves and our surroundings. So it gets us nowhere to contemplate merely external nature. Gyatrul Rinpoche, a contemporary Tibetan Buddhist master, says, "Here in the West we make a big deal of sunsets and so forth. Another way of looking at a sunset is that it's just another sign of your life passing by."[3] For some reason, we do not notice the impermanence in the natural cycles around us as related to us. We lose a great opportunity to deepen our experience of our own nature, which is not separate from that of the realms of nature.

Is Gyatrul Rinpoche telling us we are wrong to enjoy the beauties of nature? I think not, but he is pointing out that we are seeing the sunset only partially. We are like people who are given a precious medicine in a beautiful jar, and instead of taking the medicine, we admire the jar, perhaps setting it in a place of honor, but remaining lost in our sickness. Milarepa gives us an example of one use of the beauties of nature as medicine in this teaching song to his disciple Dar Bum, one of his four main female heirs:

Oh, disciple of a hundred thousand
    merits,
You, girl, who have faith and wealth,
Consider this parable of the sky
And meditate on limitless space.
Consider the parable of the sun and
    moon
And meditate on their unchanging
    clarity.
Consider the parable of the mountain
And meditate on its unmovability.
Consider the parable of the great ocean
And meditate on its bottomless depths.
Concerning the self-mind
Meditate without errors.

After having meditated according to his instructions, she returns and relates her experiences to her teacher, asking him for clarification. She is happy when meditating on the sky but a little unhappy when she meditates on the clouds, happy when meditating on the mountain but a little unhappy when meditating on the trees and bushes, happy when meditating on the great ocean, but a little unhappy meditating on the waves, happy with the nature of mind but not so happy with disturbing thoughts, and so forth. Pleased, seeing that she actually had experience in meditation, Mila sings another song to remove her doubts and obstacles:

*If you feel happy when you meditate
    on the sky,
You should know that the clouds are a
    manifestation of the sky.
Therefore, identify yourself with
    the sky. ...
If you feel happy when you meditate on
    the mountain,
You should know that the foliage
    and trees are a manifestation of
    the mountain.
Therefore, identify yourself with
    the mountain.
If you are happy when you meditate
    on the great ocean,
You should know that the waves
    are a manifestation of the ocean.
Therefore, identify yourself with
    the ocean.
If you are happy meditating on your
    self-mind,
You should know that disturbing
    thoughts are a manifestation of
    the mind.
Therefore, identify yourself with the
    mind-essence.*

Following his instructions and thoroughly contemplating the nature of mind through these examples, Dar Bum attained enlightenment in that very life. In each case he pointed her toward the essential nature of the object of her meditation, and away from the appearance. The sky is boundless and unchanged by clouds or sunsets, the depths of the sea calm and unperturbed by the activity of the waves at its surface, and so also is the nature of mind. Sky and clouds, sea and waves, mind and the nature of mind are not two, and yet not one.

The greatest of Nyingma (Old School) master/poets, Longchen Rabjam, affirms the value of the beauties of nature to beginning meditators for their ability to generate inspiration and tranquillity of mind. In his *Narrative of Joyfulness in the Forest*, he writes:

*In a forest, naturally there are few
    distractions and entertainments,
One is far from all suffering of danger
    and violence.
The joy is much greater than that of the
    celestial cities.
Enjoy today the tranquil nature
    of forests.
O mind, listen to the virtues of
    the forests. ...
In forests emotions decline naturally. ...
In forests the peace of absorption
    grows naturally. ...
Life in forests is in accord with the holy
    Dharma, and it tames the mind
And achieves the happiness of
    ultimate peace.*

We may also find nature to be an excellent instructor in mindfulness and nonattachment. In an oral teaching in July 1998, His Eminence Garchen Rinpoche spoke to us of offering such beauty as we may find anywhere; a weed growing in a crack in a city sidewalk, a nearby park, or a wilderness trail may present us with an unexcelled opportunity to make what we observe into a means of upliftment. With mindfulness, everything becomes our spiritual practice. When we see a flower, we can offer it for the benefit of all living beings. We don't need to pick it and take it with us into our rooms; we can offer it where it sits. When we see the flower and offer it spontaneously, we are really exhausting attachment and desire and thus our self-grasping ego. We become closer to the natural state of pristine awareness by eliminating what is contrived. We need only see the immovable mountain in the plant, the deep sea in the wave, the mind in the thought of offering. This transforms all places, scenes, and things, gradually opening our ordinary view into something beneficial to all beings.

The purpose of meditation on nature in the Buddhist way is not to establish an emotional relationship with it, but instead to see uncontrived nature as it is and so learn to recognize that nature in ourselves. In such moments of letting go, of relaxing the mind completely into what is in the present, it seems that the nature of nature and of one's deepest being come to rest in a single point. In that placeless place where the horizontal world of appearances meets the changeless vertical, the ineffable, nondual essence of things, we experience fully the single taste of our nature and of the realm of nature. In such experience, nature and its nature become mutually transparent.

Same old hilltop under the moon
Walked again and again
Written over and over
Its inwardness
always new

Notes:

1 Tulku Dondup, *Buddha Mind: An Anthology of Longchen Rabjam's Writings on Dzogpa Chenpo* (Ithaca, N.Y.: Snow Lion, 1989). All of Longchen Rabjam's poems in this article are from this source, recently renamed *The Practice of Dzogchen*.

2 *The Hundred Thousand Songs: Selections from Milarepa, Poet-Saint of Tibet*, trans. Antoinette K. Gordon (Rutland, VT. and Tokyo: Charles E. Tuttle Company, 1961). All quotes from Milarepa's songs are from this collection.

3 Padmasambhava, *Natural Liberation: Padmasambhava's Teachings on the Six Bardos*, commentary by Gyatrul Rinpoche (Boston: Wisdom Publications, 1998).

Parabola
Volume: 8.2
Animals

OF THE SAME ROOT

Philip Kapleau

Like many others, I grieve over the ongoing torture and destruction of millions of our fellow earthlings—the animals. In my book, *To Cherish All Life*,[1] I had a chance to express this concern and to marshal the religious, humanitarian, and scientific reasons for abstaining from flesh foods as one way of reducing the carnage. My views were based on the first precept of Buddhism: not to kill but to preserve and cherish all life. In this article I want to focus on the origin and significance of the deep relationship between human beings and animals and to show how that relation, an outcome of the fundamental laws of karma and rebirth, is demonstrated in Buddhist scripture, art, and ceremonies.

The deeply rooted belief that buddhahood is latent in all creatures is vividly portrayed in the Buddhist art of ancient China and Japan. Of such works none is more sublime than the class of paintings depicting the Buddha's "Great Demise" or his parinirvana—that is, the attainment of perfect emancipation beyond all conditioned existence. Not surprisingly, animals figure prominently in these works of art.

Before me as I write is the original of one such painting. It is a scroll measuring six feet in length and four feet in width, and like most religious art of the past, it bears no signature. The artist, obviously imbued with deep religious feeling, has succeeded in conveying the grandeur and solemnity of the occasion. The body of the Buddha, painted in golden tones, is as brilliant as the sun and as commanding. Like a magnet, the figure of the Buddha draws the upper and lower halves of the picture into the person of himself, into the Buddha-nature underlying all forms of life.

Surrounding the World-Honored-One are beings from the six realms of existence: demigods (devas), humans, fighting demons (ashuras), animals, hungry ghosts (pretas), and hell-dwellers. All have come to pay their last respects to the Buddha. Among the humans one sees monks, nuns, royal personages, and ordinary men and women. Sorrow and pain are etched on the faces of the assembled multitude. Many are weeping openly.

Occupying the bottom half of the scroll is a massed group of animals. One sees an elephant, horse, ox, dog, goat, monkey, camel, badger, fox, mongoose, deer, hare, snake, crane, tiger, leopard, duck, squirrel, chipmunk, rat, quail, eagle, dove, peacock, goose, egret, heron, crow, hawk, raven, mandarin duck, cock, tortoise, crab, butterfly, and dragonfly. Also present are the legendary dragon (representing absolute Mind) and the phoenix (symbolizing rebirth and regeneration).

Animals are represented in the painting because in Buddhism they are as integral to the life cycle as man himself. Completing the cycle, in the upper right-hand portion of the painting, a host of demigods (devas) is descending from the heavens.

Below them is the natural world of oceans, trees, and plains, with a full moon shining in the upper left-hand corner of the picture. No sun is shown because the Buddha himself embodies the Light that spreads throughout the universe and resides within all things.

The Buddha radiates sublime peace—peace within himself and with the whole world of animate and inanimate existence. The painting is a magnificent portrayal of the multiform Buddha-nature that unifies all elements of creation, and of the nobility of every creature gracing heaven and earth.

The portrayal of the status of animals in Buddhism might well begin with the Jataka birth stories, parables about the Buddha's previous animal and human existences. It is significant that the Buddha himself, narrator of these tales, regarded his own animal incarnations as no less meaningful than his human ones. Implicit in all these simple and direct stories are the Buddhist teachings of karma and rebirth—the teachings that an unbroken chain of cause and effect binds all existences, and that every creature has passed through many kinds and will pass through many more.

Writer and storyteller Rafe Martin, who has enacted these stories many times, writes:

The Jataka tales are dramatic

presentations of one of the most fundamental aspects of the Buddhist vision. They express the essential unity of all life. After entering the world of the Jatakas, one notices animals more. They live their own lives, have their own tests and purposes. And as often brief and painful as their lives can be, they are also touched with purity and clarity. The Buddha-nature, equally common to all things, can often be seen flowing transparently in them. In the Jatakas one sees their inner life revealed and finds it to be the very same as one's own. One seeks to save them all. And they too, looking out at us with golden or with black, shining eyes, yearn only to liberate us ...²

What strikes us most directly about the Jatakas is the focus on compassion, the self-sacrifice which flows from compassion, and identification of oneself with all living and suffering beings. In the Jatakas, animals freely sacrifice themselves for humans and humans sacrifice themselves for animals! Can we care this deeply? The first of the two Jataka tales which follow tells about such caring. It presents the future Buddha in a former life in which he sacrificed his body so that a starving tigress and her cubs might live. To many this may seem unbelievable. But is it? Animals often sacrifice themselves for humans—think of dogs who have gone to the aid of their masters in danger, even when to do so cost them their lives. Are the beasts nobler than we? To sacrifice oneself for another, even for a "lower" four-legged creature, is the purest form of

compassion, the noblest attribute of man or animal. For those in whom pity and compassion flow abundantly, the response to suffering, whether in man or beast, is unpremeditated and complete. Suffering is suffering, and perhaps because animals are so much less intellectual than we, they are more, not less, sensitive. Their sufferings may be greater than our own.

Of the four parts which constitute a complete Jataka—a story set in the present that gives the circumstances that led the Buddha to reveal his former birth; the story of the former birth; the original verses on which the stories are commentaries; and the Buddha's statement revealing who the characters are in their present lives—only the second is included here.

The Hungry Tigress

Once, long, long ago, the Buddha came to life as a noble prince named Mahasattva in a land where the country of Nepal exists today. One day when he was grown he went walking in a wild forest with his two older brothers. The land was dry and the leaves brittle. The sky seemed alight with flames.

Suddenly they saw a tigress. The brothers turned to flee, but the tigress stumbled and fell. She was starving and desperate and her two cubs were starving too. She eyed her cubs miserably and in that dark glance the prince sensed long months of hunger and pain. He saw too that unless she had food soon she might even be driven to devour her own cubs. He was moved by compassion for the hardness of their life. "What after all is this life for?" he thought.

Stepping forward he removed his outer garments and lay down beside her. Tearing his skin with a stone he let the starving tigress smell the blood. Mahasattva's brothers fled.

Hungrily the tigress devoured the prince's body and chewed the bones. She and her cubs lived on, and for many years the forest was filled with golden light.

Centuries later a mighty king raised a pillar of carved stone on this spot and pilgrims still go there to make offerings even today.

Deeds of compassion live on forever.[3]

The Brahmin and the Goat

A Brahmin was preparing to make an offering to his dead ancestors by sacrificing a goat, and had turned the animal over to his disciples for the preliminary bathing and garlanding. While this was going on, the goat suddenly acquired recollection of its previous existences and thereupon burst into a loud peal of laughter, like the breaking of a pot. But a moment later it fell into a fit of weeping. The disciples reported this unprecedented behavior to the Brahmin, who asked the goat, "Why did you laugh?" "Because," replied the goat, "long ago in a previous existence I was a Brahmin like you and I

too celebrated just such a sacrifice for the dead. As a result I was doomed to be reborn as a goat for 500 successive existences and in each existence to have my head cut off. I have already suffered this fate 499 times, and now when my head is cut off for the 500th time, my punishment will come to an end. Therefore in my joy I laughed." "And why," asked the Brahmin, "did you weep?" "I wept," said the goat, "when I thought of the 500 existences of sorrow which you are about to bring upon yourself by cutting off my head." "Never fear," said the Brahmin, "I shall not sacrifice you and you shall escape the pain of having your head cut off." The Brahmin, however, gave orders to his disciples to see that no harm came to the goat. Once free, the goat ran over to a ledge of rock and stretched its head out to nibble the leaves on a bush growing there. At that moment out of the clear sky came a sudden bolt of lightning, which split off a sliver from the overhanging rock, and this sliced off the goat's outstretched head as cleanly as with an executioner's knife.[4]

The bodhisattvic vow to liberate all beings, central to the theory and practice of Buddhism, emerges most clearly in two ceremonies unique to Buddhism: the rescue and liberation of living beings, and the rite of administering the precepts to them.

The Brahmajala sutra, a well-known Buddhist scripture, includes this admonition: "If one is a son of Buddha one must, with a merciful heart, practice the liberation of living beings ... and cause others to do so. And if one sees another person kill animals, he must by proper means save and protect them and free them from their misery and danger." The practice of liberating living beings is said to originate with this scripture.

Among Indian emperors who have liberated and protected beasts of every sort, the most famous was Ashoka (268-223 B.C.). In one of his Pillar Edicts he declared, "I have enforced the law against killing certain animals and many others, but the greatest progress of Righteousness among men comes from the exhortation in favor of non-injury to life and abstention from killing living beings."[5]

In Japan, too, in ancient times, when Buddhism dominated the hearts and minds of the Japanese, animal liberation was decreed by the emperors themselves. For example, Emperor Temmu, in the year 676, having commanded a Great Purification in all the provinces of his country, ordered that "all living beings be let loose." Those freed included criminals not convicted of capital crimes, as well as animals. In the year 745, Emperor Shomu ordered that all falcons and cormorants be set free, with the double aim of liberating these birds and prohibiting hunting and fishing with them.[6]

Such practices also flourished in ancient China. Chinese emperor Hsu-tsung of the T'ang Dynasty (618-906) dedicated 81 ponds for the liberation of living beings. And a well-known Chinese Buddhist monk, called "The Cloud of Compassion," in the year 1032 made the West Lake in China a pond for liberating living beings. He held an assembly of the people of the district on the Buddha's birth date (April 8) and caused them to let loose fishes and birds.[7]

While Buddhism was still a viable force in China, up until the Communist revolution of 1949, the practice of releasing living creatures was common. Holmes Welch, who has written extensively on Chinese Buddhism, says that near the main gate of almost every large monastery there was a pool for the release of living creatures, into which the pious could drop live fish they had rescued from the fishmonger. Behind the monastery there were stables for the care of cows, pigs, and other livestock similarly rescued. Sometimes thousands of animals were set free or rescued from dinner tables in mass releases intended as offerings to the bodhisattva of compassion, Kuan yin.[8]

A remarkable incident (reported in the newspapers of China in May of 1936) concerns a fox whose every hair was snow white. It had been trapped by a hunter, but appeared to be tame; later, although not confined, the fox made no attempt to escape. The hunter gave the fox as a pet to a neighbor named Lim, who treated the fox as a member of his household, a position it readily accepted. One night Lim had a vision in which he was directed to take the fox to a Buddhist monastery called White Cloud and liberate it there. Accordingly, the next morning he took the fox to the monastery. The abbot at the time was the Venerable Hsu yun, who immediately took a warm interest in the fox. The abbot suggested that Mr. Lim open the basket in which he had brought the fox. The fox hopped out, and to the amazement of Mr. Lim and several onlookers, made what was unmistakably a bow to the holy images on the shrine table.

Hsu yun explained that he felt the fox was a reincarnation of a former resident monk who, having accumulated much negative karma, had been reembodied in this manner. The abbot spoke to the fox, asking if it would like to take the Three Refuges[9] and the Five Precepts.[10] The fox seemed to understand. It bowed low before the abbot, who then recited the mantra of the Great Compassion, following this with the formula of the Three Refuges and the Five Precepts. Throughout the ceremony the white fox maintained a dignified posture, and bowed when the ceremony was finished. The abbot gave the fox a Buddhist name meaning "Towards Goodness."

Within a very short time the animal became fond of a vegetarian diet. On several occasions when the cook mixed chopped meat with its food, the fox refused to eat. Thousands of devout Buddhists came to see the animal, which by now was known far and wide as the Buddhist Fox.

Once some mischievous boys chased the fox. It took refuge in a tree in the monastery gardens. The abbot, hearing the boys' shouts, went to the tree and beckoned the fox to come down. At once it leaped onto the abbot's shoulders, taking great care not to scratch him. "A kitten could hardly have been more gentle," remarked the abbot. Observers reported that whenever Hsu yun sat too long in the cold meditation room, the fox would nuzzle his cheek until the abbot got up and went to bed.[11]

Sri Ramana Maharshi was another spiritual master who had a deep rapport with animals. Many stories are told of the dogs, cows, monkeys, peacocks, and other animals in his ashram and their unique relations with him. Speaking from his enlightened wisdom, Zen master Dogen has said, "…Those who experience this communion [with Buddha] inevitably take this refuge [in the Three Treasures of Buddha, Dharma, and Sangha] whether they find themselves as celestial or human beings, dwellers in hell, hungry ghosts, or animals. As a result, the merit that is accumulated thereby inevitably increases through the various stages of existence, leading ultimately to the highest supreme enlightenment."[12]

The purpose in administering the precepts to an animal, then, is to raise the level of its consciousness so that it may achieve a more felicitous rebirth and eventually attain full liberation. The ceremony of giving the precepts is not primarily directed to the discriminating mind, but to Buddha-mind, the Mind inherent in all creatures. In Mahayana Buddhism the precepts are more than guidelines delineating morally desirable behavior; they are an expression of ultimate reality, of the absolute Buddha-nature. On this level we cannot speak of high or low, moral or amoral, karma or akarma, birth or death, animal or human being.

Thus from the absolute standpoint of Buddha-nature, every creature, just as it is, is whole and complete, a perfect expression of buddha.[13] A mouse here is the equal of an Einstein. But from the perspective of the senses and the intellect, all things, animate and inanimate, are temporary transformations of the one Buddha- or Essential-mind—names for the ever unnameable "it"—the substratum of Emptiness (perfection) underlying all existences. "Heaven and earth and I are of the same root, all things and I are of the same substance," affirmed a Zen master of old. On this level each life, each thing is causally related to every other, forming an indivisible whole. No creature, whether it walks, creeps, crawls, swims, or flies, ever falls short of its own completeness. "Wherever it stands it does not fail to cover the ground."

Bodhi, the dog now lying at my feet, has been evolving and devolving in his beginningless and endless course of becoming through innumerable kalpas,[14] now as a mineral, now as a plant, now as a fish, now as a reptile, now as an ape, now as a demon, now as a demigod, now as one like myself—I who am what? Yet, once again, if I look at him through eyes undimmed by relativity, by such notions as karma, morality, causality, Buddha, mind, he is not a dog. Furthermore, he never evolved or devolved, was never born, will never die. Suppose he were asked, "What are you? Where did you come from? What is your relation to your fellow creatures?" How would he respond?

"Woof! Woof!"

Translated into the language of humans this reads: "Throughout heaven and earth I am the only One."

Notes:

1   Harper & Row, 1982.

2   From the introduction to an unpublished manuscript, "The Hungry Tigress and Other Jataka Tales."

3   "The Hungry Tigress."

4   W. Norman Brown, "The Unity of Life in Indian Religion," *Animals and Man in Historical Perspective*, eds. Joseph and Barrie Klaits (New York: Harper & Row, 1974).

5   "The Seventh Pillar Edict," *Sources of Indian Tradition*, trans. William T. De Bary (New York: Columbia University Press, 1958).

6 Marinus Willem deVisser, *Ancient Buddhism in Japan*, vol. 1 (Leiden: E. J. Brill, Ltd., 1935).

7 deVisser.

8 Holmes H. Welch, *The Practice of Chinese Buddhism* (Cambridge: Harvard University Press, 1967).

9 Refuge in Buddha, Dharma, and Sangha.

10 Stated from the human standpoint: 1) to refrain from taking life, 2) to refrain from taking what is not given, 3) to refrain from improper sexuality, 4) to refrain from telling an untruth, 5) to refrain from taking liquors or drugs that confuse the mind.

11 The Venerable Sumangalo, *Buddhist Stories for Young and Old* (Singapore, 1960).

12 Quoted in *Zen Master Dogen* by Yohu Yoki. (New York: Weatherhill, 1976).

13 A term used in two senses: a) ultimate truth or absolute Mind, and b) one awakened to the true nature of existence.

14 One of the sutras defines a kalpa, or world cycle, as the time it would take to empty a container of poppyseeds forty cubic miles in size if one took out just one poppyseed every three years.

•

CHAPTER TEN

On Pilgrimage

There are four places which the follower should visit with feelings of
respect and awe … the place at which the follower can say,
'Here the Tathāgata was born' … 'Here the Tathāgata attained supreme bodhi' …
'Here the Tathāgata set foot making the spot into
a kingdom of dhamma' … *'Here the Tathāgata passed away into*
the traceless passing away' …

—The Buddha

Parabola
Volume: 9.3
Pilgrimage

A NEW DWELLING

Interview with Tara Tulku, Rinpoche

*By the standards of his own rigorous tradition, the
Venerable Tara Tulku, Rinpoche, is a remarkable individual.
Born in Khams, eastern Tibet, in 1927, Rinpoche was
recognized at a very early age as the reincarnation of the
previous abbot of neighboring Sendru Monastery. Beginning
his monastic
training at Sendru at the age of three, Rinpoche in 1940
entered Drepung Monastery, the largest in Tibet, with ten
thousand monks. There he was recognized as master of all five
fields of Buddhist scholarship at the age of twenty-nine—
inordinately young for such an achievement. He proceeded for
advanced training to Gyuoto Tantric Monastery, where he
remained until the Chinese invasion—making him one of the
last monks to receive a complete Tibetan Buddhist training on
his native soil.*

*The great catastrophe of 1959 decimated Gyuoto Tantric
Monastery; of five hundred monks in residence, only seventy
escaped. After great hardships, the monastery was relocated in
India, where Tara Tulku guided it through the arduous process
of reconstruction. Following nine years as abbot—three times
the customary tenure— Rinpoche became abbot emeritus.*

But his work continues unabated. Recently, His Holiness the Dalai Lama appointed him to teach the Dharma to Westerners each year at the Tibetan monastery at Bodhgaya, and for the past year he has been teaching in America both as the Henry R. Luce Professor of Comparative Religious Ethics at Amherst College in Amherst, Massachusetts, and as scholar-in-residence at the American Institute for Buddhist Studies in Amherst.

We spoke to Tara Tulku at the home of Robert A. F. Thurman, professor of religion at Amherst College, president of the American Institute of Buddhist Studies, and the man who was instrumental in bringing Tara Tulku to the United States. Professor Thurman not only translated for us with vigor and wit, but helped illuminate difficult aspects of Tibetan teaching during the course of our long conversation. His translating skills came into play as soon as Rinpoche joined us, smiling brightly, arms spread wide in greeting, dressed in a monastic garb of maroon robes, yellow silk shirt, and red sweater bearing a portrait-pin of H. H. the Dalai Lama.

After lunch, we gathered in Tara Tulku's sunny upstairs living quarters where he sat on Western pillows. As he responded to our questions with warmth and intensity, we were aware of his openness and freedom and of our own instinctive respect toward him. His fluid attention, sense of humor, great intellectual depth—and as it seemed to us—profundity of being, gave his responses, and his silences, a rare seriousness and weight.

—Lorraine Kisly and Philip Zaleski

Parabola: *Rinpoche, perhaps we could start out by asking what connotations pilgrimage has for you.*

Tara Tulku: We believe that there are two reasons to go on pilgrimage. One is temporary, the other is ultimate. Generally, we feel that pilgrimage is very important and powerful. If we were to go on pilgrimage in the way it is recommended in the Buddha Dharma, it would be truly excellent for us. For example, the places where we live, our dwellings, are not quite right or suitable. Why is that? Because no matter how we deal with them, they become a source of suffering for us. Similarly, our ordinary body is definitely not proper as it is. Therefore, it is necessary that we contemplate the development and acquisition of a new dwelling, a new body. You can say that the Buddha

Dharma, its various techniques and arts, consists of means for developing and attaining a new body, a new dwelling. There are both ordinary and extraordinary methods for creating these; the process of going on pilgrimage should be understood as part of these methods.

Parabola: *Is Rinpoche referring to the development of a subtle body in this lifetime?*

TT: (Smiles.) We will come around to the subject of subtle bodies and such, but we haven't quite gotten there yet. Let's consider the case of Śakyamuni Buddha, to commemorate whom one goes on the pilgrimage to Bodhgaya. On the ordinary level of reality, Śakyamuni, in the series of events relating to his eating the first bit of rice, taking his bath, going to the Bodhi tree and so forth, realized a new body. He suddenly became golden, and his ascetic body filled out. He had a completely different body—it suddenly appeared on the ordinary level.

The place itself, under the Bodhi tree at Bodhgaya, was transformed as well. It became a place of diamond, a *vajra* place, a place of extreme sacredness. Why is it sacred? Because Buddha's transformative experience of unexcelled perfect enlightenment blessed it in a special way. Some people even believe that if you reach and stand on that place and take the Bodhisattva vow or make prayers to achieve Buddhahood for the benefit of all beings, then just because of the power of that place, you will never be reborn in the lower states. And if you meditate there, recite prayers, and study, the place has a special power for the mind to come to realization. It is a place of light and bliss. This is because this is the place where Śakyamuni achieved the special Buddha body, a body which has only bliss and happiness, and never suffers. He also used this place as a basis for perceiving all places as indivisible from the highest heaven of the four realms. Because this place was the basis from which he reenvisioned all reality as the highest heaven, it is extremely sacred.

That's how Buddhists explain this. But when we hear it, we have to ask ourselves whether it could really be so. There is, however, an excellent example that it really is so which the Buddhists use. We say, when we go to a battlefield, that it is a horrible, awful place. And if we go to such a place, we become uncomfortable and sad.

Parabola: *Are there actually physical forces at work in such places, or is this a result of memories connected with these places?*

TT: Both. Bodhgaya has a great special power infused in it by a person whose achievement was timeless, in the sense that the future was present. It lasts. Also, if one goes there with a strong vision of that moment, as if it were not separated from one, as if it were not past, then the power is much greater. But even when someone not thinking of its importance wanders through Bodhgaya, it has a very great power. Many people have remarked upon this.

Parabola: *Just as there are places that can be beneficial and places that can be detrimental, it can be said that there are paths that lead towards a true goal, and paths that lead toward falsehood. How can one discern whether one is on a right path—particularly if one lives outside of a traditional society?*

TT: The impact of the mind is how one judges the validity of the path. Here, again, the issue of relativity is crucial. When a path brings us into relativities, into causes and conditions that influence the mind in a positive way, we can say that the path is positive or good. But how have you asked this question?

Parabola: *We are thinking of pilgrimage as not just a physical voyage, but as the journey from ignorance to enlightenment.*

TT: Yes, you are jumping ahead of me again. (Smiles.) I am talking first about the ordinary level of pilgrimage. For example, we have Bodhgaya, a place to which anyone can go, but an especially sacred place. And if one has faith in the Buddha,

and practices and meditates and proceeds on the path from ignorance to enlightenment, the place gets a greater and greater power for one. Now, this is what we mean by ordinary pilgrimage.

As for extraordinary pilgrimage, we believe that there is a place, made by the Buddha's merits, realizations, and vows and prayers for all sentient beings, which exists on a subtle level. He has created this place from his achievement of the timelessness in which past, present, and future are equally accessible. In this place, he receives those beings who go there. But this place is practically impossible for us to encounter from our ordinary level.

The Buddha has left there an inconceivable body, an extraordinary one which has not passed away as the ordinary one has. These are the two major foci of pilgrimage on the extraordinary level. Why is that? Because the Buddha has said that if one reaches ethical, meditational, and intellectual achievements of a certain kind, then one can come to have such a dwelling, such a body and mind. One becomes a Buddha oneself. If one practices according to those teachings, one can transform one's world, one's body, and one's mind. That is the true inner pilgrimage—the attainment of enlightenment; to change the body and the world as well as the mind.

Parabola: *What is the connection or meeting point between ordinary and extraordinary pilgrimage?*

TT: You can see ordinary pilgrimage as a kind of preparation, as the creation of a paradigm in the mind, and as an accumulation of merit for the person who will then go on the extraordinary pilgrimage when he becomes capable of it. The nearer one gets to the field of those activities of the Buddha, the historical and transhistorical realities of those activities, the more one generates faith, admiration, and estimation of his achievements, and the more one prizes one's achievement of these stages oneself. The more one likes something, the more likely it is that in the future one will acquire it.

One thing that isn't well enough known is that the Buddha himself, in his own discourses, gave the recommendation to undertake ordinary pilgrimage. It's not something that others added after his death. In the Parinirvana Sutra, when the Buddha is about to die, he says to Ananda that Buddhas always die this way, and that after they die, the relics are put in a stupa, much bigger than for a king. Afterwards, there are four places where pilgrims should go: where a Buddha is born, where a Buddha attains enlightenment, where a Buddha first turns the Wheel of Dharma, and where a Buddha attains Parinirvana. Thus you recapitulate the whole life cycle of the Buddha by going around these four places. The Buddha seems to have been the first person to create such a pattern—that is, pilgrimage that is not just a journey to a local, ancestral, or tribal shrine.

Parabola: *Does this establish a physical relationship to the Buddha?*

TT: Exactly right.

Parabola: *Has pilgrimage, then, played a large role in the life of Tibetans?*

TT: Oh, yes. It has entered the ears of Tibetans that it is a great and sacred thing to go on pilgrimage. Some know what they are doing, and the context in which they do it, and the attitude which they should bring to it. Others go without knowing. At Bodhgaya, they take bits of earth and put them into amulets or charm boxes to take with them. This is a Tibetan custom.

Parabola: *Does the arduousness of the pilgrimage add to the merit?*

TT: Yes. The more suffering that is undergone—provided that suffering is borne in the positive sense—the more merit accrues. Of course, if you get mad and irritated with your hardships, that will decrease the merit. (Laughs.)

Parabola: *Has pilgrimage played an important role in your own life, Rinpoche?*

TT: Yes, it has had a great impact on my life, particularly in terms of my experiences at Bodhgaya. They have been very powerful—praying, meditating, performing ceremonies. The tremendously peaceful atmosphere at Bodhgaya has had a great effect on me. It facilitates achieving my own sense of peacefulness.

Parabola: *It's a common practice among educated Westerners to go around the world, visiting pilgrimage sites in traditions that are not their own. What do you think of, for instance, a Christian going to a Buddhist site?*

TT: It doesn't matter what religion people hold, if they are going with an open mind, if they are seeking truth. In this case, it is extremely meritorious to go to the holy sites of any religion.

Parabola: *But isn't it necessary to have a thorough training in the tradition of a site in order to fully receive the influences connected to it?*

TT: Yes, there is a question of degree of merit, but there is always some real merit. There's a famous story about a monk who was not going to be admitted to an order by some of the order's great venerable elders because he was a nasty person with a bad record. The monk complained bitterly about this, saying, "You bunch of incompetent venerables, I want to be a monk! So what if I've been mean." He scolded

them, in his typically abusive way, about how they shouldn't stand in his way, and how at least they should ask the Buddha before making a final decision. So the elders went and asked the Buddha, "Does this fellow have any redeeming characteristics, so that he might benefit himself and others by becoming a monk in our order?" The Buddha looked at the monk for a long time and then said, "Yes, indeed, he does have a redeeming feature." When the elders asked, "What is it?" The Buddha told this story: Many previous lifetimes ago, he said, this monk had been an ant. As an ant, he had been present when some pilgrims had held a picnic in Bodhgaya, near the stupa of the former Buddha. The ant had been sneaking around, trying to steal crumbs from the food of the pilgrims. Suddenly, one of the picnickers got up and started to circumambulate the stupa—with the ant stuck on his foot, hanging on for dear life! (Laughs.) He held on for several revolutions around the stupa. And by the virtue of that, the Buddha concluded, he was now deserving of become a monk in the order.

Parabola: *Could Rinpoche indicate to us what qualities a person needs to set out on the inner or extraordinary pilgrimage?*

TT: A person must have faith in the goal—faith that there is a transformed place; that there is the possibility of an evolutionary transformation of the self, of body and mind; faith that beings have done so; and that they left accurate records of how to do so. Next, effort is required. The more faith one has, and the more ambition one has in consequence of that faith, the more one's effort will increase. And in order to generate that faith more powerfully, one must have the memory, the mindfulness, of the excellence of the goal. The more one can remember what a Buddha is, the more one's aspiration for that becomes, and the more one's effort increases. The more one realizes how beneficial that achievement is, what great advantages there are in achieving such a stage, the more intensely one will wish to practice the methods leading to such a stage. Similarly, if one is aware of a really delicious meal in a particular restaurant or country, one's effort will be more intense to go get to that place to have that feast.

Parabola: *But we don't know this end state—the end of the pilgrimage—as clearly as we know the taste of food. It's something unknown by definition.*

TT: How is it that we get to know it? By depending upon the greatest of the Buddha's accomplishments—his speech. A remarkable aspect of the Buddha is that he taught and described extensively the nature of all the various stages and paths. It is by relying on these descriptions that we can come to understand it.

Two aspects of the Buddha's teaching are particularly important in this context. One is that he always spoke reasonably, providing clear reasons of why it is one must come to this or that understanding. You might call it his scientific side. And the other is his artistic side. He also spoke poetically and vividly. In his discourses, there are very vivid descriptions—evocations, you might say—of various kinds of states, of beings, heavenly realms, and so forth. So by the imagination and by critical wisdom, he has methods for both sides of the person to develop simultaneously. The initial key, of course, is to be aware that ordinary reality is the reality of suffering. And second, that suffering has a root which can be eradicated. Once that has been realized, the prospect of a state without suffering becomes tangible.

Parabola: *But what is it that distinguishes someone who comes to this understanding from someone who does not? What is the nature of that critical moment that leads one to place one's foot upon the path?*

TT: As we define it, the first step in the path is the taking of refuge. Then comes the mind of renunciation and detachment, the spirit of love and compassion. Third is the wisdom of selflessness. These are the three things that are necessary.

Parabola: *And what is it that leads one person to seek refuge and another to ignore it?*

TT: This has to do with whether the two major causes of the taking of refuge are present in the person. These causes are said to be terror and faith. By faith, we mean faith in the three jewels of Buddha, Dharma, and Sangha—that there is a community, a teaching, and an enlightened being. By terror, we mean terror of cosmic suffering, especially, at the beginning, terror of the lower states of existence—of hell, of the *preta* realm, of animal suffering, terror of future lives in an uncontrolled way. A person who has those two causes—cosmic terror of an unsaved destiny, and faith that there are compassionate beings who have the ability to give one the method of saving oneself from that terror—will automatically take refuge. That is the beginning of the path.

Parabola: *Once one is on the path, we are told that one will meet many obstacles. What is a fruitful attitude to take towards those obstacles—particularly if they seem to be other people?*

TT: We mustn't be angry with the obstacles. When obstacles arise, the key thing is to practice tolerance, one of the most transcendent virtues taught in Buddhism. One must cultivate one's patience and tolerance. Of course, there are levels wherein,

in addition to not being angry with obstacles, as far as that has to do with one's subjective attitude, there are ways of going around them. There are even methods, in the tantras for example, of removing obstacles.

Parabola: *Is there a way of transforming an obstacle, or must it always be removed or gone around?*

TT: Śantideva's book, *Bodhicaryāvatára* (*A Guide to the Boddhisattva's Way of Compassion*), is full of this sort of approach, about how your enemy is your greatest teacher—ways of turning this whole thing around. There is a very elaborate discussion in Śantideva about tolerance as a great virtue. From tolerance arises beauty. All of Buddha's beauty arises from his practice of tolerance. The more patient you become, the more you are able to bear suffering, the more beautiful you will become. To be tolerant, however, I need an enemy. I need someone to bother me, so I can practice my tolerance. Thus the enemy becomes a guru. Śantideva is full of techniques of this kind, in a very sophisticated, intricate, beautiful form.

Parabola: *So the greatest obstacle on the path is having no obstacles at all.*

TT: Śantideva will go to such extremes as making statements like that. But on the other hand, when tolerance is perfected and one has

Buddhahood, even if there are no obstacles in oneself, other beings have quite enough obstacles to go around, to provide an outlet for your tolerance. For example, the Dalai Lama is always saying that the Communists have been very kind to him, a tremendous help. But, on the other hand, he says that the Communists' destruction of his people is bad. When a soldier has beaten up an old man, or killed a monk or a child, this is bad. If you know the practice of tolerance, then an enemy can help you. But otherwise, you are simply harmed by your enemy, and experience even more harm from your own anger and bitterness at the enemy, so it's doubly bad. Nobody benefits from that. So without being angry at anyone, certainly you should try very forcefully to stop bad persons from doing bad things.

Parabola: *Is meditation in any way like a pilgrimage?*

TT: There are many ways of meditating. If one is just concentrating on a single object, then it is hard to see it as a pilgrimage. Within, however, the discursive or thematic or analytic types of meditation, some can be said to be like a pilgrimage. Again, within that, there are ordinary and extraordinary levels.

Parabola: *Even in very simple relaxation meditation, however, one encounters obstacles. One is going to a slightly* *freer place than the usual subjective state. It's a kind of inward journey, even on a very simple level.*

TT: Yes. We talk about these things in the form of remedies. For example, if one's mind is full of anxiety, then one contemplates the counting of breath. If one is excessively attached to something, the contemplation of unloveliness is considered to be a remedy. If one has anger, then tolerance is meditated on. Each mental imbalance has its particular corrective remedy.

Parabola: *To what extent is one's pilgrimage individual and solitary, and to what extent does it involve companions? If it is a group effort, what should one's attitude be towards one's companions on the pilgrimage?*

TT: There are various levels of pilgrimage, relating to the motivation involved. In an objective way, of course, there is always an individual and a collective component relating to any action. But the action changes and has a different degree of merit and power depending on the orientation of the person. For example, if a person is what is called an "inferior" person—that is, a spiritual, but "inferior" spiritual person—he is going on the pilgrimage to get merit for himself, to prevent his future sufferings and to achieve heavenly and other kinds of reincarnations in his future lives. This is somewhat narrow, but it has a certain type of merit. The middle person is going on a pilgrimage to get merit not only for the betterment of his life, but to achieve liberation and enlightenment for himself. This has a wider power. Finally, bodhisattvas go on the pilgrimage for themselves, but simultaneously wish all beings to go with them. In a sense, they visualize that they are taking all beings with them on that pilgrimage. They are including all beings as receiving the fruit of what they do. That becomes a vast root of virtue. These are the famous three types of person—inferior, mediocre, and superior—on the basis of how they are motivated in any virtuous action that they might do. If one goes on the pilgrimage just to benefit oneself in this life, it is not considered a religious action, but just an ordinary action, and yet one can receive some benefit from it.

Parabola: *Like the ant on the shoe!*

TT: Yes.

Parabola: *What aspects of Buddhism are most misunderstood by Westerners?*

TT: There's a long list. The worst is the misunderstanding of emptiness as if it were nothingness, leading to meditation on nothingness: nonthought. Relating to this, the notion that there's no ethics in Buddhism. And then, the wish and insistence on immediate practice of tantra.

Parabola: *Is it difficult for Tibetans to understand Buddhism?*

TT: Yes, it's very hard for anyone. It entails a whole process of education.

Parabola: *I know I have no understanding of emptiness.*

TT: You must make effort in the method of coming to understand it. Emptiness is the essence of the Dharma.

Parabola: *Does this have something to do with it: We have a consciousness which persists; thoughts come and go, but consciousness persists. Now, there's one consciousness which is involved in, identified with, and reacting to an external reality. Is the same consciousness, when it is freed from that identification, part of what is meant by emptiness?*

TT: (Expression of anguish.) To think about emptiness, one has to examine how, in your mind, when you let it settle a little bit, there arises a sense of "I." You have to observe that "I" and come to understand it. That's in the direction of emptiness—not just some peacefulness. The critical insight about what that "I" is. This mind of "I," "I," "I" is always, continually arising. There is a relative "I"—the conventional self really is there. But we don't understand it as a relative and conventional "I," because we have a strange way of exaggerating it, and perceiving it to be an independent thing, not part of the relativity which is emptiness. To begin to diminish that exaggeration is the purpose of contemplating emptiness. The important thing is to avoid thinking of emptiness as nothingness, which comes from thinking of it as a kind of empty space of peaceful meditation. The real meaning of emptiness is relativity, relationality, interdependency.

Parabola: *So seeing this "I" come up again and again is very important.*

Robert A. F. Thurman: Oh yes, and learning how to separate the falsely exaggerated absolute "I" from the relative "I," and getting to learn how one is exaggerating, and how the feeling arises of some sort of independence, which seems to be there but can't possibly be there. The main thing to understand is the Buddha's view, that of relativity. So, in response to an earlier question, sense-consciousness is just as much emptiness as an inner peaceful state. Subject and object—all relationships are empty. There's no place that is emptier than any other.

Parabola: *Does the ego have a purpose?*

TT: Its purpose is to organize your activity—for example, to take the pictures you are taking, to walk, to eat, to think, to achieve Buddhahood. To help other beings. Buddha has to have an "I," an ego. You need

the relative ego, you need to make it stronger, but to make it less absolute. This lets it grow more.

Parabola: *The relative ego must assume its proper place.*

TT: It's very interesting. You never lose the ego, although temporarily, because the relative ego and the hypothetical absolute ego are so inextricably intermixed, when you begin with critical wisdom to look into the absolute ego, you see through it, you see that it is just a presumption. And it seems to take the relative one with it as it disappears. You feel as if you've lost your ego. But that's an illusion. If you have a nihilistic outlook, you identify that loss of the relative "I" as a big achievement, and so you become a nihilist by experience as well—and then you are very difficult to deal with.

Parabola: *Is there any way in which the dissemination of the Dharma to the West can be seen as a kind of pilgrimage?*

TT: Since America is a new area for Buddhism, it is hard to see how one can conceive of it as a pilgrimage in the conventional Buddhist sense. However, in an unconventional sense, in the context that the metaphor of the Buddha's teaching is the Turning of the Wheel of the Dharma, and there definitely is a progression of the Dharma around the planet—it does seem that in Asia it has had a time of decline, although it is still very much there, while it is growing in the West—it can be seen as a pilgrimage. The expression for pilgrimage in Tibetan is "to turn around the place," to circumambulate a place, and we can see that the Dharma itself is circling around the globe. The whole globe is becoming a Wheel of Dharma.

•

CHAPTER ELEVEN

ALL THINGS MUST PASS: BUDDHISM AND DEATH

As Roshi Taji, a contemporary Zen master, approached death, his senior disciples assembled at his bedside. One of them, remembering the roshi was fond of a certain kind of cake, had spent half a day searching the pastry shops of Tokyo for this confection, which he now presented to Roshi Taji. With a wan smile the dying roshi accepted a piece of the cake and slowly began munching it. As the roshi grew weaker, his disciples leaned close and inquired whether he had any final words for them.

"Yes," the roshi replied.

The disciples leaned forward eagerly. "Please tell us!"

"My, but this cake is delicious!" And with that he died.

Parabola
Volume: 3.3
Inner Alchemy

"The Self"

A Convenient Fiction

Paul Jordan-Smith

When King Milinda had thus observed the venerable Nagasena seated among the Order of Arahats, he went up to him and greeted him with the respect and courtesy of friendship. Then he took his seat, and Nagasena reciprocated the courtesy so that the king's heart was pleased.

After a respectful silence, Milinda turned to Nagasena and began by asking, "By what name are you known, Venerable One?"

Nagasena replied, "I am addressed by the members of the Order as Nagasena, O king, for that is the name given by my parents. But such designations—Nagasena, Surasena, Assagutta, and so on—are no more than convenient terms of address. They are not that by which we may be known, for there is no permanent individuality implied by such terms."

Then King Milinda turned and addressed the company of Greeks and the Order of Arahats together in this wise: "This Nagasena says that there is no permanent individuality implied in his name. How is this possible? Venerable One," he continued, speaking now to Nagasena, "if this is so, who is it who tends to the needs of your Order? Who is it who has learned the articles of your faith and now guides others on the way? Who is it who lives a life of righteousness, and who is it who meditates? What is this Nagasena? Is it the hair, perhaps, that is Nagasena?"

"I do not say that, O king," replied the sage.

"Perhaps, then, the limbs of the body?"

"Most certainly not."

"Is it the nails, the teeth, the skin, flesh or bones? Is it the marrow, the kidneys, the lungs? Is it the stomach, the intestines, the brain, the spleen? Is it the phlegm, bile, urine, pus, blood, saliva, sweat, lymph, mucus or tears? Are any or all of these Nagasena? If not, is it then the form of the body that is Nagasena, or the sensation, or the ideas, or the feelings or the consciousness?" asked the king.

"No," replied Nagasena.

"Is it all of these things combined?"

"No!"

"But is there anything other than all these which is Nagasena?"

"There is not, O king."

"I conclude, then, that there is no Nagasena here at all! Where is Nagasena?" said the king, looking about him as if mystified. "And who is this man before me? Has Nagasena lied or is this man an impostor?"

At these words, the company of Greeks laughed, and the Order of Arahats was perturbed, not knowing among them how to reply. But Nagasena smiled at the laughter of the Greeks, and when the fit had passed and silence had fallen, he said, "Your majesty, no doubt, has been brought up in wealth and luxury?"

"It is so, Venerable One, whoever you are."

"Having been so brought up, you doubtless have tender feet. To have come here on foot in hot, dry weather and over rough and stony ground would have troubled your majesty much. Yet I observe that your face is not contorted by suffering. How came you here, then, Sire? On foot or in a chariot?"

Milinda replied, "I did not come on foot, Sir, but in a carriage."

"A carriage?" answered Nagasena. "Pray, what is that? Is it the shafts?"

"I did not say that," said the king.

"Perhaps, then, it is the axle," said Nagasena, as if he had concluded his question and had arrived at the answer.

"Most certainly not," said Milinda.

"Then it must be the wheels, or the framework, or the traces, or the yoke. And if not, is it perhaps the spokes, the goad, or the seat? Are any or all of these the carriage?"

"No!" replied the king.

"But is there anything else than these that is the carriage?" asked Nagasena, and still the king answered no.

"Most curious!" said Nagasena. "Here is before me a man who says he is King Milinda, who did not come by foot, and yet the carriage he says he came in does not exist. 'Carriage' is a mere empty sound denoting nothing. But since the king came not on foot, it follows that he is not here after all. Has the great king lied? Or is this man before me an impostor?"

Then the Order of Arahats applauded and said, "Let your majesty get out of that if you can."

Then King Milinda addressed Nagasena, saying, "No untruth have I spoken, reverend Sir. It is on account of its having all these things—yoke, traces, shaft, axle, wheels and frame— and because of its purpose and use as a conveyance, that it is called by the generally understood designation of 'carriage.'"

"Just so, O king, is 'Nagasena.'"

From "The Questions of King Milinda," an ancient Pali Buddhist text, as retold by Paul Jordan-Smith.

Parabola
Volume: 2.1
Death

Swimming in the Ocean of Becoming:

A Zen Perspective on Death

Conrad Hyers

Why are people called Buddhas after they die?
Because they don't grumble anymore
Because they don't make a nuisance of themselves.
—Ikkyu[1]

In traditions which equate human perfection with the loss of ego, death is not the problem it is for those concerned to perpetuate the finite self and its self-consciousness *ad infinitum*. Anxiety about death arises chiefly as fear of losing the finite self, its illusory continuity and substantiality, and all those facets of existence that are subject to change and dissolution. But to be free of ego, of its desperate striving and clinging, its "grumbling" and "nuisance-making," is to be liberated from dread of death as some dark, forbidding, perhaps evil fate lurking in the shadows of the self. At least this is how Buddhists see it.

Zen stands within the general terms of this pan-Buddhist tradition, but with some important accents of its own. One of the more unusual and revealing of these is the introduction of a sense of humor with respect to death and dying—as in these playful words of Ikkyu, noted abbot of Daitokuji. The Zen records contain many humorous anecdotes on the deaths of various monks and masters. And the presence of a sense of humor in such circumstances as this is itself testimony to a remarkable way of perceiving and experiencing both life and death. When the dying Nan-chu'an was asked by his head monk, "Where are you going after your death?" he replied, "I am going down the hill to be a water buffalo!" "Would it be possible to follow you there?" inquired the devoted monk. Nan-chu'an responded, "If you want to follow me, please come with straw in your mouth!"

This is not a matter of frivolousness or insensitivity, but of profound insight and freedom. Chao-chou, on seeing the somberness of the funeral procession for one of his monks, exclaimed: "What a long train of dead bodies follows in the wake of a single living being!" While we are inclined to associate joking and laughter in such a context with irreverence, callousness, hysteria, or even sadism, their manifestation in Zen is understood as a sign of enlightenment and liberation.

One of the more colorful examples of this spirit is that of Teng Yin-feng who, when he sensed that his time had come, asked his fellow monks, "I have seen monks die in various positions; some lying down, some sitting, some standing. But has anyone ever died standing on his head?" The monks could recall no stories to this effect. Whereupon Teng stood on his head and died. When it was time to carry him to the funeral pyre he was still

upside-down, to the wonder of those who came to view the remains, and the consternation of those who would properly dispose of them. Finally his younger sister, a nun, came to the monastery and chiding him said, "When you were alive you took no notice of laws and customs, and even now that you are dead you are making a nuisance of yourself!" And with that she poked him with a finger, felling him with a thud. And the procession took him away to the crematorium.

In this way Teng expressed his achievement of spiritual freedom, his liberation from a pathetic clinging to life and anxiety over self, and so marked his transcendence of the problem of death. Similarly, Lo-shan, feeling his end to be near, ascended the rostrum to speak. But instead of addressing his monks with some edifying discourse or parting admonitions, he abruptly dismissed them, remarking simply, "If you wish to show your gratitude for the Buddha's goodness to you, you should not be too earnest about propagating the Great Teaching." After that he began laughing loudly, and died. Or Ikkyu again:

*Though we do not preach
the doctrine,*

*Unasked the flowers bloom
in spring,*

They fall and scatter,

They turn to dust.

To be sure, this equanimity—even playfulness—in relation to death is no easy achievement. Nor, for that matter, is it an easy achievement in relation to *life*, and all those things, including ourselves, that we take so seriously. Seriousness alone is a clear sign of attachment and bondage, however "worthy of serious attention" the object or circumstance might be. The secret, in both life and death, lies somewhere between seriousness and frivolity, earnestness and silliness, attachment and detachment. Humor means freedom; to the degree that one is free, one is free to laugh.

This is by no means a cynical laughter, born of resignation and despair. Nor is it a defiant laughter, making some last gesture of rebellion against the inevitability of dying, "head bloody, but unbowed." Nor is it, certainly, a better laughter, mocking the inequities of life and the irony of all those "best-laid schemes of mice and men" that "gang aft agley." The spirit is radically different. It is a laughter of acceptance, a final "yes" to the transiency of life and the naturalness of death. It is a laughter which expresses the joy of life, without at the same time frantically clutching it. It is the laughter of non-ego and non-attachment, which is therefore free to embrace death as well as life.

In Zen, however, preparation for death is not made at the *expense* of life, as happens in so many religions of salvation. Life is not turned into a mere stepping-stone to some other,

more favorable and perhaps paradisal existence, free of suffering and sorrow. In Zen one does not reach this tranquil plane in the face of death by the essentially negative process of disparaging the circumstances of life. There is no attempt to empty life of any intrinsic meaning and value, so as to reduce desire and attachment. Life is not expended in developing a spiritualized "death-wish." One knows how to die because one knows how to live.

True, in Zen teaching one comes across quite an array of negatives from *sunyata* (void, emptiness) to a long parade of Chinese *wus* and Japanese *mus*: no-mind, no-thought, no-self, no-concern, no-seeking, no-striving, no-action, no-attachment. And such terms might seem aimed at devaluing and "voiding" life, and thus putting oneself in a better position from which to let life go in death. But in Zen such terms imply an essentially positive attitude toward both life and death. The negatives do not negate life, but rather any approach to life (and death) which leads to bondage. This is the negation of negation. It is true freedom. The way of emptiness (*sunyata*) is thus the way of fullness. The mind is not closed off from the world, but opened in the widest manner possible. "What is no-thought?" asks the Sixth Patriarch. "It is to be present in all places and yet not become attached to anything ... It is to let the six sense-robbers run out of the six sense-gates into the world of the six sense-objects, and yet not to become defiled therein, nor to get away therefrom."

Clutching to life squeezes the life out of life—that is the problem—just as clutching to life does not permit one to die with dignity and freedom. The Zen solution is not to cultivate a detachment from and disenchantment with life, but to involve oneself totally in it and to celebrate each circumstance, however lofty or lowly. Whether one eats a feast or plain rice, one eats wholeheartedly and gratefully. Whether one chants *sutras* or sweeps verandas, one does so with undivided attention as if that activity at that moment were supremely worth doing. This is emptiness. The point is not to convince oneself that life is so fleeting, vain and illusory that all energies should be devoted to "spiritual" and "eternal" matters, and therefore to a gradual "dying to the world." Rather, one is invited to take hold of each moment as it presents itself, and in the form in which is presents itself.

> *Drinking tea, eating rice,*
> *Passing time as it comes;*
> *Looking down at the stream,*
> *Looking up at the mountain.*
> —*Pao-tzu*

Zen aims at being immersed in life without clinging to life. This is the "Middle Way." All things, however simple, menial and repetitious, are to be done as *zazen*: cooking, cleaning, gardening, walking, sitting. All things, however insignificant and commonplace, are to be seen and touched in the spirit of *sunyata*: tea-bowl and summer rain, chattering sparrows and a crimson leaf, the firefly and the bullfrog, chrysanthemums and cucumbers. To do so is to be totally immersed, but without drowning. As Shan-neng counsels, "We must not cling to the wind and moon of the day and ignore the eternal void; neither must we cling to the eternal void, and ignore the wind and moon of the day."

The world of space and time, of body and matter, of eating and sleeping and drinking, is not in itself the illusory bubble of *maya* that must be burst in order to gain release. *Maya* is the world of craving and clinging, of attachment and bondage, of ignorance of the true way. Dogen, founder of the Japanese Soto sect, puts the point succinctly: "In life identify yourself with life; at death with death. Abstain from yielding and craving. Life and death constitute the very being of Buddha. Thus should you reject life you will be the loser, and yet you can expect no more if you cling to either life or death. You must neither loathe, then, nor covet ... these things."[2] To live in such a manner is to be constantly living and dying. One lives fully, yet dies to all things.

There is something here of the old Taoist view of the rhythmic harmony (*ch'i-yun*) of opposites, as well as the notion later taken up in the Zen art of spontaneity, immediacy and naturalness (*i-p'in*). Life and death, as Chuang-tzu taught, are not separate states of being that can be isolated from one another, but two aspects of the same process. The way (*tao*) therefore is that of flowing with the Tao, which is light and dark, life and death, each requiring and interpenetrating the other. Life and death are not great cosmic forces that confront one another in a pitched battle, like God and Satan or Ohrmazd and Ahriman. Existence is not necessarily a quarrel or titanic conflict, any more than nature is simply "red in tooth and claw." Life flows, as rivers flow, sometimes lazily in the summer sun, sometimes like a raging torrent; sometimes predictably and sometimes unpredictably; sometimes fertilizing, sometimes eroding; sometimes building up and sometimes destroying; but not at war with anything or anyone.

We are often deceived by our metaphors. Existence might as justifiably, and perhaps more justifiably, be seen in terms of the metaphors of play and contest—an interplay of forces, a competition, a structured game, a spontaneous dance—as in terms of the warrior metaphors of struggle and strife; adversary and enemy, hatred and enmity.

Meeting, they laugh and laugh—
The forest grove, the many
fallen leaves.
—Zenrin Kushu[3]

Are the fallen leaves "felled" in the "onslaught" of an "advancing march" of winter? Or are such the metaphors of *maya*? Meisetsu seems closer to an understanding of the interrelationship of life and death:

Butterflies
love and follow this flower
*   wreath—*
that on the coffin lies.[4]

Like classical Taoism, Zen has a surprisingly positive attitude toward time, and the transiency and ephemerality of things—especially considering the more characteristic Buddhist preachings on perishability and impermanence. As D. T. Suzuki insisted, "Zen is right in the midst of the ocean of becoming; it shows no desire to escape from its tossing waves."[5] Just because things are constantly changing, breaking, dissolving, decaying and dying does not mean that they are to be despised or shunned in favor of things judged to be eternal and immutable. Plum blossoms and cherry blossoms, as the Japanese appreciate almost to the point of a national passion, are beautiful despite the fact, and in a sense because of the fact, that their beauty is so fragile and brief. Thus Kenko could write: "If man were never to fade away like the dews of Adashino, never to vanish like the smoke over Toribeyama, but lingered on forever in the world, how things would lose their power to move us! The most precious thing in life is its uncertainty."[6]

Time cannot be measured by the yardstick of an imagined eternity, or perishability by the concept of imperishability. The beauty of time is that it is so much like time. The beauty of change is that it is so changeable. If one judges an old, cracked, misshapen *raku* tea bowl, with its irregular coloration and happenstance configurations, by the standards of finely detailed and lacquered porcelain, it is ugly. Yet, in both Zen and Japanese aesthetics generally, it is highly prized. That which is old, worn, frayed, broken; that which is imperfect, incomplete, or unfinished; that which is off-center and asymmetrical and accidental, has a beauty all its own. And no image or form of its opposite can ever negate that beauty; if anything, it can only enhance it. So too with life and death; there is a beauty of life and a beauty of death. To see things otherwise is to be imprisoned in illusory categories, and illusory uses and confusions of categories. This also is *maya*.

Given such a standpoint, a Nirvana after which one strives by developing a distaste and disgust for this world of time and change, and by fleeing impermanence and imperfection in a restless search for some eternally fixed perfection, is a limited and limiting Nirvana. Thus Chen Lung-hsin remarked: "The *Nirvana Sutra*? This is last in line for cremation!" The Zen way is not one of turning attention away from the world of passing forms,

but of seeing them more clearly and fully. Nirvana is not some distant goal. Properly understood Nirvana is Samsara (the world of life and death); Samsara is Nirvana, just as form is emptiness and emptiness is form. "When we realize the everlasting truth of 'everything changes' and find our composure in it, we find ourselves in Nirvana" (Shunryu Suzuki).[7]

In Western theological terms, Zen advocates a "realized eschatology," and it does so on the foundation of non-dualism. There can be no absolute separation of time and eternity, life and death, Samsara and Nirvana. Nirvana is a present reality, a mode of perceiving and being in the world. It is a way of dwelling in fuller awareness within the present moment. It is a way of bestowing a devoted attention upon even the smallest and lowliest and most ephemeral particulars of daily existence.

"What is the teaching of the Buddha?" Pao-fu is asked. "Come, let us have a cup of tea!" Or Lin-chi, founder of the Rinzai sect, admonishes his disciples: "The Way (Tao) consists of no artificial effort; it only consists of doing the ordinary things without any fuss: going to the stool, making water, putting on clothes, taking a meal, sleeping when tired. Let the fools laugh at me. Only the wise know what I mean … The truly noble man is a man of no concern and no ado."

Something of this spirit and understanding is reflected in the story of the late Zen master, Taji, who lay dying. One of his disciples, recalling the fondness the roshi had for a certain cake, went in search of some in the bake shops of Tokyo. After some time he returned with the delicacy for the master, who smiled a feeble smile of appreciation, and slowly nibbled at it. As the master grew visibly weaker, his disciples asked if he had any departing words for them. Taji said, "Yes." As they drew closer, so as not to miss the faintest syllable, he said, "My, but this cake is delicious!"[8]

Notes:

1   Unless otherwise noted, the Zen materials cited may be found in my book *Zen and the Comic Spirit* (London: Rider, 1974; Philadelphia: Westminster, 1974).

2   Philip Kapleau, ed., *The Wheel of Death* (New York: Harper & Row, 1971) p. 9.

3   Alan W. Watts, *The Way of Zen* (New York: Random House, 1957), p. 147.

4   Harold G. Henderson, *An Introduction of Haiku* (New York: Doubleday, 1958), p. 183.

5   D.T. Suzuki, *Studies in Zen* (New York: Dell, 1954), p. 203.

6   Donald Keene, ed., *Essays in Idleness* (New York: Columbia Univ. Press, 1967), p. 7.

7   Shunryu Suzuki, *Zen Mind, Beginner's Mind* (New York: Weatherhill, 1970), p. 10.

8   Kapleau, *Wheel of Death*, p. 67.

Parabola
Volume: 2.1
Death

THE DIAMOND VEHICLE:

Two Conversations on Tibetan Buddhism and the West

Interview with Gomang Khen Rinpoche & Nechung Rinpoche

Although holocaust may be too large a word to describe what happened in Tibet in 1959, the near-extinction of both a people and a religious tradition is exactly what took place. Then, there were internment camps, a great many dead (80,000 killed outright), thousands more sent into exile, and, to complete the act, an ultimate symbolic defilement. The monastery of Drepung, the seat of the Dalai Lama and the central locus of the Tibetan Buddhist faith, was converted by the Chinese into a municipal city hall—a change roughly equivalent to turning St. Peter's Basilica in Rome into a train station. It was from this destruction that Gomang Khen Rinpoche and Nechung Rinpoche fled, along with 100,000 other Tibetans, lamas, and other believers.

(continued on page 291)

Interview with Robert A. F. Thurman

Robert Alexander Thurman, born in New York City and educated at Harvard, has long been immersed in the study and practice of Tibetan (Vajrayāna) Buddhism. As a senior in college he took a year's leave of absence to go to India, where he first encountered Vajrayāna in the flesh. Returning to America from this initial contact, he then spent six years of study at a Tibetan Buddhist monastery in New Jersey. Having gained a footing and eager to go further, he returned to India and was formally ordained as a Buddhist monk by the Dalai Lama.

The young monk did not take full vows, however, preferring to return once again to America and pick up his academic studies where he had left them years before, as a senior at Harvard. A Ph.D in Buddhist studies and Sanskrit was attained, along with other degrees. Thurman now teaches at Amherst College.

(continued on page 299)

(Rinpoches, from page 290)

Following this termination of Buddhism in Tibet, the Tibetans charged with the preservation of the tradition realized that to survive they would need the world's help. India offered them refuge and a place to pitch their tents, but little more—certainly no help in rebuilding structures destroyed by the Chinese. Questions about transplanting a religious tradition from one culture (for example, Tibetan) to another (in this case Indian) are usually of an intellectual nature—scholars and interpreters arguing about the inevitable new forms likely to emerge, and whether the original purity of the tradition can be preserved. For Buddhists who once lived in Tibet, there is no choice and little argument. The structures must be erected in India much as they were in Tibet, because India was quite simply the only feasible place for them to go. The Rinpoches are currently in the United States to find help in the rebuilding of their monasteries and temples.

Gomang Khen Rinpoche was born in Kham, Tibet and at the age of 13 became a monk at the Pashod Monastery, which was known for its excellent training in philosophic principles. After a lifetime of study in the five-fold Tibetan division of knowledge—Logic, Transcendental Wisdom, Middle-Way Philosophy, Metaphysics, and Ethics—the Rinpoche received the highest honor awarded in his college of monks. Following the period of

hardship after the Chinese invasion, Gomang Khen Rinpoche was appointed by the Dalai Lama as abbot of Gomang College, responsible for the training of future Buddhist monks. Now 62, he is considered a Master of Tantric Studies, but the path for him was neither short nor easy: there were 41 years of study and 10 years of exile for him before he assumed the mantle of Abbot.

Nechung Rinpoche had a different path, as he is considered the incarnate Grand Lama of the monastery which was the seat of the State Oracle of Tibet. He is accomplished in ritual arts, psychic sciences, and traditional Buddhist literature, and in addition has received the most esoteric teachings of Tibetan Buddhist faith, the "hidden treasure texts" of Vajrayāna, the receipt of which marks his full ordination in the tradition. Then too, he is one of the very few lamas who will perform the ritual of Consciousness Transference, used in assisting a dying person through the first stages of the Bardo.

The two Rinpoches were traveling through the U.S., a country which did not proved to be exactly hospitable to them. Totally unfamiliar with the rigorous path of traditional Tibetan Buddhism, many Americans seem to prefer their spiritual teachings short and sweet, the Rinpoches found. Whereas it took each of these men a half-century to reach proficiency in their disciplines, many here expect to be guided "straight to the top" in a matter of weeks—or preferably at once. The great gap between this instant approach—and the teachers or gurus who espouse it—and the more sustained effort of the will which the Rinpoches exemplify made their sojourn here somewhat perplexing to them. Their task of familiarizing Americans with Vajrayāna Buddhism was not easy, and few funds were raised here for the construction of the new monastery.

Parabola: *Tibetan Buddhist teachings speak of death as a passage, a journey. But what is the essence—the word "soul" is perhaps inadequate—which makes this passage? How might we define it?*

Rinpoches: This is a difficult question, partly because it is not easy to define the Buddhist concept of "I" completely, using English terminology. But the force which goes into and through the passage of death is the discriminating force of the substance we call *mind*. This is the force which *perceives*, the force which discriminates between what is good and bad, between happiness and suffering.

But the basic definition in Tibetan Buddhism for "mind" revolves around an understanding of what we call "clear nature," and there is an analogy I can give which might help you understand this.

The clear nature is like a clear sheet of glass, without any color. So then, the glass may be put on top of another substance and whatever the color of that substance may be, the clear nature will pick it up. If it's a blue substance then looking through the clear glass you will see blue. So the clear nature is the force which perceives the different aspects of objects, it understands everything and makes discriminations. This is what we define as the mind.

Parabola: *Does this clear nature have a particular kind of energy which is organized in a certain way, which is common to every being, or does each clear nature have an individual characterization? Do you have one that is different from mine, or are all our clear natures the same?*

Rinpoches: In one sense the clear natures of all of us here are the same, but what is different and distinct about them is the potential force that each of them possesses. The potential forces are, in Buddhist terms, the karma, the accumulation of action. Action is committed and then leaves an impression on this clear nature, as a perception. And this is the force which gives us a form into the next existence, the future.

Parabola: *Could you say that the clear force, like the DNA molecule, has a code, has a plan already in it which can be transmitted? Or would you say that it is neutral?*

Rinpoches: The basic nature is neutral, but then it picks up potential!

Parabola: *To cast the question in a different light, I wonder if you could say that there is a primordial sort of beginning, a clear state which takes on these perceptions, these karmic impressions? If this were so, could you then say that the process of enlightenment is a return to an original state or is it an advance to a state that couldn't exist if you had not gone through this development?*

Rinpoches: In your question is a slight misunderstanding about what is meant by the clear nature. There is no "beginning" which can be likened to a clear aspect of mind. I am not saying that the mind can be all pure, only that there is a part of it which can perceive everything clearly, in a clear nature. So in this lifetime we did not start out with a pure mind and then lose it. In Buddhist concept there is no beginning, everything is *beginningless*. And through this beginningless current we believe that we have had innumerable previous lives, and that the stream of mind now is the same thing which was many, many years before. And since this stream has had so many of the different forces of life go through it, it has picked up a great many delusions. Then the goal of enlightenment is this: we try to get rid of all the bad impressions in the karma we have picked up along the passage of the many deaths we have experienced.

Parabola: *But if there were good impressions, one would try very hard to retain them?*

Rinpoches: Yes, you try to retain good impressions. When these good impressions are activated they get rid of the bad impressions, the bad karma: delusions.

Parabola: *If the process reaches a climax at the time of death, in leaving one lifetime behind, how does a lama help at this time, in the moments of death?*

Rinpoches: Whether or not a dying person has a peaceful death or not in general depends on his own karma. But if there is a karmic relationship between the lama and the dying person, and if the lama has received the oral transmission, the teachings of the lineage—the meditation on the transference of consciousness—then the lama will go and see this dying person. As soon as the person has externally stopped breathing, the lama will perform the meditation, to send the stream of mind which we spoke of earlier to a more favorable circumstance, an existence in one of the Buddha-fields, or else back to a human rebirth.

Parabola: *If the clear mind is able to receive an impression and hold it, is this moment of death a particularly important impression?*

Rinpoches: Yes, this moment of death has a great influence on the taking of rebirth in the future. It is not only the moment of death, it is the moment before the next life. So that if a dying person is able to have the guidance of a lama, all his previous virtues will be more powerful because they will be strengthened in this moment. Therefore he will take a better rebirth.

Parabola: *If the lama can help, what can hinder a person at the moment of death?*

Rinpoches: The person's own delusions are the forces which act as interruptions in this passage.

Parabola: *Is it possible to say that one can determine purposefully, by an act of the will, the nature of one's passage into death or one's future incarnation? In Buddhist concepts how much of a role does the will play in determining the passage and rebirth?*

Rinpoches: There are many people who can purposefully determine incarnations, but these are the meditators, the people who practice very deeply and intensely. They achieve a certain level of attainment and with it the power to determine their death and the rebirth they will take. In the traditions of Tibetan Buddhism, this is thought of as a selfless purpose, because the aim of what is called "purposeful incarnation" is to better spread the dharma, to eliminate the suffering of other sentient beings.

Parabola: *In the light of Tibetan Buddhist teachings, what is the importance of repentance at the moment of death? Does the Christian model of repentance—the thief who was crucified along with Jesus, forgiven by Him because he repented—have any resemblance to the Buddhist notion of forgiveness at the moment of death?*

Rinpoches: The force of repentance is important throughout life, not only at the moment of death. In the practice of Tibetan Buddhism, repentance certainly makes non-virtuous actions very much lighter, but it does not abolish them totally. This I would say is the principal difference: for repentance to be complete, it must be wedded to daily practices, with the three other components of daily practice of Buddhism. Repentance by itself does not destroy all the roots of bad actions. It seems that a practicing Christian can say to someone "I am remorseful," and repent. And then somebody else has the power to say "That's all right, it has been forgiven."

Parabola: *To return once again to questions relating to the nature of death and dying, I wonder if you could venture a definition of the precise moment of death. This is a question which has become quite snarled in the United States at the moment, with the civil authorities, the courts, medical doctors and spiritual leaders all venturing conflicting opinions.*

Rinpoches: I have heard this question asked quite frequently while I have been in this country. Here it seems, in most cases, that when someone dies in hospital, as soon as he stops breathing and the heart no longer registers a beat the person is considered dead. This is not how it is in Tibetan Buddhism.

Whether a person dies suddenly or whether the process of dying is slow, we have a different signal which indicates the moment when consciousness leaves the body. The dissolving of the four basic elements must occur before we consider a person to be "dead." The elements of water, air, fire and earth must dissolve into one another, and only then does the conscious mind stream leave the body. Speaking in a general way, when the mind-stream leaves the body there are physical signs. A person will bleed from one of the nostrils or there will be a white liquid which will come from the person's sexual organs. At that time only do we say that there is no longer any mind or energy in the person's system.

Parabola: *How long might that be from the time the person stops breathing?*

Rinpoches: Anywhere from a few minutes to seven days. With many lamas who have attained a high level of spiritual mastery, there has been a period where they rested in what we call "death meditation." There was recently a lama in India, who, after he had stopped breathing, held his posture in the meditation position for over a month. When the consciousness left his body, his head was seen to drop and blood came from his nostril and only at that time did we consider him to be dead. His body had remained fresh until then too, and only afterward had it begun to decay.

Parabola: *It's fairly common practice that as soon as death seems to have occurred, people want to move the body away to start processing it for burial. Is that harmful to the person who has so recently died—to be removed so quickly?*

Rinpoches: It is considered a highly non-virtuous action in the practice of Tibetan Buddhism to disturb the dying person like this—it gives him a great deal of fright and frustration. All of his senses have stopped functioning. If a person wants to communicate something, but has no power to do so, it causes a great deal of disturbance. Therefore it is considered extremely harmful and non-virtuous.

Parabola: *Is it harmful for doctors to try and maintain life by sustaining people on respirators and artificial heart-support machinery?*

Rinpoches: I feel this is harmful. When it comes to the point where a person stops breathing, completely, and there is not much hope that the person will live, then it's disturbing him in his passage, not helping him. Many Tibetans feel that when there is no hope for life, they would rather be removed from a hospital, to go home. In a hospital, you know, as soon as the person stops breathing immediately the body is thrown into a separate room, where they keep the corpses. This is something that would disturb a Tibetan greatly.

I wonder if I might ask you another question which, as Westerners, you might be in a better position to answer. Do you personally believe that with the development of medical science and technology that they will sooner or later be able to develop immortality?

Parabola: *The body living forever? Well, there are people who might think that way, but it's not really a serious aim or a goal. Scientists do study the ways in which cells degenerate, and they do recycle organs, but really so far only to learn more about how the human body functions. Immortality is not the goal.*

Rinpoches: If doctors hope they can achieve this sort of immortal life, what do your Christian theologians say?

Parabola: *Most Christian theologians would say that it is an aberration, that it should not be done. You attain perfection only with resurrection after death. And the attempt to prolong life indefinitely shows in a way, that you value the material world in a disproportionate fashion.*

But along similar lines, could you say that if a person has had vital organs transplanted from the body of another

person, a new heart, a new lung, new eyes, would that have any influence on reincarnation?

Rinpoches: No, a heart transplant, a lung transplant have no effect, no impact on the mind. When the person dies, the whole body is abandoned and the mind travels independent of the form, the body. And it has to reincarnate by itself. Right now, I eat my food using a set of false teeth, but it does not change my thinking at all.

Parabola: *There's an American medical doctor named Elisabeth Kübler-Ross who's done a great deal of work with people who are dying or about to die. Dr. Ross has also done research among patients who were considered dead, clinically, and were brought back to life through medical technology. Some very similar experiences emerged in what these people reported. Many of these people said they had a definite sensation of consciousness leaving their bodies; they reported having seen a very bright kind of light; that they saw a hand being extended to them and that the hand belonged to a loved one, or someone who had a great influence over them; that they experienced going up to a high place and being aware of what was going on below, on earth. Since these experiences occurred after these people had "died," I wonder how you might interpret them? How might Tibetan Buddhist teachings shed light on them?*

Rinpoches: These experiences that you relate do not surprise me. In Tibet there are a great many people who have returned after having been in an intermediary state of rebirth, or *Bardo*. They've returned into their own bodies and have reported similar experiences: consciousness has left the form, they have seen their relatives in their consciousness and tried to communicate with them and the relatives do not respond and the people experiencing this are frustrated, and they go through the preliminary stages of the *Bardo* and then return to their own forms. We have had very similar stories related in Tibet to what your medical doctors report in their research.

But sometimes when a person dies, as I said before, the element of air dissolves. With so many of the arteries collapsing in the channels where air is supposed to flow, sometimes the person gets extremely vivid experiences of traveling to another place, of intensely experiencing a part of their karma. And when life is restored back into the body again, they tell of these things. But this is only caused by the element of air leaving. It's an illusion, not a real experience of the *Bardo*, the death passage. The air has simply traveled in the wrong channel. Chemical things then happen in the body, and the whole experience is rather on the level of a dream.

Parabola: *Many people in the West who practice or follow the Tibetan form of Buddhism say that its traditional forms are threatened now that Tibet has been invaded by anti-religious red Chinese forces and proper monasteries have not been built elsewhere. Is this impression wrong? Is there a threat to the preservation and survival of Tibetan Buddhism?*

Rinpoches: Your impression is correct—the situation is difficult as well as desperate. The Tibetan tradition is one of the authentic forms of Buddhism in the world today, and this tradition has been preserved in a highly concentrated way in Tibet until the Communists invaded in 1959. Now of course there is no hope for Buddhism to ever return to Tibet. So the handful of people, practitioners and people trained in the teachings, the oral traditions, and the techniques of Tibetan Buddhism are trying to do their best under very difficult conditions now in India. In fact, the difficulty for a tradition to come from a center where it has developed over a period of a thousand years into a new and in many ways a hostile environment, should be self-evident to any intelligent person.

Parabola: *What does Tibetan Buddhism have to offer the world now? Are there prophecies or oracles in the tradition concerning dangers we all face at the present moment?*

Rinpoches: Materialism has taken over most of the surface of the world today, and most peoples have lost that kind of precise balance between spiritualism and materialism which sustains beneficial living. This much should again be obvious to any intelligent person; what Tibetan Buddhism can offer, especially to the West, is a definite means of achieving an equilibrium, by preserving and practicing the traditions. And the means of achieving this goal is adaptable and flexible—the forms of Tibetan Buddhism can adapt themselves wherever they take root.

Happiness is the goal of Tibetan Buddhism, and that is what we all would like—animals and insects included! Whoever has any life is included in the benefits that a knowledge of Tibetan Buddhism can bring, it is by no means limited to Tibetans, or Indians, or anyone else for that matter.

Parabola: *We'd like to understand what happened in Tibet in 1959. We know that there was some historical reason for the conflict which erupted then with the Chinese. But is there some way to understand the rupture in terms of karmic law? It might sound strange, but can a karmic cause be said to have originated in Tibet itself, through some sort of wrong action or thought?*

Rinpoches: There is no denial that the conflict was the result of a karmic consequence. But the circumstances in which these karmic results were brought to Tibet were unjustified. The atrocity, the total destruction of the faith and of the people who held it is not the way it should have happened.

Parabola: *Are you saying that there was indeed a need for reform?*

Rinpoches: There was need for reform and need for change. But the way they did it … to take away the total freedom of the people …

Parabola: *But the change should have come through a restoration of the Tibetan traditions?*

Rinpoches: Yes, we should have been allowed to do it for ourselves.

Parabola: *Just this past month (September 1976) The New York Times published a series of articles which talked about Tibet today. The series also spoke of pre-1959 Tibet, describing it as a feudal state where thousands of peasants struggled under the worst sort of conditions in order to support a handful of monks who might then live in luxury. Now, we are aware that this is a very biased view of the situation that existed then, a very materialistic point of view. But how did the peasants see themselves then—would the poorest of laborers have thought of himself as being oppressed?*

Rinpoches: No, and I am glad that you are aware of the bias in articles like the one contained in *The New York Times* series. This point of view is highly influenced by Communist hands. While it is true that the peasants in pre-1959 Tibet had to work extremely hard to support the monastery, this work was done on purely volunteer basis. The peasants pursued this labor because they felt that it was an honor to do it. It was a form of practice for them, an accumulation of merit to be able to serve the monastic community. So people did have to work hard, but they did not mind doing it. They also had their freedom.

Now, of course, there is no such thing as freedom in Tibet. Some of the peasants who remained behind, who are still in Tibet, complain bitterly about the Communist rule, and say that, if anything, the Communists have worsened their situation. So even from the materialist point of view, things are worse now in Tibet than they were.

I know the reality and the conditions of Tibet, then and now. I remained there for years after the Communists invaded and tried to work under their rule. I was put into a Chinese Communist prison camp for another three years. You must be reminded that all the claims they make for Tibet today are mere propaganda. The Tibetan people, after the Chinese invasion, simply lost their identity.

(Thurman, from page 290)

This remarkable combination of initiation and academic study has made Thurman unique as a teacher and interpreter of Vajrayāna. Able to conceptualize freely and adventurously, he seems to weigh each of his theoretical flights with the hard knowledge that only the true practitioner may gain.

Thurman is personally committed to the idea of developing an alternative approach to the teaching of Tibetan and other forms of Buddhism, a middle road between the academic and religious ways of knowing. At The American Institute of Buddhist Studies, Thurman and others are preparing just such a program, hoping to transfer it to the setting of a larger University structure.

Parabola: *What do you think, Mr. Thurman, about the Tibetan attitude towards death having some effect on our Western attitude? Do you think there's any hope for us in the West of changing our way of looking at death as being the last enemy, the final disaster?*

Robert Thurman: I certainly hope so. I can't give a valid sociological opinion but I can say that my own confrontation with Tibetan Buddhism certainly changed my attitude toward death. In the ideology of scientific materialism, the notion that there is no mind apart from the brain, or no psyche apart from the body, or that the psyche is an evolute of matter, naturally makes death the most terrifying thing of all. If all we are is a body, when the body stops, we're finished. Curiously enough, this "modern" notion of ours is also a very ancient notion as well. There were a group of philosophers in ancient India who held these views in opposition to the Buddha. Buddhism countered that view successfully then, and I think it will counter it wherever it finds it now.

Parabola: *Could you perhaps help us by clarifying what the lamas told us in answer to our question about what leaves the body at death and what is reborn in another body? And what is the essence that escapes death and rebirth?*

Thurman: Basically Buddhists speak of the mind, or what could be called the continuum of the consciousness, and in the simplest terms it is this which discards the physical body and takes on another physical embodiment in the next life after a transitional period. Buddhism teaches that the human being is composed of what are called the five aggregates. These aggregates may be called the aggregate of matter, the aggregate of sensations, the aggregate of ideation, the aggregate of volitions, and the aggregate of consciousness. You notice that the four aggregates from sensations to consciousness are non-physical and only the aggregate of matter is physical. The Buddhist teachings say that those four are not discontinued

at death, but simply separate from one particular form of the material aggregate and become ensconced in a new material aggregate after a period varying from some weeks to some moments.

Parabola: *Would the non-physical aggregates correspond to our Christian notion of soul?*

Thurman: Yes, certainly it does correspond to the Christian notion of soul. A difference however, is that the Tibetan or the Buddhist notion of mind is a notion of a non-physical process that constantly changes. Just like water flowing in a channel, the mind is described as a process that has a definite continuity, but as in the example of water, you can't say that the same water is in one or another part of the channel. So the mind is perceived as an impermanent changing process, and not as a fixed entity that travels through a medium. The Western notion of soul, then—along with the Hindu notion of *atman* or self which the Buddha took issue with in India when he brought the doctrine of non-self—is tied to the concept of a fixed entity. This concept Buddhism does not share. Let's say that Buddhism is critical of the notion of fixed self. Therefore, they don't entertain the notion of an immortal soul in the same way a Christian would.

Parabola: *I think it's right here that we run into the biggest difficulty for West-*

erners. How, for instance, can someone speaking for Buddhism say that this is a process that travels on, as you say—or as it has been described, as one billiard ball hitting another or one candle flame lighting another—and yet be able to turn to a person dying and say, "You are going to," etc.?

Thurman: I mentioned that the Buddhists had a similar difficulty talking to their contemporaries. They had to defend themselves against arguments like: if there is no fixed soul, no basic register, how can you say that karma has any coherence? How can you say there is any continuity? There are volumes and volumes of philosophical literature on the subject. One of the most effective metaphors that I've found is that of fire. A fire burns across a field. Is the fire that reaches one end of the field the same fire that was at the other end?

If you answered that it was the same, that answer could be criticized, pointing out that its fuel was different, that its location was different. And conversely, if you said it was different, it could be criticized by pointing out that it was the same fire from the point of view of the forest rangers who were fighting it and so on. Either attitude, in other words, if taken up as a dogmatic position, becomes vulnerable from the other point of view. So it is with the question of continuity versus fixed entity. It's neither the same nor different, if one has to come up with a dogmatic formula. But if a

person asks why he should be responsible for his actions or to a future life if it is just a continuum and not "me," the response to that objection has always been, traditionally, "what is it that you think is continuing from yesterday to today?" This is, perhaps, unintelligible to us at first. We think, well, we have a solid body; but if we think in biological terms of the cellular changes that are involved, the atoms that constantly change, we are really quite hard pressed to say that this body is the same one it was an hour ago or a week ago. Because of the relative stability of the material aggregate we can feel that we have a certain continuum. Our real wonderment about how the future life continuum can take place, the Buddhists tell us, is based on an overly comfortable notion of our present continuity.

Parabola: *There is another question which interests us very much. What part does spiritual love have in Buddhism? Compassion, the Bodhisattva ideal of compassion is known, but this seems to be more the part of love that goes out to other people. What part does the love for the inner life have, which seems to me the essential religious feeling? How does love for one's inner self, love for one's soul—which is what I think Christians probably mean when they talk about love of God—how does that come into Buddhism?*

Thurman: I would like just to say a quick thing about how Buddhism distinguishes between love and compassion. Love takes other sentient beings and oneself as its object and wishes for them and for oneself to be happy, truly happy in a real and permanent sense. Compassion has the opposite mode of wishing them not to suffer. It's a kind of wish to take upon oneself whatever suffering others have and alleviate it so that they may be freed of suffering and the cause of suffering. The other is trying to take in and take away suffering. In relation to love of God, if you define that in a more, say, Johannine manner, where you also say that God is love, then what you mean is a mode of existence as pure love.

Parabola: *How can the Tibetan teachings, or the ideas behind them, instruct us in the West about how to be in the face of death—either our own or that of others? The* Tibetan Book of the Dead *makes it rather clear what our concrete responsibilities are, but goodness knows they are very far from the way we generally behave and even think it right to behave. This is something we would like to have you comment on.*

Thurman: Let me say first that we tend to think of these ideas ethnically as Tibetan, and I think that will get us into intellectual problems when we approach the subject. We have to realize that Tibet is primarily the cradle of an ancient culture from India that

was lost to the rest of the world during the second millennium through the effects of materialism, the Islamic conquests all over Asia, the Christian conquests, and finally the French and British conquests. It's been a rather dark era from the spiritual point of view. But Tibet was a place where this culture was preserved, hidden away from the ravages of invasions, library burnings and so on, that took place in India and in other places. So what we can get of value from Tibet has to do with recovering something of our own heritage from the first days of the great civilizations both in the Mediterranean and Asia. That having been said, I can comfortably use the word Tibetan. From the Tibetan Buddhist teachings, what we can obtain of value about death has to do with a better analysis of the way in which our present ideologies form our attitudes towards death. Of course, the most significant one I'm referring to here is materialism—the one that makes death into such a tremendous problem for us. The Tibetan teachings can help us to analyze what it is in our make-up that causes us to have this false attitude and how we can rise above it. They have a deep understanding of the interconnection between ideology and attitude which we could well make use of. That's the first thing. There are a number of other matters that the lamas have pointed to quite adequately: for example, that we should learn to be more calm around the dead person, not to consider the death a tragedy. Our main responsibility is not to create anxiety in the consciousness of the dead person—who is said to be still in the area. Of course, they stress that the person's previous knowledge and self-control is of main importance; we can only really be a subsidiary help, and the dying person's own mental state is most significant. The root of our ability to behave in the way that is recommended, however, comes from our attitudes. Naturally one will be calm, even cheerful if one doesn't consider that the person has had the worst possible thing happen to him that ever could happen, but rather that some natural part of the process has occurred and that it might be a very good transition. Certainly we should try to think about it that way. If our attitude is not based on the erroneous notion of the pre-eminence of matter, then automatically we will take the proper behavioral paths, as will the dying person, for that matter. So, the main contribution of this culture is not in some gimmick or some rite or some procedure that we can enact. It has to do with the kind of critical analysis and reflection on our own ideological make-up that will enable us to see fundamental errors in our attitudes.

Parabola: *Speaking materially for the moment, in the West we think a person is dead when the heart stops beating or the breathing has stopped, whereas we learn from the Rinpoches that Tibetan*

Buddhists have a completely different notion of the moment of death. They say it is when blood flows from a nostril or when a fluid comes from the sexual organs, and this can happen as long as weeks after the body has stopped breathing, the heart has stopped beating.

Thurman: It can be. The rule of thumb is that an extremely good person or an extremely bad person—like a demon—departs immediately with cessation of breath. They're gone into some new experiential realm. The normal, middle range of people, neither that good nor that bad, tend to hang around a while, because they're attached to the area psychically. They think they are still there, but they can't communicate with other people, and they experience great frustration and distress. They don't understand what is happening to them. This is very vividly described in the *Book of the Dead*.

Parabola: *Are you familiar with the Kübler-Ross and Moody research on life after death?*

Thurman: Yes, a little bit.

Parabola: *The Rinpoches seemed to indicate that the experience of the individuals described by Kübler-Ross was an experience of dream consciousness, not an experience of death. Though they had stopped breathing and their hearts had stopped, they were not dead, but* *only dreaming when they reported an archetypal ...*

Thurman: Let me make one important point clear. There is no experience of death in Tibetan Buddhism. It is technically not possible. In Tibetan language or Sanskrit, life and death are not contrasted as a pair of opposites. Birth and death are a pair of opposites linguistically. In Buddhist cultures, Chinese, Sanskrit, Tibetan, birth and death are the opposition. Birth and death together make *life*, for which there are words like vitality, life-force. But what we mean when we talk about life—the joy of life—we mean what they would call the birth-and-death cycle. Therefore, death is simply an arbitrary line drawn by us. In the life process of a plant, for instance, when is this a seed, when is this a sprout? It's a flowing process that has no dividing line in its own nature. The line is our own construct. So that even when you are dying, any experience that you have, if it's previous to a certain moment of being identified with the functioning of your physical senses, then you could say that this is in the continuum of your former material aggregate. If the four aggregates that I mentioned—feeling, ideation, will, and consciousness—if they no longer have the avenues of the senses of that previous body, they still experience. But they are not experiencing death, they are experiencing the *Bardo* in the Tibetan way of seeing, which is

a kind of dream experience. So to say that those people cited by Kübler-Ross who died and were resuscitated had experienced *death* is a linguistic impossibility for the *Rinpoches*. You don't talk about experiencing death, you talk about experiencing the death/birth transitional state which is a dream-like state.

Parabola: *Thank you. I think that really clarifies it. When a person is dying, is there a certain effort they must make? In the* Tibetan Book of the Dead, *the dying person is being adjured all the time to look at one light as opposed to another, and so on. How is that effort understood, that effort to die well?*

Thurman: A point that is stressed very strongly in the *Book of the Dead* is the importance of a person having made efforts during his lifetime so that at the time of death he already has a certain skill in controlling himself. What is needed at that moment is self-control to the highest degree. The great danger in the *Bardo* state, of course, is not the *Bardo* state itself, but the danger of getting dragged into the wrong type of next life. That's the tremendous danger. What people in those cultures fear, therefore, and I would say people in the West also fear, is not death. Nobody fears death, I take it; they fear what possibly might happen subsequently. We certainly could say unequivocally that in the Buddhist cultures it is hell, or the *Preta Loka* or the animal realm, or even an inferior form of human existence that is really the cause of terror to the person who faces death. It's not the death process itself. The point is that they need to have a strong self-control so that their desire will not allow them to be attracted to one of these inferior states of existence, so that their fear or terror or hatred will not cause them to take refuge somewhere without examining where they're going and then end up in the womb of a pig, let's say. Or perhaps in the hell realm. So the effort has to do with self-control and seeing through the surface appearance of things, not being attracted somewhere undesirable. Now, as they say in the *Book of the Dead*, this is something one can do much better beforehand. Death becomes, then, a most powerful motive for self-cultivation in the Buddhist tradition because once you're at the crisis point—it's like being in a dream—once you're dreaming, and things are so fluid and changeable, and you're so unstable—it's very hard to begin at that time to make an effort at something. If you've already developed a way of not identifying with your emotions, not identifying with your hatred, not identifying with your attachments, then you can go through the kind of psychic upheaval that occurs in the *Bardo* remaining calm and concentrating on a positive result for yourself and for others. The worst thing is to go out in a state of wrath or terror and that should be avoided at all costs. There

are Buddhist laymen's prayers not to die violently, to die peacefully when they are composed and concentrated. However, even if such a misfortune should take place, if they have either (1) attained a stage of a certain type of mastery where they haven't gotten angry dying in a violent situation or (2) they have a certain cultivation of religious concentration such as devotionalism, that kind of death will not be so disastrous. If one has a deep faith in any symbol, such as the Buddha or Bodhisattva or a deity of some kind, then that concentration is something that is always going on in your mind. You may have heard of Tibetans that go around mumbling *om mani padme hum*. They have a visualization that there is a wheel turning in their heart which is a wheel of these syllables and that this wheel is turning in a constant prayer of compassion that all sentient beings, including themselves, don't go to hell or other bad places. If they have this kind of practice going on, this would save them in a somewhat artificial way. It's not like real mastery, but it's the kind of prop that will genuinely help them. It's like a homing beacon for the mind towards something positive and a way to avoid being dragged into the terrors of all the dream-like experiences. So there are two possibilities, self-mastery or some sort of symbolic focus for one's concentration that can save one from the disaster of a violent death. And first of all, of course, one will pray not to die violently.

Parabola: *Well, the Christians also.*

Thurman: Of course, these things are very similar.

Parabola: *One would then avoid battles?*

Thurman: Absolutely. There is no rationalization in Buddhism. I don't mean that there haven't been wars in Buddhist cultures, although a good thing about Buddhism is that there has never been, for instance, a holy war in its name. There is philosophically no way in which fighting is justified in Buddhism.

Parabola: *This is an instance, then, of death instructing life. To avoid a violent death, one would necessarily be a pacifist or pacific in one's thought and actions.*

Thurman: Yes, but that's a complicated question. In the former-life stories of the Buddha of which there is a vast literature—moral tales couched in terms of the former lives of the Buddha before he became a Buddha—he actually does kill during those lives when it's a question of saving more lives. If he knows, for example, that someone is going to kill 500 people, he then actually will kill that one person. He tries not to, but if he has to he will to save the 500. But he does it with a mind of compassion for the 500 people and even a mind of compassion for the person who is killed. If a tiger leaps on the Buddha, he knows the pain will be there and

then it's gone and he hasn't gotten into a violent conflict with the tiger. He prays that in the future he may feed the tiger with the doctrine, with enlightenment, now that he feeds it with his body, and boom, next life. He has a confidence that because of that detachment the next life will be better for him, you see. And this sounds strange to us unless we can really realize that to those who see the karmic nexus of former and future life it is not just an abstract theory. To them, it's just like you and me seeing this floor and feeling we could walk across it anytime. Just as we have no doubt the floor is there, they have no doubt former and future life is there, and therefore they can actually act with the confidence that they can put their foot down and it will be there. It's a kind of pragmatic thing, and not an abstruse thing they arrive at.

Parabola: *We are speaking about being reborn in a better or worse way. What, then, is the relation between different forms of life? Are there lower and higher forms? Is it bad karma to be reborn as an animal?*

Thurman: Yes, in Buddhist thinking, it is.

Parabola: *In the stories of the Buddha's past lives, wasn't he sometimes reincarnated as an animal?*

Thurman: Yes, but in his case it was a voluntary act, and that makes a critical difference. According to the Buddhist notion, there are what are called the six realms. The lowest and worst is hell, and there are many different forms of hell. It's like Dante, very elaborate: the sixteen hot hells, the sixteen cold hells, and others. There are long descriptions that are absolutely gruesome. Anyone with any sensitivity and imagination, even a convinced materialist, will genuinely feel terror reading those descriptions. The hell realms are where one is dragged if one is embroiled in anger and hatred. Total embroilment in desire or greed leads to the *Preta Loka*, one step up, which parallels the Christian notion of limbo. Sometimes this realm is translated as the realm of the "hungry ghosts" or disembodied spirits. The life there is a kind of Tantalus existence of thirst, hunger, insatiability and so on. One is attracted to the animal realm through embroilment in stupidity and ignorance. These three together constitute the three root poisons, or afflictions—desire or greed, hatred and ignorance. Then comes the human realm, with the realms of the Titans and finally the innumerable heavenly realms above. Curiously enough, however, the human realm is considered to be the best level of all. The Titans have too much power and too much easy pleasure to think about developing themselves. They have very light bodies, some of them pure mental bodies, and they experience very few difficulties. But then,

one day, their existence comes to an end, and they're in the *Bardo* again with no idea of where they are going to go. They have never developed any self control.

Parabola: *Are they like the angels?*

Thurman: Some of them are like angels, but there are many types—some are formless, energy-filled beings, others complete beings who live in a very blissful place. They tend to take things for granted, however, and when they die they suffer a great deal. So the human realm is the best, the Buddhists say, because it provides the right mixture of pleasure and pain to cause one to be able to develop freedom of will—to be close enough to the fear, terror and problems of existence to have a motivation to do that. They have a concept of the human body being a precious jewel, and it's something they take very seriously.

Parabola: *How can one person affect or help another person's karma?*

Thurman: He can help by giving you an example of the spiritual life, for instance; or by giving good advice, explaining what is right and what is wrong. But what really helps others is that which is based on compassion; in other words, your sensitivity to the feelings and needs of others to whatever degree. Obviously empathy to the highest degree is a staggering concept: to really take on the feeling of others. Supposedly that is exactly what a Buddha or someone who perfects great compassion does—he actually feels other sentient beings' feelings so he knows exactly where it hurts and what to do about it. It's hard for us ordinary people to know whether or not we're helping; the thing that we have to rely on and try to cultivate is our empathetic sensitivity to others' needs and then our help will be better and better. Does that help?

Parabola: *Yes, very much. Can you also tell us what is meant by afflictions in connection with karma?*

Thurman: You remember we spoke about the three root poisons, or afflictions: ignorance, or non-knowledge, really, which is the most important one, hatred and greed. Hatred and greed are really two reflexes of the same thing—both are based on the root poison of ignorance. That which creates the world is the interplay of one's continuing ignorance, hatred and greed with the karma one has accumulated in the past, in the events that happened to one. So, if karma is the external element, afflictions are the internal elements. Karma means causality, and includes all circumstances. The word comes from the root *ker*, meaning to do, or to work, or to make. So karma means doing or working or making, nothing more mysterious than that.

Ignorance is considered the root of it, but not the kind of ignorance as being ignorant of what's inside that file, a failure to know some discrete piece of information. The kind of ignorance that is spoken of as being the root of karma is actually knowledge—the false notion that I hold of myself, the idea that I really am what I think I am, that I am really this self against the world, that there is a subject-object duality. When this is held as a dogmatic ideology then all is ignorance and the cause of all the trouble. If you don't identify with yourself, you see, you can't desire to be a millionaire and go off on the greed path; you can't desire revenge and go off on a hatred path. You cannot feel that someone has wronged you if you don't identify first of all with "I"—with what we call "I," the pronoun, I and mine with notions of self and property. That is the fundamental ignorance, the ignorance inherent in the notion of self. Therefore they say that if you can get rid of ignorance through a cultivated critical awareness of these conditions and these notions that drive us, then you attain enlightenment. That's what it means to become enlightened: to become free of the whole causal network.

Parabola: *Something that strikes people here in the West about Tibetan Buddhism is that there seem to be so many different sects and our impression is that they aren't always on the best of terms* *with one another. One tends to wonder what is wrong.*

Thurman: The reasons for that lie in a long story of Central Asian history and have to do with the collapse of the royal dynasty in Tibet towards the end of the first millennium. At that time political power became vested in the different religious factions and created a perfect example of the mixture of the church and state from that time on. Long before the present theocracy of the Dalai Lama, different groups began to vie for political power. The Buddhist institutions, therefore, became a forum for people whose interest was not religious, with predictable results. But in spite of this, they did manage to preserve the great treasures of the teaching from India, and that is something I think not just the modern Western world, but the modern Asian world also, will in the next 50 years greatly appreciate. There are psychological techniques and scientific and artistic principles which I feel will be found to be of great value. In spite of factions and feuds, they have preserved something very significant. But sectarianism is a very unfortunate thing, it was in Tibet …

Parabola: *And it continues now in America!*

Thurman: Well, yes unfortunately, because of a certain interest in it for Americans with their fascination for the exotic. Look at Hilton's *Lost Horizons*, also Rampa's *Third Eye*, all these quaint ideas that everything about Tibet is holy. And there are some uneducated Tibetans who have this notion of themselves as the chosen people of the holy land. There is nothing in Buddhism to justify this. They might claim something unique in being the custodians of a precious cultural and philosophical heritage of mankind. Those who really understand are like the Dalai Lama himself, who doesn't climb into the cultural thing, at least not in my personal discussions with him. He even has said to me that he is very grateful for the political disaster that befell him, personally grateful, in that he now has more time to study, and the misery of it had made him more aware of the message in his own teaching.

Parabola: *We've heard it said that some of the* tulkus *who are coming to the United States and offering Americans access to these teachings are changing the forms somewhat in order to make them more accessible. Is this a corrupting influence or is it helpful or necessary?*

Thurman: Well, obviously it is inevitable at this point because of everything that has taken place. My main point here would be that we have seen an enormous number of cultural fads come in and out of the U.S. First we had swamis, then we had roshis and now we have lamas. Some of these people rely mainly on personal charisma, and many young Americans, because of a sense of alienation and many other things, tend to turn toward that sort of thing and get swept up in it. On the other hand, we have the Western educational establishment which is coming to realize that it is very important for our cultural and educational maturation to gain a better sense of Asia, to understand their culture from the inside. For that we need more linguistic training, more profound philosophical and cross-cultural work. We need real knowledge. If we put more energy into using these genuine people from these genuine traditions to teach our young people within the framework of our own liberal arts institutions where they won't get alienated from their own culture while learning about these other cultures, then we will have gained something of lasting value. It is a way between remaining closed off to it on the one hand, or on the other hand having all our young seekers running around chasing gurus. Our young people don't need encouragement to study these things, they need protection from exploitation by elements of authoritarian personalities. At the moment you can hardly find a course on Buddhist philosophy in a Western college except in specialist graduate programs. If the universities had a more open approach the young people could satisfy their personal quest while developing themselves as professionals, citizens, integrating their personal knowledge with their cultural setting so that they wouldn't go for the ethnic bag that they tend to get caught in when they go for a particular guru.

Parabola: *Mr. Thurman, don't you teach an undergraduate course in Tibetan Buddhism?*

Thurman: Right, and I am also part of a group of teachers around the country who have started the American Institute of Buddhist Studies which is working to reach the student population we can't reach in our religion and psychology departments. Our ideal is that every lawyer and doctor should be just as familiar with the real culture of China, the Buddhist thought of China and the Taoist thought of China, as they are with Plato and with France in the 18th century. Then we would have Americans who understood the world, and not just the world of European domination. What Tibetan Buddhism in particular can offer us is not magic and mystery—everybody has magic and mystery—it is their age-old academic tradition, which is quite profound. What would we give if a duplicate of the library at Alexandria was discovered buried under the sands somewhere, say some oil driller discovered it? Everybody would go nuts over the ancient Hellenic world's treasures. This is what we have found: it's not Alexandria but the library at Nalanda—the great library of Nalanda. This ancient treasure does exist in the Tibetan Buddhist teachings and it can be recovered by translation and study. It represents a very great treasure to us.

Parabola
Volume: 15.1
Time and Presence

THE EXPERIENCE OF CHANGE

Interview with His Holiness the Dalai Lama

Shortly before he was awarded the Nobel Peace Prize in 1989, His Holiness the Dalai Lama spent a few days at the Tibetan center in Washington, New Jersey, where the following interview took place. Born in northeastern Tibet, Tenzin Gyatso is the fourteenth Dalai Lama, the spiritual leader of Tibetan Buddhists worldwide. He left his native country in 1959, during the Tibetan uprising against Chinese communist rule, which was imposed in 1950. His headquarters are now in Dharamsala, India.

—Daniel Goleman

Daniel Goleman: Parabola *is trying to look at the question of time from many points of view, and we want to ask you for the Buddhist understanding of it. How can we relate our sense of the process of time to our experience of the present moment? Time passes and yet the moment seems fixed in an eternal present.*

His Holiness: In Buddhism, the concept of linear time, of time as a kind of container, is not accepted. Time itself, I think, is something quite weak—it depends on some physical basis, some specific thing. Apart from that thing it is difficult to pinpoint—to see time. Time is understood or conceived only in relation to a phenomenon or a process.

DG: *Yet the passage of time seems very concrete—the past, the present, aging. The process of time seems very real.*

HH: This business of time is a difficult subject. There are several different explanations and theories about time; there is no one explanation in Buddhism. I feel there is a difference between time and the phenomena on which time is projected. Time can be spoken of only in relation to phenomena susceptible to change, which because they are susceptible to change are transitory and impermanent. "Impermanent" means there is a process. If there is no process of change, then one cannot conceive of time in the first place.

The question is whether it is possible to imagine an independent time which is not related to any particulars, any object that goes through change. In relation to such an object, we can talk about the past of that thing, its present state, and its future; but without relation to such particulars, it is very difficult to conceive of an instant of time totally independent of a particular basis.

DG: *Can we connect what you are saying with our own experience? We experience time, we experience growth and aging, we experience that one thing leads to another.*

HH: That's right.

DG: *One thing is the cause of another thing. Now how do we explain that process of time in terms of being in the present moment? There are differences in the way each of us experiences time. Sometimes it goes very slowly, sometimes very quickly. Our sense of time seems to change with our state of consciousness. If you're fully focused—just right here, right now—then the sense of time changes. What is the relationship between the sense of time and one's own state of consciousness?*

HH: Depending on a person's spiritual maturity or realization, there could be a difference in how one sees the moment. That one could have different experiences of time is demonstrated by an ordinary fact: For instance, if two people attend a party, one person might be so absorbed in the party he would feel that time went [*snaps his fingers*] just like that! Whereas the other person who did not enjoy it very much might have felt it long, dragging, because he was thinking about when it would finish. So although both of them attended the same party, in terms of time they were different.

DG: *Let's say one's life is like that party. How can one perhaps use paying a fuller attention to the moment to expand a sense of time or to more fully enjoy the part that is one's life? Does cultivating attention play a role in this?*

HH: It does play a great role. If you have more attentiveness, if you have a fuller sense of presence, then it will make a great deal of difference in how you experience your life.

But then, you find that if you analyze time very precisely, there is no present, in the real sense of the word; only past and future, no present! The sense of present that we have is a conventional notion. Even if you employ a computer or some other instrument to divide time and analyze whether there was a present or not, you would find that there isn't. "Present" is a relative term. While in experience there seems to be nothing but the present, we actually experience only the illusion of the present.

Things are all the time moving, never fixed. So we can't find the present. This fact indicates the impermanent, dynamic nature of things, that they never remain fixed or static, they are always in the process of changing from one form to another.

DG: *But isn't it possible to be present in that movement—with attention?*

HH: Attention—yes! That's present! And present, you see, makes past and future. Without present, you can't posit future and past.

DG: *Conceptually this is very upsetting, you know; that's fine, that's okay, but … [Much laughter. His Holiness is delighted] … but now that you've upset my concepts, I've got to clarify this.*

You're saying that if you're totally present in the moment, fully attentive to the moment, the mind is attending not to a "present," but rather a future becoming a past. Is that right? That seems to follow from what you say—that in a certain state of full awareness what you see is change, simply change: the future becoming the past. Is that the case? What you are really saying is that we don't experience time at all; we experience change.

HH: Yes! My point is not to deny the existence of the present, but rather the present independent of some object that changes. If we investigate, the present is very difficult to find, but that does not mean the present does not exist. But when you talk about the concept of time, it creates confusion, because it is not based in matter. We could try to talk objectively of time as it is based in matter: anything made of matter goes through a process of change from moment to moment. Within a minute, within seconds, within one hundredth of a second, it is all the time changing. It can be spoken of only in terms of something that is subject to change. There is no independent, linear time as some kind of container.

DG: *Could we talk about that experience, then? [Laughter]*

HH: The experience of change … Yesterday I was talking to some neuroscientists about how difficult it is to say what consciousness is! On this planet there are something like five billion human beings, so there are five billion perceptions of reality. Everyone can be looking at the same object, but seeing it very differently.

DG: *The person who has the better time at the party—is it that that person is more aware of impermanence?*

HH: It hasn't so much to do with awareness of impermanence, but rather with a very instinctive nature of humans, which is that we lack contentment. When we enjoy something, we feel it has gone very fast. We are not satisfied, we want more. When we do not desire a particular experience, then that situation seems very long.

DG: *In modern life, there is a disease called "time sickness." Time sickness is the sense that there's never enough time, that time is passing too quickly. With it comes anxiety about what's going to happen. Fear and anxiety seem to be related to wanting to stop change, wanting to hold on to time. What is the cure for time sickness?*

HH: One cure is to reduce the dependence on machines! Time is moving, moving, so we feel we have to catch up ...

DG: *Catch up with the pace of technology?*

HH: I think that is the problem. But that doesn't seem practical!

DG: *If you have to live with machines, then what can you do?*

HH: Machines are okay. It is our attitude. Attitudes toward them play a great role. Generally speaking, the original idea of inventing these technologies was to serve humanity; so if you are able to retain that kind of attitude toward technology, then you will be able to command technology to do what you want, and if you find the pace of machines too fast, to stop.

DG: *To turn them off?*

HH: To change one's attitude. It is by their dependence that humans give technology the upper hand.

DG: *All of society is slave to this pace of technology, so if you're to live in society, you can't just turn it off. Is there anything you can do inside to control this anxiety?*

HH: There's a big difference one could make by changing one's attitude. Although the situation might be such that you are pressed to do something, due to your way of looking at things you might even be able to reduce that tension you would normally have otherwise. Through training of the mind, discipline of the mind, one could really reduce the anxiety that is usually associated with being pressed.

In some cases you see people who are very rushed. But they still handle the situation very slowly and very powerfully. In another case, the person remains anxious all the time, even during holidays!

DG: *It's a very big problem in modern society, an epidemic. Is there any particular remedy? What is the quality of mind a person needs to be free of it?*

HH: A lot of factors might be at play, depending on what mental attitude you have toward certain things and how you deal with it. In some people, according to the Tibetan medical system, it is due to an inner imbalance in the body that makes a person very nervous. In that case you need a treatment of the body. And in some cases the body's condition is very normal, yet the person is anxious. Each case is different and there's a different technique for overcoming it. Generally speaking, I think peace of mind plays a major role in this. Basically, the person whose mind is calm and easy, who is a giving person, has things go more easily when there's some difficulty in the situation.

DG: *Then time is manageable.*

HH: Oh, yes.

DG: *Is there a relationship between the sense of time and cultivating patience or even forgiveness? Does your sense of time have something to do with that?*

HH: There is a connection. If you are able to understand the dynamic process in the changing nature of situations, events, and things, then your tolerance and patience can offset the difficulties.

DG: *What this brings to mind is the historical urgency about the situation in Tibet, and the repression there by the Chinese. I'm struck by your ability to be so forgiving and patient. Is it because of your sense of time, of a larger historical perspective?*

HH: It does play a role in the sense that the fate of a nation is a question of generations or of centuries, not a question of months or years. And realizing that fact, you see that something that is happening now is the consequence of something that has taken place over a long period of time.

It's not so much an understanding of time, but an understanding of reality, of the forces contributing to such and such events and how they are beyond the control of the present generation. Knowing these factors plays a role in reducing the feeling of frustration.

One thing that influences my outlook is that if in any situation there is no solution, there is no point in being anxious. If the forces at work have their own momentum, and what's going on now is the product of what went before, and this generation is not in control of all those forces, then this process will continue.

DG: *So you are patient with it because of that larger perspective—you mentioned centuries, not just generations.*

HH: If there is no way out, there is no point in wasting time in worrying.

I would like to talk a little about the question of attitude in how to overcome time sickness. From a Buddhist point of view, the realization of understanding of the nature of *samsara* applies. You know, it's very bad in Tibet—an independent country occupied—there's lots of trouble and it will remain for some time. So long as the human community is also under the influence of ignorance, some sort of trouble will always be there. But there's another thing: if there is trouble, some understanding brings a benefit from it. Life becomes useful, when you confront a difficulty; it provides a kind of value for your life to have the kind of responsibility to confront it and overcome it. Whereas if you do not feel such difficulties, there's no such responsibility, no role for you to play in your life.

DG: *No meaning.*

HH: No meaning, yes. That challenge allows you to practice your ability.

Basically, the purpose of life is to serve other people, to do something of benefit for other people. From that point of view, a difficulty is really a great opportunity. I have often said that our generation of Tibetans is seeing the saddest period in all of Tibetan history. So from that angle it is, how do you say, very unfortunate; but at the same time, as bad as it is, in another sense it's a great *honor*, a great privilege, you see?—to face these times, to confront them. That is the opportunity to show the Tibetan nation's ability. So it's a great honor.

Although it's very difficult to actually find what consciousness and mind is, it is these different ways of looking at things and how it influences your experience of them that shows the elasticity of mind, of consciousness.

DG: *What I'm struck by in what you're saying is that one's perspective, one's view of things, determines how time is experienced—how one experiences change, life, and the purpose of life— whether life is empty or full. And it's not the specifics of the situation, it's how you see it. And I suppose that applies to time, too.*

HH: Yes, yes, that's good. But it does also depend on external circumstances, and how the two come together.

DG: *But if you have a view of lifetime after lifetime, of reincarnation and try-*

ing to help sentient beings, does that lead you to give more importance or less importance to the present moment?—I know, of course, that we've established the present moment doesn't exist! [Laughter.] But the English language hasn't caught up with your thinking!

HH: Of course, even if you see only one lifetime, it's the same as if you see many births, many lives. If there are many unfortunate things in your life, or if you have had a much happier life with many good opportunities, you still want one hundred years of life.

You see, the past is past, and the future is yet to come. That means the future is in your hands—the future entirely depends on the present. That realization gives you a great responsibility.

DG: *One way most people are concerned about time is how long they will live. But what about the bardo state? In the West, we think of death as a discontinuous event: you're alive and then you're dead. It seems from the Buddhist point of view that dying is a process—there's a continuity as you change from one state of existence to another.*

HH: Yes.

DG: *How long does this process take, going from this one state, life, to the other, death?*

HH: It's quite indefinite. For some people it can be as short as five minutes; I think the quickest would be within seconds. But there is quite a difference. When we talk about time now, we're talking in terms of human understanding of it. However, I think time with matter and time with consciousness, again, are entirely different. So you see, time with the rough body and time with the subtle body—it is not the same.

DG: *You mean the frame of time is different?*

HH: Yes. So for beings in the intermediate state [the bardo], from their point of view there is maybe time to do things—to evolve, to go through the process of dying and so on. But from the ordinary human point of view, it could be just a momentary instant.

DG: *You mean that within an ordinary human instant, from another point of view there's a vast amount of time?*

HH: A time which from one perspective may appear as momentary, from another perspective can appear very long.

DG: *It's like in physics, where the physical laws outside the atom differ from quantum principles within the atom. You're saying something parallel happens with time. From a human point of view, let's say time acts akin to Newto-*

nian physics, and seems very quick. But from another point of view—the subtle body, which is a consciousness not based on physical matter—it's like quantum mechanics, and the same instant can be very long. Is that so? Are there different kinds of time?

HH: Yes, that's possible. Depending on how advanced your level of mind is, your perception of time changes. Something that ordinarily appears as momentary may appear very long. And as you're dying, there can be both normal time and this expanded time. As you shift to the subtle body, time expands. Consciousness is not tied down by the physical body. For the subtle body, things can move faster than the speed of light. There are two kinds of time: physical time and inner time.

In Buddhism, there are many realms, each with its own scale of time. There are infinite universes and infinite time scales.

Contributor Profiles

Robert Aikten: A retired master of the Diamond Sangha, a Zen Buddhist society he founded in Honolulu in 1959. In 1974, he was given approval to teach by Yamada Roshi, Abbot of the Sanbo Kyodan in Kamakura, Japan, who gave him transmission as an independent master. He is the author of more than ten books on Zen Buddhism, including *Taking the Path of Zen.*

Pema Chödrön: An American Buddhist nun and the resident teacher at Gampo Abbey in Nova Scotia, the first Tibetan monastery in North America established for Westerners. She is the author of several books, including *When Things Fall Apart, Start Where You Are* and *The Wisdom of No Escape.*

Karlfried Graf von Dürckheim: (1896-1988) Trained in psychology and philosophy, von Dürckheim became a student of Zen when he was sent to Japan by the German government in 1937. After the war, he returned to Germany, where he founded the Existential-Psychological Training Center at Todtmuss-Rutte in the Black Forest. He brought a synthesis of Eastern and Western spiritual understandings and developed a practice of "Initiatory Therapy". He is the author of *Zen and Us, Hara* and *The Way of Transformation.*

Frederick Franck: Artist, sculptor, writer and the creator of the non-sectarian sanctuary, *Pacem in Terris*, in Warwick, New York, a center which is dedicated to Pope John XXIII, Albert Schweitzer and D. T. Suzuki. Frederick Franck was born in the Netherlands in 1909. He began his career as an oral surgeon and later followed artistic pursuits. Between 1958-1961, he served as a doctor on the staff of Albert Schweitzer in Africa. He is the author of over thirty books, including *The Zen of Seeing, The Awakened Eye* and *Zen Seeing Zen Drawing* and the award-winning *Pacem in Terris: A Love Story,* and he has been a Contributing Editor of *Parabola.*

Herman Hesse: (1877-1962) German poet, novelist and thinker, who became a citizen of Switzerland in 1923. He loved music and the beauty of nature, admired Goethe and was influenced by Indian and Chinese philosophy and by the work of Carl Jung. His books, which include *Siddhartha, Steppenwolf, Narcissus and Goldmund* and *The Glass Bead Game*, were suppressed in Nazi Germany but have had a great influence throughout the world. Hesse was awarded the Nobel prize for literature in 1946 "for his inspired writings which, while growing in boldness and penetration, exemplify the classical humanitarian ideals and high qualities of style."

Conrad Hyers: Professor and Chair of Religion, Gustavus Adolphus College, Saint Peter, Minnesota. He is the author of *The Comic Vision and the Christian Faith* (1981), *The Meaning of Creation* (1984) and *God Created Laughter: The Bible as Divine Comedy* (1987). He has extensively studied and interpreted the works of Mircea Eliade.

Philip Kapleau, Roshi: (1912 –2004) An American Zen teacher of Zen Buddhism in the Harada-Yasutani tradition, which is a blend of the Soto and Rinzai schools. After he was ordained by Hakuun Yasutani-Roshi in Japan, the first Westerner to become a roshi, he returned to the United States where he established the Rochester Zen Center in 1966. Author of *The Three Pillars of Zen, The Zen of Living and Dying* and *Awakening to Zen,* among others.

Thomas Merton: (1915-1968) A Trappist monk of the Cistercian Abbey of Gethsemani. He died in an accident in Thailand while attending an ecumenical council of Catholic and Buddhist monks. As a writer, he is perhaps best known for his autobiography, *The Seven Storey Mountain.* Other books include poetry, *The Strange Islands*; works on contemplation *Seeds of Contemplation, The Silent Life* and *New Seeds of Contemplation*; and journals, *The Journals of Thomas Merton* and *The Asian Journal of Thomas Merton.*

Philip Novak: The Sarlo Distinguished Professor of Philosophy and Religion at Dominican University of California in San Rafael, where he has taught for twenty-five years. He is the author of *The World's Wisdom,* a widely used anthology of the sacred texts of the world's religions; *The Vision of Nietzsche;* coauthor with Huston Smith of *Buddhism: A Concise Introduction* and editor of the current volume in the Parabola Anthology Series. He is a long-time practitioner of Vipassana meditation as taught by S. N. Goenka.

E. F. Schumacher: (1911-1977) A British economist and writer. Although he was born in Germany, he first came to Britain as a Rhodes scholar and returned there permanently before WWII. When he traveled to Burma in 1955, he developed his economic principles based on the belief that work is an important aspect of human development and that production from local resources for local use is the most appropriate economic way of life. He was founder and chairman of the Intermediate Technology Development

Group. He wrote *Roots of Economics, Small is Beautiful* and *A Guide for the Perplexed*.

William Segal: (1905-2000) Publisher, artist, writer, spiritual seeker. He met P. D. Ouspensky and G. I. Gurdjieff in the late 1940s and continued to follow the teachings of Gurdjieff throughout his life. After meeting D.T. Suzuki he spent periods of time in the main Soto and Rinzai monasteries in Japan. His paintings include many self-portraits by means of which he made a study of the inner landscape. Some of his essays, poems and interviews are collected in the book, *Opening*. His memoir, *A Voice at the Borders of Silence: The Autobiography of William Segal*, gives an overview of his life and his search.

Miranda Shaw: Assistant Professor of Religion on the faculty of the Department of Religion at the University of Richmond, Virginia. She has made a study of the theory and practice of Tantric Buddhism, especially as a path for women. She is the author of *Passionate Enlightenment, Women in Tantric Buddhism,* and *Her Waves of Bliss: Buddhist Goddesses of India, Tibet, and Nepal*.

Mary Stein: Instructor of aikido at Aikido In, in San Francisco, California. She is also a teacher, a writer and a doll maker.

Robert A. F. Thurman: Scholar, translator, author, former Tibetan Buddhist monk, founder (with Richard Gere) and Director of Tibet House in New York, a non-profit institution devoted to preserving the living culture of Tibet. He is the Jey Tsong Khapa Professor of Indo-Tibetan Buddhist Studies at Columbia University, the first endowed chair in Tibetan Buddhism studies in the United States and a widely respected proponent of Tibetan Buddhism.

Janwillem van de Wetering: A Dutch student of Zen, a novelist and an accomplished storyteller who has written accounts of his experiences at a Zen monastery in Japan in *The Empty Mirror* and at a Zen monastery in the United States in *A Glimpse of Nothingness*.

J. L. Walker: Lives and writes in hermitage in the hills of western Maryland. She is co-translator of *Grass Mountain* by Master Nan and assistant editor of *The Paintings of Xugu and Qi Baishi* by Jung Ying Tsao, and she has done Chinese ink painting in Taiwan and America. She is a practitioner in the Tibetan Drikung Kagyud tradition of Vajrayana Buddhism.

FOR FURTHER READING

General Accounts

Bhikkhu Bodhi, *The Noble Eightfold Path* (Seattle: BPS Pariyatti Editions, 1994).

Michael Carrithers, *The Buddha* (Oxford: Oxford University Press, 1983).

Edward Conze, *Buddhism: Its Essence and Development* (Birmingham, England: Windhorse Publications, repr. 2002, 1959).

Roger Corless, *The Vision of Buddhism* (New York: Paragon House, 1989).

Peter Harvey, *An Introduction to Buddhism* (Cambridge: Cambridge University Press, 1990).

Trevor Ling, *The Buddha: Buddhist Civilization in India and Ceylon* (New York: Scribner's, 1973).

Pankaj Mishra, *An End To Suffering: The Buddha in the World* (New York: Farrar, Strauss & Giroux, 2004).

Walpola Rahula, *What the Buddha Taught*, revised and expanded ed. (New York: Grove, 1962).

Richard Robinson and Willard Johnson, *The Buddhist Religion*, 4th ed. (Belmont, CA: Wadsworth Publishing Co., 1997).

Nancy Wilson Ross, *Buddhism: A Way of Life and Thought* (New York: Random House, 1981).

Bhikkhu Sangharakshita, *A Survey of Buddhism* (Glasgow: Windhorse Publications, repr. 1987, 1957).

Huston Smith and Philip Novak, *Buddhism: A Concise Introduction* (San Francisco: Harper, 2003).

The Buddha's Life

Edwin Arnold, *The Light of Asia* (Philadelphia: Altemus, 1879).

David Indrani Kalupahana, *The Way of Siddhartha: A Life of the Buddha* (Boston: Shambhala, 1982).

R. A. Mitchell, *The Buddha: His Life Retold* (N.Y.: Paragon House, 1991).

Bhikkhu Nanamoli, *The Life of the Buddha* (BPS Pariyatti Editions, first U.S. ed., 2001).

E. J. Thomas, *Life of the Buddha as Legend and History*, 3rd rev. ed. (New York: Barnes and Noble, 1952).

Scriptures: The Buddha's Discourses

The Buddha's Discourses are grouped in five large *nikayas* or collections: the *Samyutta*, the *Majjhima*, the *Digha*, the *Anguttara* and the *Khuddhaka*. For example:

Bhikkhu Bodhi, *The Connected Discourses of the Buddha*, a translation of the *Samyutta Nikaya* (London: Wisdom Publications, 2002).

An excellent brief anthology of this literature is:

Nyanatiloka Thera, *The Word of the Buddha* (Kandy, Sri Lanka: Buddhist Publication Society, 1981).

Eknath Easwaren, trans., *The Dhammapada* (Tomales Bay, CA: Nilgiri Press, 1985, 1996). Perhaps the single best known Buddhist text, the *Dhammapada* is a collection of some 400 sayings attributed to the Buddha. It is available in many translations.

A superb website for surveying all of the Buddha's discourses is accesstoinsight.org.

Other Buddhist Scriptures

Edward Conze, trans., *Buddhist Wisdom Books* (London: Allen & Unwin, 1958). This is a translation of the Heart Sutra and the Diamond Sutra, the best known scriptures in the vast Mahayana canon.

Philip Yampolsky, *The Platform Sutra of the Sixth Patriarch* (New York: Columbia University Press, 1967). An important text from the Zen Buddhist tradition.

Scripture Anthologies

E. Conze, trans. and ed., *Buddhist Scriptures* (Baltimore: Penguin Books, 1959).

William T. De Bary, ed., *The Buddhist Tradition in India, China, and Japan* (New York: Modern Library, 1969).

John Strong, ed., *The Experience of Buddhism: Sources and Interpretations* (Belmont: Dickenson, 1973).

Buddhist Philosophy

Masao Abe, *Zen and Western Thought* (Honolulu: University of Hawaii Press, 1985).

Stephen Batchelor, *Buddhism Without Beliefs* (New York: Riverhead, 1997).

_____. *Verses from the Center: A Buddhist Vision of the Sublime* (New York: Riverhead, 2000).

Steven Collins, *Selfless Persons: Imagery and Thought in Theravada Buddhism* (Cambridge: Cambridge University Press, 1982).

Edward Conze, *Buddhist Thought in India* (London: Allen and Unwin, 1962).

Mark Epstein, *Thoughts Without a Thinker: Psychotherapy from a Buddhist Perspective* (New York: Basic Books, 1995).

Bernard Faure, *Double Exposure: Cutting Across Buddhist and Western Discourses* (Stanford, CA: Stanford University Press, 2004).

Jay L. Garfield, *Empty Words: Buddhist Philosophy and Cross-Cultural Interpretation* (New York: Oxford University Press, 2002).

Anagarika Govinda, *The Psychological Attitude of Early Buddhist Philosophy* (London: Rider, 1969).

Nolan Pliny Jacobson, *Understanding Buddhism* (Carbondale, Illinois: Southern Illinois University Press, 1986).

David Kalupahana, *Nagarjuna: The Philosophy of the Middle Way* (Albany: SUNY, 1986).

_____. *A History of Buddhist Philosophy: Continuities and Discontinuities* (Honolulu: University of Hawaii Press, 1992).

D. Keown, *The Nature of Buddhist Ethics* (London: Macmillan, 1992).

David Loy, *Lack and Transcendence: The Problem of Death and Life in Psychotherapy, Existentialism and Buddhism* (Atlantic Highlands, N.J.: Humanities Press, 1996).

T. R. V. Murti, *The Central Philosophy of Buddhism* (New York: Macmillan, 1955).

Frithjof Schuon, *Treasures of Buddhism* (Bloomington, Indiana: World Wisdom Books, 1993).

Nyanaponika Thera, *The Vision of Dhamma* (York Beach, Maine: Samuel Weiser, 1986).

A. K. Warder, *Indian Buddhism* (Delhi: Motilal Banarsidas, rev. ed. 1970).

Richard Welbon, *The Buddhist Nirvana and Its Western Interpreters* (Chicago: University of Chicago Press, 1968).

Vipassana Meditation

Joseph Goldstein, *Insight Meditation: The Practice of Freedom* (Boston: Shambhala, 1994).

Henepola Gunaratana, *Mindfulness in Plain English* (London: Wisdom Publications, 1993).

William Hart, *The Art of Living: Vipassana Meditation as Taught by S. N. Goenka* (HarperSanFrancisco, 1987).

Nyanaponika Thera, *The Heart of Buddhist Meditation* (London: Rider, 1962).

Zen

Robert Aitken, *Mind of Clover: Essays on Zen Buddhist Ethics* (North Point Press, 1884).

William Barret, ed., *Zen Buddhism: Selected Writings of D. T. Suzuki* (Garden City, New York: Doubleday, 1956).

Hubert Benoit, *Zen and the Psychology of Transformation,* formerly *The Supreme Doctrine* (Rochester, Vermont: Inner Traditions International, 1990).

Carl Bielefeldt, *Dogen's Manuals of Zen Meditation* (Berkeley: University of California Press, 1988).

John Blofeld, *The Zen Teaching of Huang-Po* (New York: Grove Press, 1958).

Heinrich Dumoulin, *A History of Zen Buddhism* (Boston: Beacon Press, 1963).

Thich Nhat Hanh, *Miracle of Mindfulness: A Manual on Meditation* (Boston: Beacon Press, 1992) .

_____. *Peace Is Every Step* (New York: Bantam, 1991).

_____. *Zen Keys* (New York: Doubleday, 1995).

Philip Kapleau, *The Three Pillars of Zen* (New York: Anchor Books, 1989).

Isshu Miura and Ruth Fuller Sasaki, *Zen Dust* (New York: Harcourt, Brace & World, 1966).

Irmgard Schloegel, *Wisdom of the Zen Masters* (New York: New Directions, 1975).

Shunryu Suzuki, *Zen Mind, Beginner's Mind* (New York: John Weatherhill, 1970).

Vajrayana / Tibetan Buddhism

Walt Anderson, *Open Secrets: A Western Guide to Tibetan Buddhism* (New York: Penguin, 1979).

Lama Anagarika Govinda, *Foundations of Tibetan Mysticism* (York Beach, ME: Samuel Weiser, 1969).

Tenzin Gyatso, the 14th Dalai Lama, *The Buddhism of Tibet and the Key to the Middle Way,* Jeffrey Hopkins trans., (London: George Allen and Unwin, 1975).

_____. *The Way To Freedom* (HarperSanFrancisco, 1994)

_____. *Ethics for a New Millenium* (New York: Riverhead, 1999).

Donald S. Lopez, *Prisoners of Shangri-La: Tibetan Buddhism in the West* (Chicago: University of Chicago Press, 1998).

John Powers, *Introduction to Tibetan Buddhism* (Ithaca: Snow Lion, 1995).

Reginald Ray, *Indestructible Truth: The Living Spirituality of Tibetan Buddhism* (Boston and London: Shambhala, 2000).

Sogyal Rinpoche, *The Tibetan Book of Living and Dying* (HarperSanFrancisco, 1992).

Robert Thurman, *Inner Revolution: Life, Liberty and the Pursuit of Real Happiness* (New York: Riverhead Books, 1998).

_____. *Infinite Life: Seven Virtues for Living Well* (New York: Riverhead, 2004).

Chogyam Trungpa, *Cutting Through Spiritual Materialism* (Berkeley: Shambhala, 1973).

_____ and F. Freemantle, *The Tibetan Book of the Dead* (Boston: Shambhala, 1975).

Tsong-kha-pa, *The Great Treatise on the Stages of the Path to Enlightenment*, Vols. 1, 2 and 3, ed. J. W. C. Cutler, G. Newland et al (Ithaca: Snow Lion Press).

B. Alan Wallace, *The Bridge of Quiescence: Experiencing Tibetan Buddhist Meditation (Chicago: Open Court, 1998).*

Buddhism in the West and America

Stephen Batchelor, *The Awakening of the West: The Encounter of Buddhism and Western Culture* (Berkeley: Parallax Press, 1994).

Martin Baumann, "The Dharma Has Come West: A Survey of Recent Studies and Sources," *Journal of Buddhist Ethics* 4, 1997.

James Coleman, *The New Buddhism: The Western Transformation of an Ancient Tradition* (New York: Oxford University Press, 2001).

Rick Fields, *How the Swans Came to the Lake: A Narrative History of Buddhism in America*, 3rd ed. (Boston and London: Shambhala, 1992).

Charles Prebish, *Luminous Passage: The Practice and Study of Buddhism in America* (Berkeley: University of California Press, 1999).

C. Prebish and K. Tanaka, eds., *The Faces of Buddhism in America* (Berkeley: University of California Press, 1998).

Richard Hughes Seager, *Buddhism in America* (New York: Columbia University Press, 1999).

Women in Buddhism

Tessa Bartholomeusz, *Women Under the Bo Tree: Buddhist Nuns in Sri Lanka* (Cambridge: Cambridge University Press, 1994).

Sandy Boucher, *Turning the Wheel: American Women Creating the New Buddhism* (HarperSan-Francisco, 1988).

_____. *Opening the Lotus: A Women's Guide to Buddhism* (Boston: Beacon, 1997).

Pema Chödrön, *When Things Fall Apart* (Boston: Shambhala, 1997).

Rita Gross, *Buddhism after Patriarchy: A Feminist History, Analysis and Reconstruction of Buddhism* (Albany: SUNY Press, 1993).

Anne Klein, *Meeting the Great Bliss Queen: Buddhists, Feminists and the Art of the Self* (Boston: Beacon, 1996).

Miranda Shaw, *Passionate Enlightenment: Women in Tantric Buddhism* (Princeton: Princeton University Press, 1995).

Karma Lekshe Tsomo, *Buddhism through American Women's Eyes* (Ithaca: Snow Lion, 1995).

Websites

A magisterial compilation and discussion of the Cybersangha, i.e., Buddhist websites, can be found in Chapter 4 of Charles Prebish's *Luminous Passage: The Practice and Study of Buddhism in America* (Berkeley: University of California Press, 1999). As most websites contain links to numerous others, we name only a few that we have found particularly helpful:

1   http://www.accesstoinsight.org

2   http://www.baumann-martin.de/, the homepage of Martin Baumann, a European Buddhist scholar who chronicles the global Buddhist scene.

3   http://www.dharmanet.org

4   http://www.buddhanet.net

5   http://jbe.gold.ac.uk

Chapter Citations

Call of The Tradition

1 *Udana 5, 5, Uposatha Sutta.*
   (ack: accesstoinsight, John D. Ireland)
2 *Digha Nikaya,* 16
   (ack: accesstoinsight.org)
3 *Dhammapada* 1, 2. (ack: Nilgiri)
4 *Samyutta Nikaya,* 38.1 (ack: Nyanatiloka's
   Word of the Buddha)
5 *Majjhima Nikaya* 1, (editor's free
   rendering)
6 *Dhammapada* 183 (editor's free
   rendering)
7 *Fundamentals of the Middle Way* 25, 19.
8 Opening line of *On Trust in the Heart*
   (editor's free rendering).
9 From Dogen's *Bendowa.*
10 Untraced source.

Chapter 1

1 Edwin Arnold, *Light of Asia,* 138. (ack:
   public domain)

Chapter 2

1 *Dhammapada* 42-43
2 *Dhammapada* 80
3 *Kayagata-Sati-Sutta*

Chapter 3

1 "Kayagata-Sati-Sutta," in *Further
   Dialogues of the Buddha*, trans. Lord
   Chalmers (London: Humphrey Milford/
   Oxford University Press, 1927,).2

Chapter 4

1 Sayings of Buddha derived from *The
   Gospel of Buddha,* translated by Samuel
   Beale (Mt. Vernon, NY: Peter Pauper
   Press, 1957).

Chapter 5

1 *Zen and Japanese Culture,* by D. T. Suzuki
   (New York: Bollingen Series LXIV:
   Pantheon Books, 1958).

Chapter 6

1 *The Buddha* (Majjhima Nikaya, I.36)

Chapter 7

1 *Buddha and the Gospel of Buddhism* (New
   York: Harper and Row, 1916) 18-19
2 *Dhammapada* 393-94, translated from
   the Pali by Thanissara Bhikkhu, courtesy
   of Access to Insight

Chapter 8

1 Padmasambhava
2 Peter Matthiessen, *The Snow Leopard*

Chapter 9

1 Zen Master Dogen

Chapter 10

1 The Buddha, Mahāparinabbāna Sutta, in
   Agehananda Bharati, "Pilgrimage in the
   Indian Tradition," *History of Religions,*
   vol. 1, no. 3, 1963.

Chapter 11

1 Untraced source.

Photography Credits

Cover Photo
Chris Bland/Corbis

Pg. 138-140, Ten Oxherding Pictures
Jugyuzu attributed to Shubun. Shokokuji-Temple, Kyoto, Japan

Color Plates: (left to right)
Pg. 109, Standing Buddha
Photo © 1993 The Metropolitan Museum of Art, Gift of Cynthia Hazen Polsky, 1991.423.5. MMA/Metropolitan Museum of Art. Standing Buddha, 5th century Chieng Sen style, Thailand

Pg. 110-111, Buddha Heads, Row 1
Martin Westlake. Getty Images. Shwedagon Paya. Yangon, Myanmar (Burma).
Punch Stock. Bali, Indonesia.
Glen Allison. Getty Images. Wat Suthat Temple. Bangkok, Thailand.
Rob Atkins. Getty Images. Vancouver, British Columbia, Canada.
Grant Faint. Getty Images. Kamakura, Japan. 1252.

Row 2
Peter Adams. Getty Images. Kunming, Yunnan, People's Republic of China.
Pete Turner. Getty Images. Thailand.

Row 3
Glen Allison. Getty Images. Wat Bowonniwet. Bangkok, Thailand.
Sylvester Adams. Getty Images. Kanzeon Temple. Okinawa Prefecture, Japan.
Stephen Studd. Getty Images. Shwedagon Paya. Yangon, Myanmar (Burma).
Ric Ergenbright. Corbis. Detail of eyes of an Indian golden Buddha sculpture. Thikse Gompa, Ladakh, India.
Yann Layma. Getty Images. Baima Temple. Luoyang, Henan Province, People's Republic of China.

Row 4
Martin Moos. Getty Images. Face of Daibutsu. Kamakura, Japan.
Glen Allison. Getty Images. Sha Tin. Hong Kong, New Territories, People's Republic of China.
Glen Allison. Getty Images. Jade Buddha Temple. Shanghai, People's Republic of China.

Corey Wise. Getty Images. Shwedagon Paya. Yangon, Myanmar (Burma).
Chris Bland. Corbis. Statue of Buddha within a pagoda. Battersea Park, London, England.

Pg. 112-113, Buddha's Footprints
Photo © Linda Connor, *Buddha's Footprints*, Mahabodhi Temple, Bodhgaya, State of Bihar, India

Pg 114-115, Practitioners, Row 1
Gavin Hellier. Getty Images. Wat Xieng Thong. Luang Prabang, Laos.
Colin McPherson. Corbis. *Buddhism in Britain.* Scotland. June 12, 2002.
Plush Studios. Getty Images.
Punch Stock. Katmandu, Nepal.

Row 2
Getty Images.
Punch Stock. *Monks Walking with Umbrellas.*
Paula Bronstein. Getty Images. Reportage. Sri Lanka. January 2, 2005.
National Geographic Society. Getty Images.

Row 3
Peter Adams. Getty Images. Xian, People's Republic of China.
Michael Freeman. Corbis. *Young Nun Reading in Convent.* Sagaing, Myanmar (Burma).
Chris Cole. Getty Images.
Angelo Cavalli. Getty Images. Wat Sri Chum. Sukhotai, Thailand.

Pg 116-117, Zen Garden
Macduff Everton. Corbis. *Japanese Rock Garden at Ryoanki Temple*

Pg 118-119, Thankas, Row 1
Photo courtesy of the Rubin Museum of Art. Shelley & Donald Rubin Collection. *Guhyasamaga – Akshobhyavajra.* 46. Central Tibet. 1500-1599.
Photo courtesy of the Rubin Museum of Art. *Buddha Shakyamuni – Shakyamuni.* 39. Eastern Tibet. 1500-1599.
Photo courtesy of the Rubin Museum of Art. *Vaishravana (Protector) – Red, Riding a Blue Horse.* 103. Tibet. 1800-1899.
Photo courtesy of the Rubin Museum of Art. Shelley & Donald Ruben

Collection. *Buddha Shakyamuni – Life Story*. 699. Buryatia. 1800-1899.

Row 2
Photo courtesy of the Rubin Museum of Art. *Buddha Shakyamuni – Shakyamuni*. 509. China. 1700-1799.

Photo courtesy of the Rubin Museum of Art. Shelley & Donald Rubin Collection. *Yamari, Rakta*. 8. Tibet. 1600-1699.

Photo courtesy of the Rubin Museum of Art. Shelley & Donald Rubin Collection. *Padmasambhava – Longku Totreng Rig Nga*. 45. Tibet. 1800-1899.

Row 3
Photo courtesy of the Rubin Museum of Art. *Buddha*. 230. Tibet. 1300-1399.

Photo courtesy of the Rubin Museum of Art. Shelley & Donald Rubin Collection. *Shri Devi (Protector) – Magzor Gyalmo*. 105. Central Tibet. 1700-1799.

Photo courtesy of the Rubin Museum of Art. *Avalokiteshvara – Chaturbhuja (four hands)*. 80. Tibet. 1800-1899.

Photo courtesy of the Rubin Museum of Art. Shelley & Donald Rubin Collection. *Lama (Teacher) – Milarepa*. 180. Tibet. 1700-1799.

Pg 120-121, Reclining Buddha
Hugh Sitton. Getty Images. Gal Vihara rock shrine. 12th Century. Polannaruwa, Sri Lanka.

Pg 122-123, Mudras, Row 1
Chris Lisle. Corbis. Buddha Statue with Vitarka Mudra. Nakhon Pathom, Thailand.

John Banagan. Getty Images. Seokguram (Sokkuram) Grotto. Bulguksa, South Korea.

Chris Hellier. Corbis. Wat Pha Kaew.

Row 2
Dennie Cody. Getty Images. Gangarama Temple. Colombo, Sri Lanka.

Miho.

Row 3
David Vall. Index Stock Imagery, Inc. Thailand.

B. S. P. I. Corbis. *Hands of Buddha*. Kamakura, Honshu, Japan.

Ernest Manewal. Index Stock Imagery, Inc. De Lat, Vietnam.

Photos.com. Stone Mudra. 19026037.

Pg 124, Buddha
Araldo de Luca. Corbis. 17th-century Japanese cannon figure. 1673. Japan.